The Krajina Chronicle

A History of Serbs in Croatia, Slavonia and Dalmatia

SRDJA TRIFKOVIC

The Krajina Chronicle

A History of Serbs in Croatia, Slavonia and Dalmatia

The Lord Byron Foundation for Balkan Studies
Chicago-Ottawa-London
2010

Printed and bound in the United States of America by
The Lord Byron Foundation for Balkan Studies
Chicago-Ottawa-London

ISBN 978-1-892478-10-8

Table of Contents

Note on Pronunciation

Most linguists outside the Balkans regard the Serbian and Croatian (as well as 'Bosnian' and 'Montenegrin') as one language with minor structural, lexical and idiomatic differences. International linguistic authorities continue to refer to it as 'Serbo-Croat' or, less contentiously, as 'Serbian/Croatian.' Both are based on the *Shtokavian* dialect. They are mutually intelligible. The Serbian Cyrillic alphabet was devised by Vuk Karadžić and its Latin equivalent is based on Ljudevit Gaj's reform. The orthography is consistent and reflects the norm "Write as you speak, read as it is written." Serbian/Croatian words and names used in this book are given in the Latin script and commonly should be pronounced as follows:

a – *a* as in f*a*ther (long), ab*o*ve (short)
c – ts as in ra*ts*
ć - 'soft' ch, as in Pacino, chilli
č - 'hard' ch, as in chalk, cello
dj or đ – g as in gender, or j as in juice
dž – 'dzh' as in jam, edge
e – as in p*e*t (short), or grey (long)
g – as in go (never as g in 'large'!)
h – 'kh' (gutteral), as in loch
i – as in p*i*n (short) or mach*i*ne (long)
j – y as in yet or yes
lj – li as in million, halyard
nj – ni as in dominion, canyon
o - o as in up*o*n
s – as in hi*ss*
š - sh as in shawl, sugar
u – u as in rule
ž - zh, as in French *jour*

Preface

I n August 1995, the television news showed roads jammed with tractors and horse-drawn carts fleeing a region known as the Krajina. It was the largest episode of ethnic cleansing in the wars of Yugoslav succession. A quarter of a million Serbs inhabiting the western parts of the old Habsburg Military Border passed into exile.

Krajina in various versions is a Slavic toponym which means 'borderland.' The Military Border, the Habsburgs' *Militärgrenze,* was once the name of a string of territories whose history is far older and longer than the short history of the South Slav state. It was an essential link in the chain defending Europe from the Ottoman onslaught at a time of supreme peril in the 16th and 17th centuries.

The tourists have returned to the Dalmatian coast, but most Serbs have not come back to their homes in the towns and villages of the Adriatic hinterland. Even more lived in the districts of Lika, Banija and Kordun, which lie across the Dinaric Alps, along rivers that run into the Sava, and in two pockets of western and eastern Slavonia further down the Sava, where the river flows east towards the Danube and Belgrade.

The Krajina Serbs rose in arms to defend their districts in 1991 and held them for four years, just as they had fought in the same places, and against worse odds, in 1941. Many of their ancestors had been settled there centuries before by Hungarian kings, Austrian kaisers and Venetian governors for the express purpose of defending their lands against Ottoman invasion, and – in Habsburg lands – with the express liberty of not being subject to Croatian laws and taxes. In August 1995 they fled en masse, and few have come back.

For many generations the Serbian population of these regions was periodically decimated by warfare in the service of the Austrian Emperor. In 1941-1945 the Serbs were subject to a genocidal attack after the Germans put the Croatian Ustaša movement in power in Zagreb. Their resistance to this slaughter and the ensuing epic struggle is a large part of the story both of the royalist Četniks and of their bitter rivals for post-war power, Communist-led 'Yugoslav' Partisans.

In 1990-1991 Croatia seceded from Yugoslavia a second time. Once again the Serbs of the old Krajina took up arms against the Croatian secession and a short-lived *Republika Srpska Krajina* emerged. It covered part, but not the whole, of the old Military Frontier, as well as some former Venetian possessions in Dalmatia that had not been included in the Habsburg Military Border. This latter-day Krajina perished in August 1995, when the order came from Belgrade to withdraw, rather than fight, in the face of a well-signalled Croatian offensive. The result has been devastating for the community. A quarter of the population of today's Croatia was Serbian before 1914; a fifth before 1941; a sixth before 1991; today it is but five percent.

It is sometimes said that the bitter quarrels of Serbs and Croats in the 20th century are a modern phenomenon, no older than the creation of Yugoslavia in 1918. It is true that the Serbs of Serbia, when it was a small state south of the Sava and the Danube, as yet untied from the Ottoman empire, had no direct or traditional quarrel with the Croats of Croatia, the Habsburg territory whose principal concern was with imperial masters in Budapest and Vienna. More exactly, the Croats living in 'Civil Croatia' – the heartland around Zagreb that did not belong to the Military Frontier – and Serbs living in the former Ottoman *pashaluk* of Belgrade had nothing to quarrel about before 1918. But the seeds of the legendary quarrel between Serbs and Croats in the Yugoslav era were sown in the Krajina long before. The legal status and privileges of the Military Border were detested by the Croatian nobility from the moment the Border was formed in the 16th century to the time it was dissolved in 1881.

From the moment of its creation, on the ruins of the old Europe at the end of the Great War, until its final disintegration almost seven and a half decades later, Yugoslavia was beset by national problems. Those national problems proved impossible to solve, in the 'first,' royalist Yugoslavia (1918-1941) no less than the 'second,' Communist one (1945-1991). Structural deficiencies of Yugoslavia, as a state and as a polity, were fundamental, which precluded the emergence of a viable political system. From the outset the issue of Serb-Croat relations was at the core of the problem. Those relations were plagued by an ambivalent legacy of the previous three centuries in the Krajina. Serb-Croat relations could have remained ambivalent but tractable, had the two nations not been placed under the same roof.

In some ways the Krajina was the nursery of Yugoslavia. Both the acute anxieties of nineteenth-century Croatian nationalists about the Serbs and the possibilities of 'Illyrian' or South Slav co-operation are hard to comprehend if the history of the Krajina is not understood. This book is presented in the hope that it can and will be better understood. The only way we can meaningfully judge the present is by the example of the past.

On those rare occasions when the Serbs and the Croats worked together, Austria or Hungary hastened to pull them apart again – to divide and conquer. The Military Border, though it lost its traditional legal status in 1881, had a personality too marked by warfare and identity not to persist in political life, in rebellion and occupation. Without the Military Border, the venom of Croatian genocidal fascism in 1941 is inexplicable; without the fighting instinct of the Krajina Serbs, the two resistance movements in Yugoslavia would have been deprived of a major fighting component.

The war of 1991-1995 in the Krajina was a curious affair. Belgrade was itself in turmoil in 1991. It encouraged the Krajina's rejection of the new Croatia, but that is as far as it went. The Krajina become a pawn to be advanced or sacrificed as needed. The Krajina Serbs, a poor people many of whom lived in poor territories, were always a bargaining chip in the unstrategic mind of Slobodan Milošević. The war, as conducted on the part of the post-Communist, quasi-nationalist political establishment in Belgrade, was devoid of any strategic sense. For four years, under military discipline, the Krajina Serbs were obliged to sit still as their enemies grew stronger. Finally, in the summer of 1995 – still under military discipline – they were ordered to abandon their homeland, to which but a few have returned over the past 15 years.

This book is dedicated to the memory of their forefathers and to the hope that their homes and their lands will be restored, in the fullness of time, to their rightful owners.

Chicago, Easter 2010   The Author

The Setting

The history of the Balkan Peninsula is the history of migrations. It is commonly accepted that the most important one – the great movement of Slavs into the region – took place in the late 6th and the first half of the 7th centuries. Unlike their Germanic predecessors, however, the Slavs, as agrarian settlers, came to stay. Within decades they were to be found in compact settlements from the foothills of the Julian Alps to the Isthmus of Corinth. Their tribal self-rule replaced imperial Byzantine authorities, but their statehood was slow to develop.

The Balkan peninsula is the area of Europe south of the line extending from Istria (on the Adriatic) in the northwest along the Kupa, Sava and Danube rivers in the north, to the Danube Delta and the Black Sea in the north-east. Unlike other south European peninsular regions – Iberia and Italy – the northern boundary of the Balkans is not marked by mountain ranges that sharply separate the peninsula from the heartland of Europe. On the contrary, the boundary is long and wide open, marked by easily fordable rivers, and criss-crossed by several key transit corridors that connect Central and Western Europe with the Middle East and eastern Mediterranean.

Hauntingly beautiful in many parts but relatively poor in natural resources and, south of the Danube and the Sava, with few large tracts of fertile soil, the region is significant mainly because of its location. Its geographic position has been the bane of its history, inviting invaders and turning the region into an object of competing designs and interests of the great powers for much of its history. The key transit route runs along the Sava, Morava and Vardar rivers from the Julian Alps to Greece. This key corridor has been deemed worthy of considerable investment in blood and treasure, from the times of the empires of Rome,

Byzantium, Turkey and Austria to both world wars, and on to our own time.

The Serbs' Balkan heartland, their first known political entity, was the region of Raška, in today's southwestern Serbia. It gave them a geographic name, *Rascians*, by which they were often known for many centuries thereafter. How and when they came there is still a matter of some dispute. In most parts of the Balkan Peninsula, they, like the Croats to their northwest, and Bulgarians to their southeast, expelled or assimilated the native population. On the Adriatic coast, however, the Slav newcomers were confronted by the affluent maritime city-states. They were highly civilized and able to rely on the support, cultural no less than material, of their kin in Italy.

While the rural districts were soon populated by the Slavs, the late Roman, proto-Italian population moved for safety to the walled cities of Ragusa (Dubrovnik), Zara (Zadar), Spalato

Slavic groups in the Balkans (7th–8th century c.e.)

(Split), Trogir (Trau), and other coastal towns. The western Balkan region between the Germans in the Alps and the Greeks of Epirus was shared between three ethnicities: Serb, Croat and Albanian. Their modern rivalries are partly rooted in the clash of Roman and Byzantine ecclestiastical jurisdictions. That clash contributed to the schism between Eastern and Western Christianity that was made final in 1054. The Albanians, Croats and Dalmatian Latins were to be mostly Catholic, and the Serbs mostly Orthodox – until Islam arrived to complicate the picture.

The presence of the Serbs in many parts of today's Croatia – notably in Dalmatia and along the Adriatic littoral – harks back to the early medieval times. A host of ancient toponyms, contemporary chronicles and historical monuments relating to the Serb name antedate by hundreds of years the major  population shifts across the Western Balkans induced by the Turkish onslaught in the 15th and 16th centuries. The earliest specific reference dates from the early 9th century. In 822 the annals of the Frankish chronologist Einhard (c. 775-840, shown l. in a contemporary miniature) referred to the uprising of the Lower Pannonian prince Louis (Ljudevit, 818-823). Einhard relates that Louis escaped from Sisak and went south, "towards the Serbs, who are said to inhabit the greater part of Dalmatia."[1] The Byzantine province of Dalmatia extended at that time from the Adriatic coast over a hundred miles inland, covering much of the hinterland and western Bosnia.

The Croats, who settled the neighboring territories to the north, are conspicuously absent from Einhard's account. They are mentioned for the first time some three decades later, in 852, in the *Charter of Prince Trpimir*. Their language was Slavic, although their origins are still a subject of debate; Gothic,

---

[1] *Liudevitus Siscia civitate relicta, ad Sorabos, quae natio magnam Dalmatie partem obtinere dicitur, fugiendo se contulit.*

Sarmatian, and even Iranian 'theories' have been advanced over the years. Their early Balkan heartland, ruled by *Bans*, extended from Istria in the northeast to the Cetina river in the southwest, and as far as the Vrbas river (in today's Bosnia) to the east, with additional settlements soon spreading into today's Slavonia.

Two early Croat states came into being in the ninth century, in the Panonian plain and along the Adriatic coast. They were merged into a single domain by Duke (*dux Croatorum*) Tomislav Trpimirović, who is said to have received letter from the pope granting him the royal title in 925. He was able to raise his rank and increase his holdings at a time of trouble in all neighboring states. Byzantium was weakened by Arab attacks, iconoclasm, and dynastic disputes; the heirs of Charlemagne were unable to hold local magnates in check; the newly arrived Hungarians – still pagans – were wreaking havoc in the heart of the continent; and Pope John X needed local allies to keep Dalmatia, which he had only recently gained from the Byzantines. The facts of the case are uncertain, however, as there is no primary evidence, reliable documents and eyewitness accounts. What we know of Tomislav comes from chroniclers who may have had a political axe to grind. Tomislav vanished from history after 928 and some historians suggest that he might have been poisoned on orders from Rome. At the time of his death the discord over whether the liturgical language of the Roman Catholic Church in Croatia would be Latin or Slavic was still unresolved.

The names 'Serb' and 'Croat' implied supra-tribal entities, groups that were early 'nationalities,' yet far from state-defined nationhood. In the 10th century Byzantine Emperor Constantine VII Porphyrogenitus (r. 913-959), in his *De Administrando Imperio*, offered a wealth of information (not uniformly reliable) on the Slavic peoples – *hai Sklabeniai* – of the Balkans.[2] The Croats, he relates, came to the northeastern shores of the Adriatic in the early 7th century led by five brothers and two sisters. They

---

[2] Constantine Porphyrogenitus: *De Administrando Imperio*. Dumbarton Oaks Texts, 2009.

killed their Avar overlords on the advice of Emperor Heraclius and took over the land. It is noteworthy that Porphyrogenitus does not mention Tomislav. The Serbs, he says, were granted land by Heraclius in the vicinity of Salonica but were not satisfied with it and moved "beyond the Danube." Heraclius subsequently asked them to settle along the Adriatic Coast, in the areas ravaged by Avar raids in two preceding decades.

In Chapter 32, "On the Serbs and the lands in which they live," Porphyrogenitus placed them in Bosnia and along the Adriatic littoral. The rather vague description of the Byzantine Emperor can be validated with greater precision by the rise of a Serbian Prince, Bodin, in the area of Knin in the Dalmatian hinterland, and by the presence of ancient Orthodox churches built in the Zeta-Zahum style in that region. The western boundary of Serbian Cyrillic tombstones ran at that time from Poljice near Split to Benkovac and thence due north to the area of Kordun which adjoins, on the Croatian side, Bosnia's northwestern tip.[3]

The Hungarians staked a claim to the northeastern Adriatic after a weakened Croatia was taken over by King Koloman of the Hungarian Arpad dynasty in 1102. The agreement regulating the personal union of Hungary and Croatia, known as *Pacta Conventa*, preserved certain privileges of the Croatian nobility. They were taken, in subsequent centuries, to imply the unbroken continuity of Croatia's distinct statehood..

In 1166-1168 Stefan Nemanja, the founder of the medieval Serbian state, took control of the coastline from northern Dalmatia to today's Albania. His younger son Sava, subsequently canonized as the founder of the autocephalous Serbian Orthodox Church, established the diocese of Hum in this region in 1219. Its seat was in the city of Ston, linking the Sabioncello (Pelješac) peninsula with the Hum mainland. By the late medieval times, compact settlements of Serbs were

---

[3] Cf. Djordje Janković. *Tradicionalna kultura Srba u Srspkoj Krajini i Hrvatskoj.* Beograd: Etnografski muzej, 2000.

established further north, in central and northern Dalmatia, along the Krka and Cetina rivers. The oldest major Orthodox monastery in the region, Krupa (r.), dedicated to the Ascension of the Mother of God, was founded in 1317. Its building was paid for in part by two prominent Serbian kings, Dragutin and Milutin, and it was later endowed by the most powerful medieval Serbian king (later *Tsar*, 'Emperor') Stefan Dušan.

By the middle of the 14th century, Serbs were present in and around the fortified cities of Clissa (Klis) and Scardona (Skradin) in central and northern Dalmatia. Their settlement coincided with the arrival of Jelena, King Dušan's sister, who was married to a local prince, Mladen II Šubić of Bribir. A detachment of her brother's Serbian soldiers accompanied her to Dalmatia and remained there, initially as her retinue and then as her husband's mercenaries. By that time one's denominational allegiance had already become largely synonymous with national identity. Along the Balkan fault line between Orthodoxy and Roman Catholicism the struggle for this allegiance has only intensified in subsequent centuries.

Princess Jelena, a Serb, was a patron of several Orthodox churches and monasteries in the region, although her husband, a Croat, was a Roman Catholic. Her spiritual advisor was one monk Rufim, who accompanied Jelena to her new abode and soon thereafter invited three monks from the heartland of Orthodoxy at Mt. Athos to join him. They are believed to have been the first occupants of the current seat of the Serbian Orthodox Bishop of Dalmatia, the monastery dedicated to Archangel Michael (*Krka,* next p. r.), built in 1350.

The influx of Serbs continued under Tvrtko I (1354-1391), who in 1377 was crowned 'King of the Serbs and Bosnia.'[4] By the 15th century the entire region of Knin, with the villages of Golubić, Padjene and Polača, had an Orthodox majority.

Dalmatia was never fully Italian, and largely Slavic by the eighth century. The coastal communes were born with Greek names and their loyalty was Roman. They spoke a Romance language which died out in the medieval period to be replaced with Italian, or with Italian-Slav bilinguality. Political appetites soon followed linguistic and cultural penetration. Venice showed its hunger for Dalmatia by diverting the Fourth Crusade to sack and subdue the rich city of Zara in 1202 (repeating the crime on a grand scale in Constantinople in 1204). From the north, Croatian magnates sought to impose themselves in the name of

the Hungarian king. Hungary wanted to tax the rich Dalmatian communes, while the cities tried to play Venice and Hungary against each other. The medieval and renaissance culture of Slavic Dalmatia is undifferentiated in terms of later national identity. In Italian and Serbian historiography it has been alleged that the designation 'Croat' is absent from all known Venetian and Ragusan records; in Venice's case it may have been due to censorship.[5]

---

[4] "Hic [Tvartkus] inplicitus cura esset erroribus et schismate Graecorum, a patrui virtute ec religione longe multumque degeneravit, haereticis perfugium ac patrocinium praebuit, catholicos quinuscumque potuitmodisvexavit." Daniele Farlati, *Illyricum Sacrum*, IV, p. 172. The religion in medieval Bosnia is still a contentious issue; it was syncretic and without distinct character.

[5] [Venice] 'destroyed every document which could have thrown doubt upon her rights over Dalmatia, as against the Hungaro-Croatian Crown. Above all she set herself to discover and destroy at Zara all charters of the twelfth century, down to the most insignificant copies.' Louis Voinovitch, *Dalmatia and the Yugoslav Movemen.* London: George Allen & Unwin, 1920, p.63.

While the presence of the Croatian magnates was undeniable, neither submission to the Ban of Croatia nor opposition to his authority had any proto-national significance or 'ethnic' meaning at the time. Through the following centuries 'Croatia' was but a medieval memory.

While Hungary recognised a *Regnum Dalmatiae* and conferred charters and liberties, Venice grew stronger and had the better grip on Dalmatia by the early 15th century. The Serenissima's control of the Adriatic was reflected in its designation as 'the Bay of Venice,' *Golfo de Venetia*, in contemporary Italian maps. In 1409 the Republic purchased all Hungary's rights in Dalmatia for 100,000 ducats. It remained in Venice's possession for almost four centuries. That possession was threatened by the Turks after the fall of Bosnia in 1463, but never interrupted. By that time both Serbia and Bosnia were conquered, which pushed Hungary into the front line as the chief Christian opponent of the Ottoman empire. It also enabled Venice to emerge as the master of the eastern Adriatic shore.

In the 1500s its supremacy was sometimes challenged from a new quarter. The Turkish conquest of Bosnia drove large numbers of Orthodox Christians into Venetian territory. A body of these *Uskoks*, as they were called (from Serbian for 'intruder') established itself in Klis, and thence staged sporadic cross-border attacks upon the Turks. In the 1530s they moved into the Habsburg realm, to Senj (Segna, Zengg), further north along the Adriatic coast. They were welcomed by the Emperor Ferdinand I and promised an annual subsidy in return for fighting the Turks. Unhappy with the spoils of cross-border raids and only sporadically paid by the Crown they soon turned to piracy, however, preying upon the commerce of the Adriatic. The Uskoks continued causing endless tensions between Venice and Austria until their activities were finally curtailed in 1617.[6]

---

[6] See C.W. Bracewell, *The Uskoks of Senj: Piracy, Banditry and Holy War in the sixteenth-century Adriatic* (Cornell U.P, 1992), p.40.

The Military Border

The first Islamic invasions of Europe were stopped thirteen centuries ago. One failed at the walls of Constantinople where the Byzantines withstood the great Arab sieges of 674-678 and 717-718. The Arabs also crossed the Straits of Gibraltar, took most of Spain, and were turned back at Tours by Charles Martel in 732. The defence of Constantinople saved the Greek empire for another seven centuries; the battle of Tours protected the Latin West from destruction before its own medieval civilization had developed. The Arabs controlled Sicily for a time and threatened mainland Italy and Dalmatia, but the Normans took Sicily just before they conquered England. At sea, Byzantium, and then Venice, were strong enough to keep Saracen piracy in check, although the Barbary corsairs remained a problem for centuries.

The next great Muslim attack by land came centuries later, and it was Turkish. This assault developed slowly after the Byzantines lost Anatolia in the late eleventh century. In 1354, the Turks, led by the new Ottoman (Osman) dynasty, crossed the Dardanelles from Asia Minor and established a foothold on the European shore. The line of the attack went from Thrace via Macedonia to Kosovo; through Rascia (later known under the Ottomans as the 'Sanjak') into Bosnia, and all the way to the Una river. It was finally stopped by Venice and the Habsburgs in the 16th century.

The Ottoman conquest all but destroyed a rich Christian civilization in the Balkan peninsula. Although Byzantium was, after 1354, a spent force as an empire, Serbia and Bulgaria, its dynamic and creative Slavic offspring, were flourishing states and Hungary was a major power. The Dalmatian communes – Ragusa, Zara, Spalato, Sebenico, Scardona and many others – kept the South Slav world in contact with Italian culture and commerce. But the Ottomans at their zenith ruled all of the

Balkans except the outer fringe of Hungary and a few of those fortified Dalmatian cities which Venice could support. Ragusa (Dubrovnik) only retained its independence by paying tribute to the Sultan. The destruction caused by Turkish conquest was phenomenal; recovery was slow and partial.

The conquest was never secure, however, and it remained contested both internally and externally. The conquered towns became largely Muslim, the countryside remained largely Christian. The subjugated Christian populations became second-class citizens (*dhimmis*) whose security required obedience to the Muslim masters. They were heavily taxed (*jizya*, or poll tax, and *kharaj*) and subjected to the practice of *devshirme*: the 'blood levy,' introduced in the 1350s, of a fifth of all Christian boys in the conquered lands to be converted to Islam and trained as janissaries. In the collective memory of the Balkan Christian nations, half a millenium of Turkish conquest and overlordship – with all their consequences, cultural, social, and political – are carved as an unmitigated disaster:

> If any single factor made the Balkans what they were in history – and what they still are today – it was the ordeal of the Turk... The image of Turkey was that of a rotting empire, of a corrupt, incompetent and sadistic national elite preying on the subject Balkan peoples – of a cynical government whose very method of rule was atrocity.[7]

The dynamism and effectiveness of the early Ottoman system were undeniable. In the middle of the 16th century Turkish military forces were more undeniably more effective and in many respects more "professional" than their European opponents. In the Balkans they grew stronger, becoming as Slav and Albanian as Turkish in the process. Perpetual warfare was supported by a huge taxation base of Christian *dhimmis* subjected to the rigors of sharia.

---

[7] Edmund Stillman, *The Balkans*. New York: Time-Life, 1967, p. 43.

The host set out every year to defend or extend that base. The Ottoman army was strong in highly skilled light cavalry (*akinci*, raiders, shown in a contemporary gravure) who could campaign on their own when they were not attached to the main Ottoman host. The *akinci* were more numerous than the janissary infantry and more important in securing consistent military success.

As the Turks moved northward over the two centuries after the battle of Kosovo (1389), they pushed ahead of them a no-man's land known as *serhat*. Turkish conquest was usually preceded by decades of *akinci* raiding to seize Christian slaves and goods and designed to lay waste to enemy territories and weaken resistance to eventual conquest. This was the crucial feature of Ottoman warfare and has left a lasting mark. It created wastelands on both the Turkish and the Christian side of the imperial borders. In the course of the fifteenth century Serbia, Albania, Bosnia and Hercegovina were annexed one by one setting off waves of emigration into Croatia and Dalmatia. Tens of thousands of mostly Orthodox Christians, escaping the onslaught, moved into depopulated lands between the Pannonian plain and the Adriatic that were ravaged by constant Turkish intrusions. Others were settled by Ottomans on their own side of the expanding border as privileged Christian groups (*martoloses;* Greek: *armatolos*), but many switched sides and emigrated when their privileges were withdrawn by Sultan Suleiman.

Some Ottoman raids reached as far as Friuli and Austria. In 1493 a Croatian force of 8,000 infantry and 2,000 cavalry tried to intercept an *akinci* raiding force of 8,000 and was destroyed at Krbava. Areas of today's southwestern Croatia, badly devastated after this Turkish victory, were referred to as *desertum primum;* the area further north, periodically attacked throughout the 16th century, was known as *desertum secundum*. Attempts were made from the beginning to repopulate the territories. Christian settlers from Turkish-controlled lands, mainly of Orthodox faith, became a majority population in both by the early 16th century. The need to use them in defense against Ottoman incursions required the Hungarian-Croat kingdom, and later the Austrians, to consider grants of privilege designed to give them a personal stake in their lands. It was also necessary to create areas of discipline which protected more settled areas further north and west from an influx of refugees from Turkish territory. The result was a series of measures to defend the border against the Turks, to control flight beyond the border belt, and to restore economic life and political authority in a wasted no-man's land.

When Bosnia fell to the Ottomans, resistance was continued in Dalmatia by Venice and in Croatia by the Kingdom of Hungary. A captaincy to defend the Border was created at Senj as early as 1469. The defensive system later called the Border predates the famous Austrian-sponsored instituton. The first version was Hungarian and consisted of two lines of fortresses between Magyar lands. The first line passed from the Danube, focused on Belgrade, to Klis in Dalmatia; the second terminated at Senj. Janos (John) Hunyadi's famous victory at Belgrade (Nándorfehérvár) in 1456 saw the breaking of an Ottoman siege meant to unpick the strongest point line of forts. The church bells were rung all over Europe. Hungary was unable to conserve its resources, however, while the Ottoman empire was becoming an economic giant. The first line of Hungarian defences started to founder after Suleiman captured the Belgrade fortress in 1521. In 1521-1522 the Imperial Diet, meeting at Nuremberg, authorised the Archduke Ferdinand of Austria (r.) to take the fortresses of Klis, Knin and Senj and keep troops in Croatia. This reinforced Hungarian defences already in existence.

The crisis soon deepened: Scardona and Knin fell in 1522, with additional strongholds falling one by one in later years. Pope Hadrian VI received a melancholy report from Spalato:

> We are troubled by daily attacks of the infidel Turks; they harass us incessantly, killing some and leading others into slavery; our goods are pillaged, our cattle are led off, our villages and settlements are burned; the fields from which we drew our livelihood are in part laid waste to and in part deserted, for those once worked them have been carried off; and instead of fruit they bear brambles. We defend our safety with our walls alone, and we are content that our Dalmatian cities are not yet besieged ... But only the cities are spared, and all else lies open to pillage and rapine.[8]

Suleiman's army destroyed the main Hungarian army and killed the king at Mohacs in 1526. The Habsburgs competed for the Crown with a Magyar candidate and a protracted succession crisis began. The issue of dynastic succession was not a foregone conclusion since the Crown was elective. The contest was destructive, and the House of Austria did not win quickly. Indeed, after 1526 the Ottomans might have left Hungary alone for a time if there had not been the succession struggle to tempt them further. While Croatia (unlike Transylvania) opted for a Habsburg king, the clergy and nobility made a symbolic point of asserting that they were submitting to him of their own free will.[9]

Over the next thirty years the Hungarian kingdom nearly collapsed. In Croatia, Obrovac and Udbina fell in 1527; in Bosnia, Jajce and Banja Luka fell in 1528. The Turks raided Istria and Lower Austria, and briefly laid siege to Vienna in 1529. In central Hungary they took Buda in 1541 and there was inconclusive warfare in 1543-62. Central Hungary was lost. Transylvania became tributary to the Sultan, who was remarkably keen to tolerate Calvinism in his new domains. What

---

[8] Bracewell, *The Uskoks of Senj* (1992), p. 22.

[9] Cf. Ferdo Šišić, *Povijesti hrvatskoga naroda*. Zagreb, 1916.

remained as Royal Hungary was a thin buffer covering the many possible approaches to Vienna. What remained of Croatia was the western half of this buffer. Klis, a strong castle near Spalato (Split) in Dalmatia, was the strongest point and furthest forward in the chain. It finally fell in 1537 after the Croatian prince Petar Kružić had held it for twenty-five years.

Having taken over the military responsibility and financial burden of defense of the newly-acquired Hungarian lands, the Austrians decided to go beyond the existing system of fortresses and settlers by placing both inside special territorial units under their direct control, known collectively as the Military Border. The Austrian commitment to what was left of the Hungarian military defence system – the second line of fortresses – thus became essential and permanent. The settlers who were encouraged to come in, farm and take up warfare were mostly Orthodox Christians fleeing from Serbia or Bosnia. But they did not all come at once. The first wave came after the fall of Serbia (1459) and Bosniab (1463), and was mainly directed northward, into the Panonian plain. The influx lasted two hundred years: warfare was more nearly continuous than recurrent. The Grenzer were mainly Slavs: Orthodox and Catholic *graničari* who were settlers and paid only when mustered. The Habsburgs were willing to grant them certain privileges to encourage settlement and ensure loyalty: they were typically exempt from taxation for the first 20 years, allowed to keep the loot plundered on cross-border raids into Ottoman territory, and as free soldiers exempt from the authority of the Croatian nobility, or feudal obligations to it. A small number of German soldiers hoping for regular wages manned the key forts. Taken together, they were the backbone of *Antemurale Christianitatis*. This title was given to Croatia by Leo X in 1519, just before the storm struck. (The same optimistic pontiff hailed England's Henry VIII as *fidei defensor*).

Initially there were two Croatian captaincies in the system, Senj and Bihać. In the 1530s there were three: Maritime, Croatian and Slavonian. By that time two former captaincies had been much reduced: Senj had lost what the Ottomans called the Sanjak of Lika, and Slavonia had lost the Sanjak of Pakrac. In 1553 their remnant came under one command. The military zone, between 30 and 50 miles deep, ran the entire length of the frontier by that time, and rested on a chain 12 major and 130 minor fortified posts manned by 5,000 soldiers and relying on 20,000 Grenzer militiamen available for action at a short notice.

The German overlay on Hungarian-Croatian territory, at the very moment of the Ottoman Empire's zenith (map below), proved successful. This time the line held. The Turks were kept out of Italy, Germany and Bohemia, during the rest of the sixteenth century, by the power of Austria and Venice acting behind a screen provided by the Dalmatian Krajina, by the Croatian and Hungarian Military Border, and by the settler-soldiers. In 1568 the Border was divided into two commands (*Krajinas*), Croatian and Slavonian, and administered by the *Hofkriegsrat* in Graz. Archduke Charles of Inner Austria as General of the Frontier reorganized it into two generalcies in the 1580's, the northern, with headquarters at Varaždin (Windische

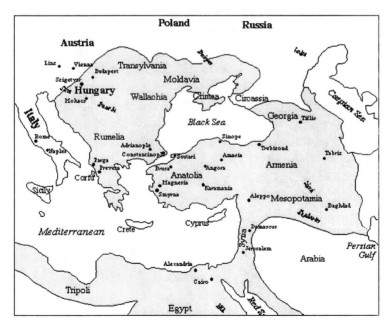

or Warasdin Gränitz), and the southern, which had its command post in the newly fortified town of Karlstadt (Karlovac), built in 1579. Varaždin was the largest Croatian town at that time, and outside the military area when it was defined. In this section of the Border Catholics were the majority but the Orthodox element was large and and growing, especially after the Ottoman conquest of Srem and eastern and central Slavonia in the 1580s.

The Karlovac generalcy (the *Krabatische Gränitz*) had an Orthodox majority from the outset. It faced its Ottoman counterpart, the *Bihaćka Krajina*, at the northwestern tip of Bosnia-Herzegovina. The strategic importance of this area to the Turks is reflected in the fact that, unlike most other parts of the former Ottoman frontier in the Balkans, it has had a majority Muslim population, consisting of local converts and Muslim settlers, ever since the first half of the 17th century. The burning of the relics of St. Sava, the founder of Serbia's autocephalous Orthodox Church, by Sinan Pasha in Belgrade on 27 April 1594, marked a symbolic turning point: the end of a century-long period when many Serbs served as auxilliaries in the Sultan's army and were used as settlers along the western borders of the Ottoman Empire. From the 1590's century onward the Ottomans could no longer rely on local Serb *matrologs* along the Austrian border. The allegiance of the latter became strictly confessional. The Emperor in Vienna was not always reliable as a defender of their privileges, but he was still a Christian, and an enemy of the hated Turk.

Defending the realm was a costly endeavor for the Habsburgs. In 1554, for example, only 1,327 forints was collected as war levy in Croatia, while the cost of maintaining the border exceeded 200,000 forints. There were dozens of forts along the border that local impoverished nobles could no longer man, let alone defend. Some sections were placed in local hands, notably akong the southern or maritime border based around Senj and populated by the Uskoks (see p 16 above):

This mountainous region could not support the growing number of refugees who were supposed to be paid by the government to defend the frontier with Ottoman Bosnia. Chronic indebtedness forced the Habsburgs to tolerate Uskok raiding and piracy instead.[10]

The crown lands that became military borders were almost totally depopulated by Turkish warfare and repopulated by mostly Orthodox peasant-warrior settlers. In 1535 and 1538, for instance, Ferdinand I issued two decrees authorizing their free movement into abandoned villages in the area of Žumberak. Their settlement was often resisted by the Croatian-Hungarian magnate families such as Zrinyi (Zrinjski) and Frankopan, resentful of the newcomers' Imperial and military patronage and exemption from feudal obligations. They received little help from the Austrian treasury, however, and were expected to supplement their modest land resources with cross-border raids into Ottoman Bosnia.

As soldiers these settlers were Grenzer; as semi-nomadic pastoralists they were *Vlachs*. This term was generally used to refer to the members of an upland economy of wandering shepherds not settled in a fixed locality.[11] Some were Vlach by ethnicity and language, too, pre-Slavic proto-Romance speakers; but the issue was complicated by the tendency of Austrian and Turkish authorities to refer to all newcomers from the south and east as 'Vlachs,' referring to their socio-economic status and lifestyle rather than national origin. When the latter was specifically alluded to, however, the Vlach designation was often absent. In the earliest Habsburg charter for the Border, issued by Ferdinand I on September 5, 1538, the settlers were referred to as "Serbs or Rascians" (*Serviani seu Rasciani*).

---

[10] Peter H. Wilson, *The Thirty Years War: Europe's Tragedy*. Cambridge, MA: The Belknap Press, 2009, p. 82.

[11] The word *Vlach* in Bosnia is colloquially used by Muslims for Christians regardless of denomination. In Dalmatia it is still used in coastal towns for the people who live inland, regardless of religion or ethnicity.

Subsequent Austrian documents, in German and Latin, refer interchangeably to 'Ratze' and, in a letter by Ferdinand I to the Croatian Ban, *Rasciani sive Serbiani atque Valachi*.[12] Whether this particular document refers to two categories or one may be textually uncertain, yet a century later a similar designation – "Vlachs or Rascians, or better still Serbians" (*gens Valachorum sive Rascianorum vel potius Servianorum*) – was used by the Roman Catholic Bishop of Zagreb, Petar Petretić. He also referred to them as "Vlachs, or Rascians, or correctly speaking Serbs originally from the Kingdom of Serbia."[13] The language they spoke, according to the bishop, was the "Serbian language, which is by us here known as Vlach" (*Lingua Serviana quae apud nos Valachica dicitur*).

In the end most of the Orthodox Christians could be identified as Serbs, athough for generations they were called Vlachs. The name was known throughout the Balkans, but it is the Vlachs of Serbia, Bosnia, Dalmatia and Croatia that concern us. Nineteenth and early twentieth-century historians argued whether such people were Latin Vlach, Albanian Vlach, Serbian Vlach, or another proto-something Vlach. For the past half-century the modern historian has declared a stylish indifference to such issues; though perhaps the display of approved, liberal attitudes would sustain the style even if the indifference were more apparent than real.

The idea that Balkan peasantries were uniformly pre-national before their 'awakening' – or indeed, that nationalism, or 'bourgeois nationalism,' kicked into action circa 1789 to astonish an unsuspecting world with new energies and narrowness – is one of the oddest conjectures ever to have captured historical attention. Some identities may be far older than the continuous evidence for them. The soup of nationality was certainly thicker in the 19th century, after Danton and Herder

---

[12] Archduke Mathias, writing to the Emperor in 1604, refers to them as 'Serbs.'

[13] *Valachi siue Rasciani uel ut verius dicam Serviani nam ex regno Serviae prodierunt*, in a report to the Crown Council dated April 21, 1662.

and Scott.[14] The medieval world knew something about *nationes*, even perhaps that *natio* could gather force and direction over time or lose it; but are we to suppose that the nations of Christian Europe have been largely reinvented from one generation to another? Even as a sophisticated suspicion, this is implausible. As an idea, it carries an unacknowledged bourgeois prejudice against the culture of peasants. Serbian Orthodox peasants, at least, had an extensive religion-supported oral history and a grasp of deep family history. This was always rare, and is so today more than ever. But it would have been understood for Scotland and Ireland by Scott and Synge.

It is therefore wholly possible that Serbs were already *Serbs* before they emerged from the Vlach chrysalis; that the same may be true of smaller numbers of Croats, Bosnian Muslims, and even Albanians; that Romance-speaking Vlachs in Bosnia and the Croatian Military Frontier, were likely to emerge as Serbs; that some Serbs may have gone into the Vlach social condition in one century only to re-appear decades later as re-Serbifying Orthodox settlers or Greek-rite Uniate Slavophones destined to become Croats. We do not know whether the Vlach economy was a melting pot or a cooking pot in which *nationes* were stirred and warmed and then re-congealed as they came out of it.

The debate has been sterile at times, but not in principle: it would be worthwhile if mention of Vlachs were more than a deliberately provocative sneer, as it had been in 19th and 20th century Zagreb, and if there were evidence enough. The Balkan peninsula might seem to be, between 1400 and 1700, a fringe of settled areas defining the edges of a space and an economy which itinerant pastoralists could navigate by adopting Vlach customs and manners. But whatever identity went into that space, something came through or came out.

---

[14] But also after Milton's *Areopagitica* (1644) and Shakespeare's *Henry V* (1599), and the Scottish Declaration of Abroath (1320). Nationality – a name, its memory and loyalty – is plainly older than 1789, however important that date in the history of the French.

Although the borders were fairly well delineated in the northwest, the edges were less certain further south and east, where the relations between peasant and Vlach herdsman were not marked by the urban contempt for Vlachs noticeable in Dalmatia and 'Civil' Croatia. This raises a different point: the clash of culture, the West and the Rest.

A tendency in Vlach communities to shift from Latinate speech to a Slavic dialect, already in evidence in the 16th century, was accelerated by the Ottoman conquest. Slavs, mainly Serbs, entered the upland economy of migrant pastoralists to escape share-cropping and Islamized landlords. Every South Slav group has some pre-Slavic, 'Vlach' component in its ethnic mix. Their full slavicisation was complete by the end of the 17th century.[15] But even before the restoration of the Orthodox Patriachate at Peć in 1557, the trend was clearly towards the identification of Slavic-speaking Orthodox with Serb. That most Grenzer of Orthodox faith referred to themselves as *Serbs*s was reflected in countless records of their reverence for the saga of Kosovo and Prince Lazar's sacrifice, by an implacable hostility to the Turk and strong adherence to their faith.

Austria found in its Grenzers (r.) an effective bulwark against further Ottoman incursions. By 1600 all administration of the Border was firmly in the hands of the Inner Austrian Estates (Styria, Carinthia and Carniola), with the district regiments synonymous with the administration of the district. Two central districts known as the 1st and 2nd Banal regiments (Petrinja, Kostajnica) were nominally commanded, but

---

[15] T.J. Winnifrith. *The Vlachs: The History of a Balkan People,* London: Palgrave Macmillan, 1987, p.129

not controlled, by the Ban of Croatia. Senior appointments in all regiments were reserved for the *Hofkriegsrat*. Although the Croatian nobility continually struggled to maintain their own control of the region, the Military Border was kept explicitly separate from the legal, administrative and political system of the Hungarian provinces of Croatia and Slavonia.

In places scarcely thirty miles wide, the zone covered the southern flank of 'Civil Croatia' and shielded it from Ottoman territory. The Border divided Civil Croatia from Slavonia, reaching northwards to touch Austria. From the 1550's until the late 1680's, the Habsburg defensive zone passed eastwards through the Magyar parts of Royal Hungary. After Ottoman Hungary was recovered following the second siege of Vienna, the Border achieved its final form. It now included the Velebit highlands just north of Knin and passed west of the border of Bosnia and north to the Kupa, and in a northward extension west of the Ilova to the Drava, flanking the city of Zagreb.

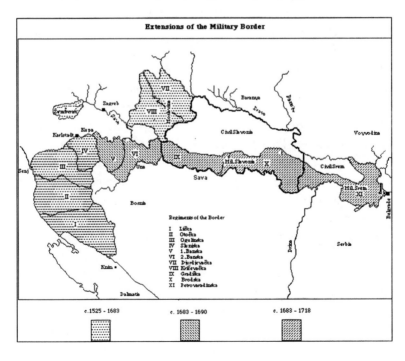

Extensions of the Military Border

Regiments of the Border

I Lička
II Otočka
III Ogulinska
IV Slunjska
V 1.Banska
VI 2.Banska
VII Djurdjevačka
VIII Križevačka
IX Gradiška
X Brodska
XI Petrovaradinska

c.1525 - 1683   c. 1683 - 1690   c. 1683 - 1718

The chief fortress in Syrmia was at Petrovaradin across the Danube from Novi Sad (Ger. Neusatz, Hung. Ujvidek, Lat. Neoplanta). East of the Croatian Border a new section was added in 1702: the Slavonian Border, which ran due east along the northern bank of the Sava until it reached Syrmia (Srem) and came within sight of the Turkish garrison in Belgrade.

Civil Croatia was scarcely bigger than the Croatian Border, and even narrower between Karlstadt and Austria. The laws and most administration remained under local control. Though their jurisdiction was overriden by the administration and liberties of the Military Border, that was an Austrian dispensation in favor of the Grenzer and not a real or legal submission to Hungary. This is far from being a theoretical distinction. At every stage in the history of Austria's relationship with Hungary, Vienna counted on local Croatian support to moderate or oppose the endless truculence of Hungarian magnates and politicians.

Croatia was the focus of a double imperative. The first was military: the Serbs were needed to fight. But the second was political and never diminished: the Croatian Sabor, and those it represented, was needed to manage Hungary successfully. In 1102, as we have seen, Croatia had entered a personal union with the crown of St. Stephen, not a legal union with Hungary. Its statehood (*Pacta Conventa*) was not extinguished. This continuity was reiterated in 1527 when the crown of St. Stephen passed to Archduke Ferdinand of Austria. Austrian monarchs and Hungarian officials tried, at times, to curtail Croatia's self-rule, but the legal entity of 'Croatia' survived under the Habsburgs since the dynasty had every reason to retain it, ensuring that there was no discontinuity in the nominal claim to statehood. The notion of *state rights* helped form the nation in the modern era. It included the key claim that no inhabitants of Croatia should escape the jurisdiction of the elite, the Croatian 'political nation.'

For the upholders of Croatia's *state rights* the Serbs were unwelcome and alien intruders for as long as they insisted on retaining their name, privileges, and Orthodox faith. An obsessive aristocratic resentment at Grenzer privilieges was passed on from generation to generation of Croatia's social and political elite, and continued to wield a strong influence even after the collapse of feudalism in 1848. At the historical root of ethnic cleansing in twentieth-century Croatia lay a determination – four centuries old – to impose legal and religious homogeneity and to re-establish political obedience.[16]

For much of the early-modern era the Austrians could afford to ignore the grievances of the Croatian gentry in respect of the Border, but the Crown came to the defense of the Grenzer if the pressure from the Croatian Estates became oppressive. An effective Habsburg line of defense against the Turks demanded not only a chain of fortified strongpoints but also a reliable population settled around them. A grant of royal land and legal status superior to the peasantry of Civil Croatia in return for life-long loyal military service was a mutually attractive and straightforward deal. That the combative Serbian settlers in the borderlands were rewarded for their military services to the Crown by being relieved of all feudal dues ('contributions') to the Croatian-Hungarian nobility was of no consequence to the authorities in Vienna or Graz. The latter were happy to let the *Krajišnici* elect their own captains (*voivode*) and magistrates (*knezovi*). Their obligatory labor service (*rabota*) was limited to the maintenance of fortifications, and the Kaiser might intervene to ensure it was not abused by local commanders. They could engage in trade, including in cattle and even salt, without paying customs. Since the land was mostly infertile this was necessary, though there were also some damaging commercial restrictions which kept the *Vojna Krajina* economically underdeveloped.

At a critical moment of the Thirty Years War, in 1630, Grenzer privileges, primarily religious, were codified by Ferdinand II in the *Statuta Valachorum* and repeatedly

---

[16] Cf. E.A. Hammel, "Demography and the Origins of the Yugoslav Civil War." *Anthropology Today* 9 (1): 4-9 (February 1993), Royal Anthropological Institute of Great Britain and Ireland.

confirmed thereafter. They came as the Crown's response to the refusal of the Croatian Diet to recognize Ferdinand's earlier privileges granted to the Orthodox in the Varaždin Generalcy. In 1627 the *Warasdiner Grenzer* responded by asserting that they "would rather be hacked to pieces than separated from their officers and made subjects of the Croatian nobility."[17] The Statutes finally removed the Grenzer from the judicial authority of the Croatian Diet and formally placed them under direct Crown jurisdiction.

Under the Statutes each village was to have a head (*knez*) elected annually at the popular assembly. The heads were obliged to maintain the lists of trained able-bodied men liable for military service, to adjudicate minor disputes and to refer more serious cases for trial by the 'Great Judges' or captaincy tribunals. Village heads and prominent men in each captaincy chose from among their own one Great Judge and eight deputies, also on an annual basis.

The *Statutes* effectively granted the Krajina an extensive local autonomy. They were a carefully crafted document which took into account the traditions, aspirations, and way of life of the Grenzer community. They also reflected the desire of German officers to keep that community supervised and to deploy its human resources for military purposes as efficiently as possible. All males were entered on their Regiment's muster roll at birth and were liable for service from 16 to 60 years of age. In view of the life expectancy at that time, the Grenzer were effectively liable for life-long service. The *Militärgrenzrechte* required that "all able-bodied male inhabitants have an obligation of service and are subject to military discipline… the laws bind them to drill periods and a willing acceptance of the relevant orders given to them by their senior officers."[18]

[17] Gunther E. Rothenberg, *The Military Border in Croatia 1740-1881*. Chicago-London: University of Chicago Press, 1966, p.10.

[18] David Hollins. *Austrian Frontier Troops, 1740-98*. Oxford: Osprey Publishing, 2005.

With the Statutes the Austrian authorities finally vetoed the establishment of neo-feudal institutions in the Military Frontier. Emperor Leopold I issued a new decree in July 1659, confirming the privileges contained in the Statutes, when he allowed a fresh group of Orthodox settlers into the Karlovac Generalcy. Another similar document followed in 1666. The decisive intervention of the Crown meant that overwhelming majority of Serbs in Croatia *had never been serfs*. The Grenzer had no share in the feudal and neo-feudal habits of thought, institutions and social structures imposed on their Croat neighbors. They saw those institutions and structures, reasonably enough, as a threat to their status and identity. Until the end of the Border they insisted on remaining under the jurisdiction of the Imperial military authorities and the spiritual authority of their own Orthodox Church.

Emperor Ferdinand was fortunate that, following the end of the 'Long War' in 1606, the Turks were kept busy fighting Persia in today's Iraq and quelling internal revolts. The long border truce, coupled with the codification of Grenzer privileges, enabled him to mobilize a total of 25 regiments for use as Imperial line troops on the battlefields of Germany and Bohemia during the decisive 'Swedish' phase of the Thirty Year War.

The maintenance of the Grenzer way of life and traditional culture was enhanced by a specific form of their family organization and land tenure. The Military Border was an agrarian society whose members were defined by two social roles, those of the free peasant and the lifetime soldier. The greater part of their lives, however, was spent making a living as farmers. They lived in extended farming households (*zadruga*, *Hauskommunion*), typically comprising three to five married couples and their offspring, in which the *pater familias* and his wife exercised the final authority. The land was owned not by those who farmed it but by the authorities, and classed as Imperial *Lehen* (feuds). Plots measuring 8-12 *Joch* (12-18 acres) were granted to households in lieu of pay. Each family in turn was obliged to provide the army with a fixed number of soldiers, subject to a maximum of three for infantry and two for hussars.

The *zadruga* was a community based on blood, kinship, culture and economics. It was a traditional Serbian institution: there is no evidence for joint family structure among the medieval Croats, but there are numerous documents from the 14th and 15th centuries showing that joint family organization was well established in Serbia. Its value as a source of good soldiers and the backbone of a stable order was recognized by the Austrian military authorities. In 1737 *zadruga* ownership and common law inheritance practices were codified by Joseph Friedrich, Herzog zu Sachsen-Hildburghausen, general commanding Karlovac and Varaždin. The military approved the joint household organization, "especially since the regions west of Karlovac were then, as now [early 1995], preponderantly Orthodox, among whom joint family organization is clearly traditional from the mediaeval Serbian evidence."[19] Because the zadruga was based on a patrilocal system, when a girl married, she left her parents' zadruga and joined that of her husband. Within the zadruga, all of the family members worked to ensure that the needs of every other member were met. No zadruga could be split without prior approval from the captaincy or regiment to which they belonged.

Such land tenure format had a major weakness, however: a successful defense of the Border by the Grenzer was bound to lead to a growing population in an area of limited capacity, and the demands of military service would keep farmers away from agricultural work and make new technologies hard to introduce. The result was a chronic economic crisis in the Military Border, starting in the 1750s. It was evident in the rise in landlessness and the stagnation of agricultural production, which coincided with the expansion of a standardized administration.

The combination of frequent military service and subsistence agriculture guaranteed economic stagnation. The Grenzer prided themselves on their freedom from feudal

---

[19] E.A. Hammel and Kenneth W. Wachter, *The Slavonian Census of 1698*, pp. 145-166 (University of California at Berkeley, 1995)

obligation, but it meant that – unlike in the villages of Civil Croatia – there were no market-oriented landlords to force serfs to adopt new farming methods.[20] The Grenzer were caught in a social and economic bind. In the 18th century, since the Turks were still in Bosnia but a declining threat, they were increasingly used not merely as local militia for border patrols and quarantine enforcement, but increasingly as infantry in line regiments.[21] Their farmsteads stagnated, or declined.

The increased demands of the military administration for soldiers meant that Grenzer communities needed large families to cover for the frequent and prolonged absence of fighting men from the fields. Warfare did not cease as the Ottomans became less powerful. A border tradition continued with the 'Turks' of Bosnia, mostly Slavic converts to Islam, as the local enemy.

---

[20] Lohr Miller's review of Karl Miller, *Freier Bauer und Soldat: Die Militarisierung der agrarischen Gesellschaft and der kroatisch-slowanischen Militargrenze 1535-1881* (Vienna, 1997) <www.Habsburg.com> April 1998.

[21] The Grenz regiments were based on three battalions. The first two battalions went to war; the third formed the reserve. The Croatian Border gave 11 regiments during the Napoleonic Wars. They were: 1. Liccaner-Gospić; 2. Otocaner-Otočac; 3. Oguliner-Ogulin; 4. Szluiner-Karlstadt; 5. Warasdiner-Kreuzer-Belovar; 6. Warasdiner-St.Georger-Belovar; 7. Brooder-Vincovce; 8. Gradiscaner-Neugradisca; 9. Peterwardiner-Mitrovitz; 10. First Banal-Glina; and 11. Second Banal-Petrinja. See map on p. 29.

The Great Serbian Migration of 1690

Throughout the 16th and 17th centuries thousands of Serbs migrated each year from Bosnia and other Ottoman lands into the Military Border. All previous population movements were dwarfed by the mass migration from southern Serbia, Kosovo and northern Macedonia in the spring of 1690, led by Patriarch Arsenije III Čarnojević (depicted in a 19th century painting by Paja Jovanović, below). This exodus was the result of political and military developments in distant lands. The French threat to the Habsburgs' western flank at the beginning of the the Nine Years' War caused the Austrians to withdraw from the Balkans the forces which had taken Belgrade in 1688. The Austrians had recovered Hungary and were willing to consolidate their gains by marching south. On their advance into Serbia – they reached as far as Peć in Metohija – Habsburg troops had been joined by thousands of Serbian volunteers, encouraged by Austrian promises of liberation and deliveries of arms. In the winter of 1689-1690 they grasped that they were about to be left in the lurch. They also knew that they would be regarded by the Turks as rebellious *dhimmis* whose very lives, families, and property were forfeit under the Islamic sharia law.

Fearful of Turkish retribution, between 50,000 and 80,000 Serbs – volunteers, their family members, and other civilians – withdrew in a single column from Kosovo and other southern Serbian lands with the Austrian army in early spring of 1690. They reached the right banks of the Sava and the Danube three weeks later. In April of that year Emperor Leopold I (1658-1707) issued his *Letter of Invitation*, in which he called on them to cross the rivers and settle in the Habsburg realm. The Patriarch called an ecclesiastical and national assembly in Belgrade (*Beogradski sabor*) on June 18 at which it was decided to accept Leopold as 'Serbian King' and to continue the war against the Turks. (The Croatian gentry were not alone in their political nostalgia.) War against France became the Emperor's chief priority, however, and the regular forces withdrawn from Serbia were transferred to the Rhine.

In urgent need of soldiers to defend and farmers to settle the newly acquired southern borderlands, Leopold I (l.) issued his first Charter on Privileges on August 21, 1690 – others followed in 1691 and 1695 – in which he pledged to take the Serbs 'into royal protection.' He recognized their status within the Monarchy as a separate political entity (*corpus separatum*), under the authority of the Serbian Orthodox Church. Leopold's grants were the pillar of the the 'Serbian Privileges,' the foundation for the autonomous corporate development of the Serbian community in the Habsburg Monarchy.[22] Leopold guaranteed its right to "a free exercise of rite and religion, with no fear, danger, or harm to body or property."

[22] Jovan Radonić and Mita Kostić. *Srpske privilegije od 1690 do 1792.* Belgrade: Naučna knjiga, 1954.

Having received the guarantees on September 29, 1690, the Serbs – led by their Patriarch – started crossing the Sava and Danube. This migration significantly increased the number of Serbs in the Monarchy and changed the character of the Military Frontier. This change was reflected in the detailed Slavonian Census, undertaken by the Austrian authorities in 1698.[23]

A similar process was under way in Dalmatia, too, where Venice, after two hundred years of sustained commitment to the defense of the coastal communes, had enjoyed military success against the Ottomans. The Venetians were willing to accept 'Morlachs' as settlers in newly acquired but largely depopulated Dalmatian hinterland. The reason of state which guided Austria and Venice in granting privileges could not, however, shape a full and final religious settlement. Religious toleration conceded in Protestant Europe tended to become permanent, but in Catholic Europe it did not. The Roman Catholic hierarchy in Croatia and Dalmatia was never reconciled to the 'schismatics' being legalized or to Orthodox bishops operating freely on the territory of Catholic bishoprics.

Within months of leaving Serbia, Patriarch Arsenije started receiving reports that Roman Catholic clergy were exerting pressure on the newly-arrived Serbs to convert or accept the Union. Upon complaining to the Emperor, he was granted the *Diploma of Protection* for the Serbs and their religion (December 11, 1690). The following year the Patriarch was able to obtain from Leopold a new, explicit confirmation of the right to exercise authority over all Orthodox Serbs in the Habsburg lands. That right was granted at a time when the Great Turkish War was far from over and the Serbs' military service was considered essential to the success of Austrian arms. The war had taken a favorable turn for the Austrians in preceding years. The Ottoman Empire was showing signs of political, economic and cultural decrepitude which were reflected on the battlefield.

---

[23] Mažuran, I. *Popis naselja i stanovnistva u Slavoniji 1698. godine*, vol. 2, JAZU, Osijek, 1988.

The Turks were decisively beaten at the Battle of Senta on September 11, 1697, in which the Serbian light cavalry played a key part (Franz Eisenhut's 19th century painting, below). The Treaty of Karlowitz[24] was signed on January 26, 1699, thus ending the Great Turkish War. The Treaty came at the end of a two-month congress between the Ottoman Empire on one side and the Holy League, a coalition of European powers created in 1684, after the second siege of Vienna, that included the Habsburg Monarchy, Poland, Venice and Russia.[25]

The Great Turkish War and Prince Eugene of Savoy's subsequent victory at Belgrade in 1717, marked the end of Ottoman military advantages in Europe. The Sultan's realm now began to shrink. The Turks were forced to relinquish Hungary, Transylvania and Slavonia to Austria. Most of Ottoman-ruled Dalmatia passed to Venice, including the heavily Serb-inhabited Dalmatian hinterland centered on the Krajina of Knin. Belgrade and central Serbia returned to Turkish control, however. (Belgrade would be captured three more times, only to be surrendered again, in 1739, 1791 and 1813; the Ottomans finally handed over the keys of the Kalemagdan fortress in 1867.)

In 1702 the Military Border was extended eastward with the creation of the Slavonian District, in addition to the three 'Generalcies' established earlier (Karlovac-Karlstadt, Varaždin and Petrinja). In 1712 Lika-Krbava were added to the Karlstadt Generalcy. The Hungarian and Croat Estates, as always, continued to object to the existence of this exception to their authority. After the Peace of Karlowitz they argued that the diminishing threat from the Turks no longer justified its existence. The Grenzer, as always, resisted any change with protests and violence. The Habsburgs were on the whole supportive of the maintenance of their privileges, but remained in two minds about the ecclesiastical concession to followers of the 'non-Uniate Greek rite.' Vienna knew the value of its Orthodox subjects, not only as reliable soldiers but also as a weapon against the unruly nobles; yet it was clearly hoped that they would become Roman Catholics in the fulness time.

Despite their origins as border guards the Grenzer gradually became an important element of the Austrian army, notably so after the reforms of the 1740'sunder Empress Maria Theresa. In the wars of the 18th century they appeared on battlefields all over Europe as line regiments, after 1769 formally so, outfitted in new uniforms. They were best used as a mobile skirmishing force, a role for which they required no tactical training. In the wars of Spanish and Austrian Succession and in the Seven Years' War their losses routinely reached 25-30 percent per campaign, well in excess of those of other Imperial troops. In the Seven Years' War the Military Border contributed 88,000 soldiers in all, an enormous number considering its population base. They were the best soldiers in the Habsburg army. Military historians have noted that, "[f]ar from being passive conscript hordes, the Grenzer had a lively sense of their dignity and what was due to them, and in this respect they may be compared with the yeoman archers of late medieval England."[26]

---

[26] Christopher Duffy, *Instrument of War: The Austrian Army in the Seven Years War*. Emperor's Press, 2000, p 304

The Grenzer were tough and used to living off the land, hostile or not; often they were left with no choice in the matter. This inevitably created serious command problems: "Officers were unable to restrain the Grenzer, whose passion for drink and plunder was ungovernable and who, even in friendly territory, were a terror to the inhabitants."[27] They were unruly, admitted a sympathetic 19th century observer, but often unfairly maligned:

> Day and night they carried their rifles and, until 1872, guarded the frontier against the age-old enemies of Christianity. In addition, they kept away the deadly epidemics from our Monarchy. Indeed, this soldier-people, in a self-sacrificing manner, impacted the fortunes of our Royal House and the Emperor... through much bloodshed willingly endured. No branch of the Austrian-Hungarian family of nations is so little known and at the same time so wrongly judged as this soldier-people... judged only on the basis of the tradition of excesses by the embittered Grenzers in the field of battle.[28]

Though the Croatian feudal and clerical establishment regarded the Serbs as an alien group and a threat, relations among the frontiersmen of Orthodox and Catholic faith were mostly correct. They had a common interest in not being feudalized, and "there were cases where protesting against feudal encumbrances, homesteaders of Catholic and Orthodox religion acted in solidarity."[29] Although they were deliberately isolated from Croatian society, the relatively favourable social situation of the Serb frontiersmen encouraged bonded peasants of Catholic faith to demand equality of rights with the frontiersmen.

---

[27] Rothenberg, op. cit., p.20

[28] František Vaníček, *Specialgeschichte der Militärgrenze: Aus Originalquellen und Quellenwerken geschöpft*. Vienna: Kaiserlich-Königliche Hof- und Staatsdruckerei, 1875.

[29] Vasilije Krestić, *Through Genocide to Greater Croatia*, Belgrade: BIGZ, 1997, p.20.

The 1699 Treaty of Karlowitz (octagonal 18th century building commemorating the famous tent, r.) registered a shift in military power. The Ottomans retained the ability to mobilize impressively large armies and support them in the field, but they had plainly lost their old military advantage. Prince Eugene of Savoy scored a string of striking victories which suggested that the Ottoman grip  on the Balkans would have unravelled in the 18th century if the balance of power among Christian powers of Europe had not continued to favour the Turks.

The destruction of Hungary as a great power in 1526 had presented Austria a challenge which, with the assistance of Venice, it was able to meet. The recovery of Hungary ensured that the Habsburg Monarchy, as the leading power in Central Europe, would remain the major force in the western Balkans until 1918. The subsequent treaties of Passarowitz (Požarevac, 1718) and Belgrade (1739) set the borders in the Western Balkans for over a century to come.

Habsburg Austria and Hungary, 'Indivisible and Inseparable'

Religious Pressure

Medieval Serbia, baptized with other Slavs into Christianity by ss. Cyril and Methodius, was firmly Orthodox by the time of her glory in the late 13th and the first half of the 14th centuries. It was not affected by the Union of Florence (*Laetantur caeli*) of 1439 which caused such destabilizing turmoil in the final decade of Byzantium. Quite the contrary, the spirit of 'fighting Orthodoxy' was prevalent among the newcomers and the cult and folk-poetry of the Kosovo battle was firmly entrenched in their collective memory as they crossed the rivers into Habsburg lands:

> Cultural, ideological and religious homogenization was their collective response to the collapse of the Serbian state and the resulting dispersion. The sense, rampant after the fall of Smederevo [the huge and powerful Serbian fortress on the Danube which fell in 1459], that the emerging Serbian diaspora cannot find peace and quiet unless the Kingdom is re-conquered and rebuilt, that it is doomed to endless blood-letting, acquired a higher meaning in the willing martyrdom of Prince Lazar.[30]

Faced with a massive influx of 'schismatic' Serb warriors, the nobility and Roman Catholic clergy of Civil Croatia became closely allied in seeking to preserve the feudal privileges of the former and the religious monopoly of the latter. For different reasons they were equally loath to accept the special status of Serb frontiersmen as permanent. Almost from the moment the Military Border was established they subjected the *Grenzer* to a constant double pressure: to turn them into serfs subject to feudal law and the nobility, and to force them to accept the authority of the Roman Catholic hierarchy. That pressure took different forms over the centuries yet remained the same in its key goals.

---

[30] Hemmel, op. cit. (1993)

The Croatian Diet (*Sabor*) passed a law in 1608 saying that only Roman Catholics could live and enjoy rights in Croatia. This measure was the result of the 'Long War' Austria fought with the Turks from 1593 to 1606, during which thousands of Serbs moved into the area of the Varaždin Generalacy of the Military Border. The area of modern-day western Slavonia and Podravina became known as Nova Rascia, and its spiritual center was at the Marča monastery built by the Serbian Orthodox Archmandrite (from 1607 Bishop) Simeon Vretanja. He went to Patriarch Jovan in Peć to have his status confirmed in 1607. Immediately upon his return Bishop Simeon came under intense pressure from the Bishop of Zagreb, Petar Domitrović, to accept the Union, meaning Roman authority and a licence for Orthodox rites. Vretanja succumbed to the pressure, and in 1611 went to Rome to accept the confirmation of his episcopal status from the pope. In the end he severed all links with the Patriarchate at Peć.

Vretanja's successors, bishops Maksim and Gavrilo Predojević and Gavrilo Mijakić, after periods of hesitation, returned to the fold of Orthodoxy. Bishop of Zagreb Benedict Vinković was compelled to ask Rome in 1640 to appoint a bishop 'of Roman faith' instead of Maksim Predojević, and to order the Austrian military authorities to prevent Orthodox priests and monks from crossing into Habsburg lands. Vinković also advocated the establishment of a seminary for Uniate priests who would bring the Serbs into Rome's fold. He asked the authorities to set aside a special budget to encourage conversion, with money rewards for those who become Catholic. Vinković recommended the Canon of Zagreb, Raphail Levaković, as the new Bishop of Marča, quoting as his qualifications his knowledge of the Cyrillic script and Eastern liturgy.

Vinković's successor Bishop Petar Petretić complained that it was wrong "to establish a diocese for the Serbs and to allow their priests and monks to come into the Empire as they are the biggest obstacle to the Union." A 19th century Croatian historian noted of Petretić that the Union was the main focus of his life:

In that endeavor he was tireless, working publicly and privately at Hungarian and Croatian Diets. He got the Orthodox living in the Varaždin and Križevci regions to succumb to him, because the appointment of their bishops depended exclusively on him ... Much more could be said of this, but it would not be to the credit of the upper Croatian clergy, who greatly fanned the religious hatred in the land. Their proselytizing zeal could only be justified by the fact that they were being constantly egged on by Rome to persist in the endeavor of the Union.[31]

The resistance of the flock was so strong that Uniate bishops of Marča, appointed from Zagreb after 1670, were reluctant to take possession of their see. The issue remained unresolved until 1734, when the Crown sent a commission to examine the Varaždin Grenzers' religious allegiance and found that hardly any supported the Union. It subsequently allowed the appointment of Simeon Filipović as the Orthodox Bishop in the Generalcy of Varaždin. Marča remained under Uniate control, but devoid of the flock. The integration in the early 1700s of newly-acquired territories into Austria's legal and administrative system displayed the Habsburgs' opportunistic attitude toward their new Serbian subjects. This task was entrusted to the Archbishop of Esztergom and Primate of all Hungary, Count Leopold Graf Kollonitsch.

Cardinal Kollonitsch was determined to ensure that tens of thousands of Serbs who had crossed into the Habsburg domain during the war should become Uniates, that is, accept Roman Catholic ecclesiatical authority with a licence to use Orthodox rites. In 1706 he advised the Court that any future confirmation of Serb privileges – customary when a new monarch ascended the throne, as was about to happen that year – should be "qualified by unclear terms and ambiguous words, which may be understood and interpreted in different ways at different times."

---

[31] Ivan Kukuljević Sakcinski, *Književnici u Hrvatah u prvoj polovini XVII vieka.* Zagreb 1868.

In Kollonitsch's view Serbian Patriarch Arsenije III was the very son of the devil (*solius diaboli filius*) and his flock were but the devil's dependents, *diaboli asseclas,* and as such the enemies of God and Emperor.[32] It was therefore necessary to ensure, "quietly and with little fuss," that these people be unified with the Church of Rome "even against their will." The Roman Catholic Bishop of Senj (Segna), Martin Brajković, went further and demanded the right to arrest and punish any Orthodox Bishop who would dare enter his diocese without prior approval. This was of course contrary to the privileges granted to the Serbs by Leopold I, while the war was still going on. It specifically violated his decree of March 4, 1695, giving the Patriarch the right to bring all Serbian Orthodox dioceses in Croatia, Slavonia and Hungary under his authority. But far from being treated as permanent, such concessions were viewed as expedients determined by *raison d'etat*: As long as the services of the Orthodox Grenzer were needed, their religion was respected;

> but when the need had passed, the throne did nothing to restrain the efforts of the Catholic hierarchy, which, with the zealous collaboration of the military, attempted forcibly to convert the Orthodox or at least to coerce them to accept the Uniate rites.[33]

Once the Great Turkish War was over, the default assumptions soon revived. They were not confined to Roman Catholic prelates like Kollonitsch or Brajković. The Crown Commission for newly acquired lands – a secular body – also saw the Serb newcomers unsympathetically as "schismatics who are headed by the man we know as the Archbishop of the Serbs and whom they call Patriarch, and follow him in all matters." In the same spirit, Governor of Slavonia Guido Wald Rüdiger Count von Starhemberg (a cousin of Ernst, the celebrated

---

[32] *Istorija srpskog naroda*, Beograd: Srpska književna zadruga, Vol. IV-1, pp. 39-40.

[33] Rothenberg, *The Military Border in Croatia* (1966), p. 29.

commander of Vienna during the siege of 1683) submitted a report on the Military Frontier on August 29, 1699, in which he singled out Serbian Orthodox priests as potentially dangerous elements because of their influence on the common people. He suggested that the right of the Serbian Patriarch to appoint bishops and ordain priests should be terminated.

After the Peace of Karlowitz the resentment of the Croatian-Hungarian aristocracy and ecclesiestical hierarchy of the Serbs' privileged status became more sharply pronounced than before. The Turks were on the defensive, they argued, and the privileges granted to the 'schismatics' had become an intolerable anomaly. The overseer of the Zagreb diocesan landholdings, Ambroz Kuzmić, in a report dated November 13, 1700, suggested that they should be "slaughtered, rather than settled down," as they were "more of a nuisance to the noble state illumined by the Emperor than an advantage... neither the Emperor's radiance nor the noble state will ever be at peace with them."[34] This may have been the first proposal of its kind for a radical and final solution of the 'Serb problem' in Croatia: it was by no means the last.

In October 1701 the Emperor tried to limit the authority of the Patriarch to the Serbian Orthodox cathedral of Szentender (Sentandreja), just north of Budapest. Arsenije promptly responded by asking for the right to take his people to the jurisdiction of "another Christian king" (a clear allusion to Russia) where they would be free to practice their faith. The growing climate of intolerance was such that in early 1702 a thousand Serbian families moved back to Turkish territory without seeking prior Austrian approval. The following year Leopold ordered Arsenije to stop using the title of the Patriarch: he was reduced in rank to the 'Metropolitan of Szentendre' (Sentandreja), a title which was never accepted by Serbs. Also in early 1703, Cardinal Kollonitsch wrote to Pope Clement XI that his goal to impose union on all schismatics was "within reach."

---

[34] Patrick Barriot, Eve Crépin, *On assassine un peuple: les Serbes de Krajina*. Paris: L'Age d'Homme, 1995, p. 33.

The pressure on the Serbs to convert – growing after the Peace of Karlowitz – came to a sudden halt in June 1703, however, when Ferenc (Francis) II Rákóczi started the Hungarian uprising against the Habsburgs. Austria suddenly needed the Grenzer again, especially since a major part of the Imperial army was busy fighting the French in the War of Spanish Succession. On November 2, 1703, the Imperial Cabinet

asked Patriarch Arsenije III (l.), who was in Vienna at that time, to tour the southern regions. His brief was to ensure that the Serbs not only stay faithful to the Emperor, but also agreed to fight Rakoczi's forces. In return, their privileges granted between 1690 and 1695 would be reinstated and reiterated. In the event most Serbs remained loyal to the Imperial authorities, although their settlements were subjected to attacks by bands of Hungarian insurgents. Rakoczi's insurrection was still in full

swing in May 1705 when Leopold I died and was succeeded by his son Joseph I (1705-1711). The new Emperor confirmed all previous privileges of the Serbs in August 1706, emphasized their services in fighting both Turks and Rakoczi, and promised to extend those privileges in the future.

Following Patriarch Arsenije's death in October 1706, the issue facing the Serbs in the Habsburg Monarchy was whether to set up a separate ecclesiastical authority or to maintain their link with the Patriarchate of Peć (below), which was under Ottoman rule. The former was the option favored both by the court in Vienna and by the Roman Catholic Church. The alternative was to accept the nominal authority of the new Patriarch of Peć, Kalinik I, whose appointment had to be approved by the Porte. A diplomatically astute Greek who understood the art of the possible, Kalinik resolved the issue by issuing an edict in 1710 which granted *de facto* autonomy to the 'Metropolitans of Krušedol,' Arsenije's successors. (Krušedol was the foremost Serbian Orthodox monastery in Srem.) At the same time, however, Kalinik retained the nominal canonical hierarchy, even though his authority remained only notional for the rest of the 18th century.

In 1741 the Banal authorities of Civil Croatia succeeded in having some Orthodox rights abrogated and the westernmost Orthodox monastery at Gomirje (r.) was taken over by Uniate priests escorted by Ban's soldiers. The decision was soon reversed, following a revolt of Serb Grenzers posted in Bavaria during the War of Austrian Succession. Another mutiny broke out during that same war in 1744 when soldiers got the news – which eventually proved to be wrong – that their families were to be forcibly converted to Catholicism while they were fighting in Germany. For some exasperated officers and their men, the only permanent solution appeared to be emigration to the only Orthodox Christian power, Russia. Several thousand eventually made the move under Catherine the Great, settling a tract of land optimistically called 'New Serbia' in today's southern Ukraine.[35]

The numbers of people eventually known as 'Serbs' and 'Croats' in the Military Border has been for decades, and still is, a politically charged question. It remains a matter of dispute among modern historians. In 1785 and in 1797, Austrian census takers counted some 380,000 Orthodox inhabitants in the Border. They and their Roman Catholic neighbors shared the traits of a common *Grenzer* identity but they lived in separate communites. They shared a common freedom from serfdom and a common history of military accomplishment, but they remained Orthodox

---

[35] This is a key theme in Miloš Crnjanski's epic novel *Migrations* (*Seobe*).

or Catholic and thus divided. It has been argued that their identities had remained 'pre-national' until the early 1800s, but that is not correct. The people crossing into Panonia with the Patriarch in 1699 did not belong to an ethnically undifferentiated multitude. They were politically and proto-nationally Serbs, and they were bringing the soul of their future nationhood with them. Having obtained self-governance from the Emperor they were most unlikely to be converted to something different, either confesionally or nationally. Once nationality was politicised, however, they became adherents of one of the two rival national movements. The root cause was religious:

> Throughout the Border there was a sharp and permanent division along confessional lines. Serb refugees moving up out of the Ottoman lands found their Orthodoxy to be a major means of maintaining any village-level cohesion. And in a region where villages were often isolated from one another, where roads were more often used to move troops than goods and ideas, local churches and clerics, both Catholic and Orthodox, enjoyed leadership roles.[36]

There were few diversified economic interest groups or social classes in the Border that could provide an alternative basis for integration. Local identifications with village, family, and church were not eroded by military service. Quite the contrary: given the territorialization imposed by the canton system, local bonds were solidified by regimental service. Isolated by geography and deliberately kept apart from Civil Croatia by the military administration, the Grenzers' identity was ready to develop from a confessional base of the early modern era into the spirit of 1848 and its aftermath.

---

[36] Lohr Miller's review of Karl Miller, *Freier Bauer und Soldat,* published on Habsburg.com in April 1998.

Dalmatian Serbs Under Venice, France and Austria

T he large Serb community at the southwestern end of the Krajina crescent was centered on Knin. Once the Turks had lost it, Knin remained under Venetian sovereignty until the abolition of the Republic in 1797. Venice's Slavic subjects in the Dinaric hinterland, both Orthodox and Roman Catholic, were collectively referred to as 'Morlacchi.'[37] This term was originally used to describe the pre-Slavic nomadic population of early-medieval times, but it continued to be applied well into the modern era, long after the South Slav identity of most of them was beyond doubt, and so became a misnomer: an old ethnic name for a large social category.

In the 18th century Abbe Alberto Fortis visited the 'Morlachs' of Dalmatia. In his famous travelogue, which was widely read all over Europe, he noted that they sang epic poetry in Serbian, to the sound of *gusle,* about the Battle of Kosovo and the glories of medieval Serbian kings.[38] Fortis also noted social and religious tensions throughout 'Morlacchia':

> A most perfect discord reigns ... as it generally does in other parts, between Latin and Greek [Orthodox] communion, which their respective priests fail not to foment, and tell a thousand little scandalous stories of each other.

The long struggle for supremacy along the eastern shore of the Adriatic between the Republic of Venice and the Ottoman Empire ended in Venice's favor at the beginning of the 18th

---

[37] See Larry Wolff. *Venice and the Slavs: The Discovery of Dalmatia in the Age of Enlightenment.* Stanford University Press, 2001. The territorial militia composed of the Morlacchi was known as the *Craina* (p. 133)

[38] *Viaggio in Dalmazia* (1774), recently re-published in English as *Travels Into Dalmatia,* New York: Cosimo Classics, 2007. A true man of the Enlightenment, Fortis saw the superior Italian civilization of Venice as a corrupting influence on the primitive and natural customs and culture of the *Morlacchi* – the noble savages of the Eastern Adriatic.

century. All of Dalmatia – the Slav Catholic coastal strip, with its now Italian-speaking urban elites, and the Slav Orthodox hinterlands – became a Venetian possession. The Signoria of Venice, not unlike Leopold of Austria, made concessions. The Serbs were placed under the spiritual jurisdiction of the Ecumenical Patriarch of Constantinople and his Greek 'Archbishop of Philadelphia' who resided in Venice. But in subsequent decades Venice exerted a great deal of pressure on the Orthodox. The pressure was often uneven, however, reflecting a lack of consistent state policy in the Republic's eastern territories. Just as in Austria, the Serbs were under stricter limitations in peaceful times, and freer to practice their religion unhindered when their military services were needed in time of war.

In 1686 the Republic decreed that all Orthodox priests in its territory should submit to the authority of local Roman Catholic bishops. The order proved impossible to apply, however, and it was not enforced. A decade later, at the height of the Great Turkish War, the decision was reversed and Serbian Patriarch Arsenije III was allowed to send Bishop Basil of Bosnia to manage the affairs of the Orthodox Church in Dalmatia. Dalmatian Governor-General (*provveditore generale*) Danielle Dolfino initially granted the Serbs in the city of Šibenik (Sebenico) full religious freedom. In 1702 the grant was extended to the entire province: the Senate confirmed Nikodim Bušović – a valued ally of Venice in the war that ended with the Peace of Karlowitz three years earlier – as Bishop of Dalmatia and gave him tracts of state land in Bukovica.

Three years later, in 1705, with the Turkish border peaceful once again, the edict was rescinded and Bishop Nikodim was ordered to submit to the Roman Catholic bishop of Split – effectively to become a Uniate.[39] When he refused and seven

---

[39] Nikodim Milaš: *Documenta spectantia historiam Dalmatiae et Istriae a XV usgue ad XIX saeculum* (Zara 1894), pp. 63-64 and 76-78. His Latin title was *Archiepiscopus Jadertinus*. Jadera is better rendered as Zadar than as Zara. But this city, above all, was Italian-speaking.

thousand Serbs gathered to protest the order, Bishop Nikodim was accused of instigating a rebellion and had to flee. He returned to Dalmatia many years later, at the end of his life. The pressure was further increased when the new Roman Catholic bishop of Zara (Zadar), Vincenzo (Vicko) Zmajević, took over the see in 1713. He was a determined upholder of the principle that only one bishop – in this case, he – could exercise authority in any one diocese. Nikodim's successor, Bishop Savatije Ljubibratić of Hum (Herzegovina), often had to stay in seclusion at Nikodim's monastic cell in Vrlika when visiting Dalmatia. Only Savatije's income from his diocesan lands in Herzegovina enabled him to finance the building and reconstruction of numerous Serbian Orthodox churches all over Dalmatia.

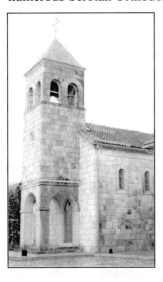

In 1716 Bishop Savatije died and was succeeded at the diocesan see by his nephew Stefan Ljubibratić. Another war against the Turks was under way (the eighth, 1714-1718). Stefan supported the war effort by calling on the Serbs of Dalmatia to fight for the Republic. In turn Governor-General Alvise Mocenigo III (1717-1720) supported Stefan's formal elevation to the rank of Bishop and arranged for his seat at Dragović (l.) to be given additional state lands along the banks of the Cetina river.

The war ended with the Peace of Požarevac in 1718. Almost immediately Bishop Zmajević asked the Venetian authorities to prevent Stefan from visiting his flock in Dalmatia. The governor-general was opposed to such a drastic move but reluctant to confront an influential Roman Catholic hierarch. In 1722 the Senate of Venice revoked the privileges previously granted to the Orthodox in Dalmatia. Harrassed and unable to perform his duties Bishop, Ljubibratić was forced to leave Dalmatia for the

Austrian Military Border where he was confirmed in the rank of Bishop of Kostajnica by the Emperor. The Serbs refused to be cowed, however. They were ably led by Simeon Končarević, Orthodox parish priest in Benkovac. Fr. Simeon was educated in Venice, spoke Italian fluently, and inspired respect with Venetian officials. In 1728 when Bishop Zmajević with two Catholic priests and a company of Venetian soldiers came to Benkovac and attempted to carry our "an official canonical visit and inspection," Končarević confronted them and was taken to Zadar in chains. He spent several months in jail, but his fame and popularity grew during that time.

Two years after his release, with the diocesan see still vacant, Fr. Simeon organized in 1731 a major assembly of parish delegates from all over Dalmatia in Benkovac. The assembly, attended by Venetian officials, confirmed Simeon's unofficial position as leader of all Serb Orthodox subjects of Venice. Under his guidance it issued a statement which asserted that the Serbs were not subjected to the Church of Rome, did not recognize the authority of Catholic bishops, would not accept their canonical visitations to Orthodox parishes, and rejected the Union. While reasserting their loyalty to Venice, the Serbs requested the Senate to allow an Orthodox monk to be consecrated as Bishop of Dalmatia and swear an oath of allegiance to the Doge. It was a strong statement:

> The Benkovac Declaration expressed the Serbs' feelings so clearly and so faithfully, that it quickly became an important platform, a Serb-Orthodox position vis-à-vis the Roman Catholic Church of the time, and remained as such for generations to come... [It] showed the Dalmatian Serbs a way to argue and fight for their religious freedom peacefully. It created a sense of unity among the Serb communities throughout the region.[40]

---

[40] Paul Pavlovich, *History of the Serbian Orthodox Church*. Toronto: Serbian Heritage Books, 1989, p. 170.

In the meantime Zmajević's successor in Zadar, Bishop Matteo Karman, was developing a new approach. Having visited Russia, he was well aware of Moscow's rising importance as the source of spiritual and cultural inspiration for Orthodox Slavs in his diocese. He proceeded to publish books in Serbian Cyrillic, including a Catholic missal (liturgical handbook) and a tract attacking the 'schism' in Dalmatia. He next asked the Venetian authorities to remove from Orthodox churches all liturgical books published in Russia and replace them with the ones printed in Cyrillic by him and by the Congregation for the Propaganda of Faith in Rome. In a 1750 memorandum Karman warned Venice that any compromise with the Serbs was harmful to the Republic, and demanded that they should be prevented from electing their own bishop.

The government in Venice supported Karman's proposals in late 1750 with a decree under which "no Orthodox priest can be appointed to a parish unless he is interviewed by the Roman Catholic Bishop in whose Diocese the Serb parish is located." Two months later the Serbs responded by naming Simeon Končarević – a widowed priest and monk by that time – as candidate for their bishop at a popular assembly at St. Ilija's church in Dalmatian Kosovo. This *Kosovo Sabor* was organized by Abbot Nikanor Rajević of Krka Monastery, this time without prior knowledge or approval of the Venetian authorities. It emphatically reaffirmed all of the key points of the Benkovac Declaration. Patriarch Atanasije II Gavrilović of Peć apporved the appointment and Simeon was consecrated as Bishop of Dalmatia in September 1751.

After his elevation Simeon continued to reside in Benkovac and serve liturgy in his old parish church, which became known locally as 'Bishop's Church.' He proceeded to appoint new priests to vacant parishes and to open elementary schools using Serbian books and language in several large parishes. A contemporary Venetian survey lists 190 Orthodox churches and around 200 Orthodox priests serving over 50,000 people. In April 1753, however, Bishop Simeon had to seek refuge in Lika, that is in Habsburg territory, just like his predecessor Stefan Ljubibratić over two decades earlier. Yet again, he and his followers addressed earnest petitions to Venice, asking to return and not to be subjected to Catholic bishops. Their demands were supported by Governor-General Francesco Grimani, but rejected by the Senate of Venice.

From the Military Border Bishop Simeon travelled to Russia seeking the intervention of Empress Catherine on behalf of his flock. The Russians obliged in 1760 and presented a note to Venice expressing displeasure at the treatment of their Orthodox co-religionists. The Senate reacted in a characteristically devious manner. It issued a proclamation pledging freedom of observance to its 'Greek Rite Christians.' The problem was that by this term Venice meant eastern-rite Uniates, which is exactly what the Serbs did not want to become. Between Bishop Simeon's exile in 1753 and the long-overdue granting of full religious tolerance to the Orthodox by the Venetian authorities in 1780, the Serbs of Dalmatia were without a bishop. Bishop Simeon Končarević did not live to see that day, however. He was destined never to set foot in his beloved Dalmatia again, having been proclaimed an enemy of the state by Venice. He died in August 1769 at Petropavlovsk monastery near Kiev. Perhaps the most important part of his legacy is a history of the Serbs in Dalmatia, *The Annals of Lay and Church Events* ("Ljetopis"), written during his exile in Russia.

Between 1753 and 1780 Venice's pressure on the 'schismatics' drove thousands of Serbs into the neighboring Habsburg Military Border, and hundreds of them as far as Galicia, in the Austrian-ruled parts of Poland, and southern Russia ('New Serbia'). Particular pressure during this period coincided with the lean years, when the delivery of the Venetian grain dole was made conditional upon conversion. The adage *prodao vjeru za večeru* ('he sold the faith for a dinner') dates from those days. Some Venetian administrators remained well aware of their Orthodox subjects' military valor and overall loyalty to the Republic, and advocated tolerance.

Governor-General Grimani remarked that every Morlacco lost to Venice took with him the "seed of able soldiers," thus diminishing Venice's military potential. He urged his successor Alvise Contarini (1756-1759) to govern the Morlacchi (in traditional dress in a contemporary gravure, l.) "with a  maximum of tolerance and gentle tact."[41] During the final decade of the Republic the balance had nevertheless shifted: the Venetian census of 1781 counted 263,674 inhabitants of Dalmatia, of which around one-fifth (just over 51,000) were Orthodox. Neither group was described by a national name.[42]

In 1797 Austria took possession of Dalmatia following the collapse of Venice and the peace of Campo-Formio. The first period of Austrian rule lasted only eight years and was uneventful: there were far more pressing issues to attend to elsewhere in Europe. The subsequent equally brief period of French rule (1805-1813) was far more significant, politically, culturally and economically. The Orthodox were finally granted equality and tolerance. The 'Illyrian Provinces' (Dalmatia and the Littoral), to which the defunct Republic of Ragusa (Dubrovnik) was added in 1808, were not constituted as a tributary kingdom ruled by one of Napoleon's relatives. It was annexed by France, entrusted to a strong-willed soldier, and subjected to rapid reforms.

French rule was marked by the imposition of modernity from above. It was a period of accelerated development coupled with economic hardship for the common folk. Old feudal obligations were terminated, wreaking havoc on the social and economic hierarchy. The introduction of 'Slavic' language in

---

[41] Wolff, op. cit. (2001), p. 143.

[42] *Srbi u Hrvatskoj: Naseljavanje, broj i teritorijalni razmeštaj.* University of Belgrade, 1993, p. 29.

primary schools further weakened the position of the Italian element. Napoleon's Governor, Marshal Auguste Marmont (r.), embarked on major road building and other public works projects. It was also marked by the establishment of full legal equality between the Roman Catholic and Orthodox churches. The new Orthodox Bishop Benedict Kraljević – an  obscure person of uncertain background – was appointed by Napoleon himself on March 26, 1810. Another Orthodox cleric rose to prominence during this period, the illustrious and much-travelled Archimandrite of Krupa Monastery, Gerasim Zelić. Fr. Gerasim attended Napoleon's wedding to Princess Marie Louise of Austria, representing the Emperor's Orthodox subjects from Dalmatia. Zelić was to enter a bitter conflict with Bishop Kraljević, however, following the return of Austrian rule in 1814, its final codification at the Congress of Vienna. and the proclamation of the Habsburg Kingdom of Dalmatia (1817). Dalmatia's reincorporation was followed by another attempt to effect the Union, with elements of a thriller and a farce.

In 1815 Bishop Kraljević succumbed to the pressure from Emperor Francis I to accept the Union. He did so without a rite and without informing his clergy. In 1818, at government expense, he travelled secretly to Vienna with his secretary to discuss future plans. The Austrian Governor of Dalmatia, General (*Feldzeugmeister*) Baron Franz Tomašić – a Croat – promised him state funds and four Ukrainian Uniate priests as teachers for the proposed seminary in Šibenik. In December 1819, however, Tomašić warned Kraljević that the Orthodox clergy were becoming suspicious. Chancellor Saurau, writing from Vienna, also urged Kraljević to be "discrete and cautious." The operation had the character of an elaborate conspiracy. With the arrival of Uniate priest-teachers in 1820 the cat was out of the bag, however. Kraljević's services were boycotted and he was verbally abused by common people. The prefect of Zadar and one Ukrainian were killed on May 10, 1821, in an attack on the coach in which the Bishop was mistakenly believed to be travelling. Primarily concerned with the maintenance of stability and order, Vienna finally abandoned Kraljević. He was forced to leave Dalmatia for good in late 1821. (He died in Italy in 1862 at the age of 97, claiming that he was still Orthodox.)

The Austrian authorities were weary of further problems and controversies over the Union. The need for stability, law and order took precedence in their priorities over the old preference for religious uniformity. In Kraljević's successor, Bishop Josif Rajačić (1829-1834, l.) who later became the Metropolitan of Karlovci and Patriarch, the imperial government found a loyal Austrophile who studied law in Vienna, spoke fluent German, and was ready to swear an oath of loyalty to the Emperor as a precondition of his ordination. Rajačić was firmly Orthodox, however, and he obtained state approval for his diocese to come under the jurisdiction of the Metropolitanate of Sremski Karlovci. In 1833 a seminary was opened in Sebenico (Šibenik). In 1841 it was moved, with the Bishop's residence, to the provincial capital in Zara (Zadar).

The formal end of pressure on the Orthodox in Austria finally came in the midst of revolutionary turmoil, when the Crown issued, on March 4, 1849, the Decree on Religious Tolerance, which helped secure the loyalty of its Serb subjects. During the subsequent long tenure of Bishop Stevan Knežević (1853-1890), new Orthodox churches and schools were built all over Dalmatia. Along the way, the 'Morlacchi' disappeared from the anthropological equation, leaving Orthodox Serbs and Catholic Croats instead.

Six years before the Decree, Slovak ethnographer Pavel Jozef Šafárik in his Slavic Ethnology (*Slovanský národopis*, Prague 1842) treated 391,000 Slavs of Dalmatia as 'Serbs,' regardless of religious affiliation. A generation later such a conflation was impossible. By the late-19th century, Austrian census figures reflected emerging, or newly clarified, ethnic divisions. Pre-

modern religious affiliation shaped early-modern culture and national consciousness, which produced modern nationalism. The tensions and rivalries had ceased to be ostensibly religious and became nationalist.

Coat of arms of the Habsburg Dalmatia

The Serbs' Disputed Name and Identity

During the period of national awakening in the first half of the 19th century, the remnants of Croatia's political integrity were threatened by the centralist tendencies of the Hungarian political class, which continued to regard Croatia as a semi-autonomous province of the Crown of St. Stephen. With the rise of popular, Jacobin nationalism, fully mature by the time of the Revolution of 1848, the idea of a unitary Hungarian state from the Carpathians to the Adriatic – inhabited by people whose designations and claimed identities might differ but all of whom belonged to a Hungarian political nation – became the *leit-motif* in Hungarian politics. This idea did not diminish after the suppression of the revolution in 1849, and was able to assert itself again after the *Ausgleich* of 1867.

In the run-up to 1848, this increasingly aggressive Hungarian integralism fostered the rise of the *Illyrian* idea in Croatia. This was a quaint misnomer for the notion of wider South Slav unity, based on common background and language. From its inception this early brand of 'Yugoslavism' was limited to Croatia, popular among a narrow segment of its educated elite (civil servants, clergy, members of free professions), and defensive in character. It was born out of the perception that the development of a specifically Croat identity needed a broader South Slav context in order to assert itself and to withstand the onslaught of stronger, more dynamic nationalisms to the north and west. It engendered the notion of Slavic unity with proto-Yugoslav overtones, as manifested in Ilija Garašanin on the Serbian and Ljudevit Gaj on the Croatian side. Its local champions were often members of the upper social stratum, like Lovre Monti, a landowning lawyer of Italian origin from Knin and a leader of the mid-19th century 'national awakening' in Dalmatia that was intended to provide a common framework for Serbs and Croats. He advised both "to turn East, where our Sun

61

is rising, to the future that will bring us happiness together with other brothers who live from the Black to the Adriatic Sea."[43]

Roman Catholic Bishop of Djakovo in Slavonia, Josip Juraj Strossmayer (r.), was the most prominent champion of the Illyrian idea. He had no intention of 'turning East.' The political ideas of this Catholic Liberal (notable for his opposition to the doctrine of papal infallibility) rested on the assumption that the yet-to-be integrated Croats would be the ones to give the tone and flavor to any future process of South Slav integration. He  expected this process to take place inside the Habsburg monarchy. Strossmayer did not seek to replace the Croatian identity by a 'Yugoslav' one, nor to sink it into the South Slav amalgam. His Illyrism was born out of the need to defend Croatian identity and interests by harnessing the energies of other South Slavs at a time of political weakness and national underdevelopment of the Croats. Its clearly Croat character became apparent in the 1860s when the 'Illyrian' movement morphed into the People's Party (*Narodna stranka*).

The upholders of the Illyrian idea seemed to opt for linguistic unity with the Serbs by introducing, in the 1830s, the štokavian (*štokavski*) dialect, based on the pioneering work of Serbia's language reformer Vuk Karadžić. The two distinctly Croat dialects, kajkavian (*kajkavski*) and čakavian (*čakavski*), fell into disuse. Transliterated from the Cyrillic to the Latin script, *štokavian* was adopted as the Croat literary standard. In 1850 Serbian and Croatian writers and linguists signed the Vienna Literary Agreement, declaring their intention to create a

---

[43] Dušan Plenča. *Kninska ratna vremena 1850-1946*. Zagreb: Globus, 1986, p. 36

common supra-national language. Thus a complex bi-variant language appeared. The variants of the conceived common literary language served as different literary variants, however, chiefly differing in lexical inventory and stylistic devices. The common phrase describing this situation was that Serbo-Croatian or 'Croatian or Serbian' was a *unified* language. In practice it provided the Croats with the linguistic base for their own national integration. It also enabled the nationalist intelligentsia, in the fullness of time, to claim the heritage of distinctly non-Croat traditions (including self-declared Serbs of the Renaissance Dubrovnik), and to stake audacious territorial and ethnic claims based on the use of 'Croatian' language.

The category 'Croat' was virtually unknown in many parts of today's Croatia, let alone in Bosnia-Herzegovina, until the 'Illyrian Awakening.' The Hungarian 1840 census, and subsequent studies based on it, listed 504,000 Serbs (31.4 percent) in Croatia-Slavonia alone. There were 1.6 million Serbs "of both Orthodox and Roman Catholic faith," and just under 1.3 million Croats, in the Monarchy as a whole.[44] Mid-19th century Austrian sources did not find any Croats in Dalmatia, which was listed as 96.18 percent Serb.[45] The 1857 census counted 1.5 million Serbs and 1.4 million Croats in the Monarchy as a whole.[46] According to that census there were hardly any Croats in Dalmatia, which was listed as 88.9 percent Serb.

A decade later a Croatian 'annexationist' aspirations were asserted in full. The key variable was Vienna. For much of the nineteenth-cenury, Vienna wanted Dalmatia to stay out of Hungarian reach – it was to remain imperial, not become royal. In this period Dalmatia's Italian-speaking elites were exposed to the cultural-political force of Italian nationalism, at a time when

---

[44] Elek Fenyes. *Magyarország statisztikai, birtokviszonyi és topographiai szempontból*. II. 2. Pest, 1859

[45] Joseph Hain, *Handbuch der Statistik des österreichischen Kaiserstaats* (2 vols), Vienna 1852-1853.

[46] Adolf Ficker. *Bevölkerung der österreichischen Monarchie in ihren wichtigsten Momenten statistisch dargestellt*. Gotha, 1860.

much of Italy was still 'Austrian.' When the Italian provinces were lost in 1859 and 1866, Vienna acted to prevent Dalmatia sliding in the same direction. Calling Slavs 'Serbs' had been a contribution to keeping Dalmatia safe from Hungarian ambitions; calling Slavs 'Croats' made, at a later stage, a contribution to keeping the province within the Empire at a time when Italy and Serbia were growing stronger. The inherently contentious character of the national rivalries and claims in the 19th century enabled the Austrian authorities to fine-tune their approval and displeasure, rewards and punishments, as tools of imperial-royal patronage.

Within a generation, the fruits of the 'Illyrian' linguistic legerdemain became visible in the rising number of Croats in the Habsburg censuses carried out between 1880 and 1910. They used the criterion of *Umgangsprache*, the 'language of daily use,' in Austria, and mother tongue, *Muttersprache*, in Hungary. As modern identities gelled, the term *Morlacchi* was no longer used yet the debate lingered on. As late as 1892 an Austro-Italian author wrote that "the scientific struggle still fluctuates, since some viewed them as Romans (Mavro-Vlahos, 'black Latins'), and others *as true Serbs*."[47] [emphasis added] The Morlacchis' Serbian character was generally taken for granted by Western sources well into the 20th century:

> The Morlachs wear a picturesque and brightly-coloured costume, resembling that of the Serbs. In appearance they are sometimes blond, with blue or grey eyes, like the Shumadian peasantry of Serbia; more often, olive-skinned, with dark hair and eyes, like the Montenegrins, whom they rival in stature, strength and courage; while their conservative spirit, their devotion to national traditions, poetry and music, their pride, indolence and superstition, are typically Serbian.[48]

---

[47] Tullio Erber, quoted in Wolff, op.cit., p. 339.

[48] "Dalmatia," *Encyclopaedia Britannica*, vol. vii, p. 773, 11th Ed. (1911).

The adoption of the štokavian form written in Latin script as the Croat linguistic standard was a formula to claim that all Roman Catholic Slavs using that standard (variously known as *Bunjevci, Šokci, Slavonci, Dalmatinci*, etc) are Croats. The process was probably unintentionally aided by the Austrian authorities, which sought to suppress the use of the term 'Illyrian' in 1843 as a potentially subversive euphemism for centrifugal South Slavdom. The 'Croat' designation readily stepped into the vacuum, and soon established itself as the cornerstone of a nascent 'imagined community' *par excellence*.

The process was still far from complete, however, when the revolution of 1848 shook the Habsburg Empire. During the revolution the provincial authorities in Zagreb, supported by Vienna, propagated commonalities and the common interests of

Serbs and Croats. It was a small price to pay for the willingness of Grenzer Serbs to fight loyally – starting on September 11, 1848 – for the Crown under Croatian Ban Josip Jelačić (l.). A total of 120,000 Grenzer were mobilized; close to one third never came back. One notable decision was to allow the use of Cyrillic script in elementary schools in Croatia and Slavonia. This was a major step towards the recognition not only of the Serbs' religious rights but also of their cultural, linguistic, and therefore national distinctiveness. On the issue of language, which until 1847 was formally known as *zemaljski jezik* (i.e. pertaining to territory rather than nation), Jelačić expressed preference for the non-ethnic appellation 'Slavic,' rather than Serbian or Croatian.

In the aftermath of the revolution, however, the idea of the 'political' Croatian people – a carbon copy of the much-resented Hungarian claim – became the *leit-motif* of Croatian politics. Whereas in feudal society only the gentry (often tenuously

'Croat' by blood) made up the 'political' people, after 1848 all inhabitants of Triune Croatia (i.e. Croatia, Slavonia and Dalmatia), irrespective of their socioeconomic status or self-perceived national identity, were supposed to constitute the Croatian 'political nation.' Put differently, no one inside the territory claimed for Croatia was to be allowed to constitute a *different* 'political nation.' Inside a well-established state this is not a problematic doctrine; inside a complex territory of potential national states, it is a call to territorial controversy.

Young Croatian nationalism, in the stage of its 'awakening' in the 1850s, was fast becoming both democratic and assimilationist. This process matured at the end of the absolutist regime of Alexander von Bach and the rise of liberal institutions in the Monarchy, following the military defeats of 1859.[49] The Serbs in Croatia were given civic rights, but not the right to national individuality, in the same year in which thousands of them died at Solferino vainly defending Austria's title to the Italian land of Lombardy.

The new, shrill assertion of integral Croatianism was in evidence barely a year after the Revolution. On March 19, 1850 Colonel Josef (Josip) Maroičić, Commander of the Third Ogulin Regiment and in subsequent years a prominent political figure, wrote (in German!) to the Serbian Orthodox Bishop of Plaški, Evgenije Jovanović, that in Croatia there existed only one 'Slavonic tribe,' which is Croatian. That 'tribe,' Maroičić asserted, practised two religions, Roman Catholic and Orthodox, but spoke one language, Croatian. To Maroičić, the Serbs in Croatia – regardless of what they felt or claimed – were Croats of Greek Orthodox faith who spoke Croatian.

In Dalmatia the same thesis was launched by Fr. Mihovil Pavlinović, a Catholic theologian and one of the leaders of the neo-Illyrian People's Party (*Narodna stranka*), founded in 1864.

---

[49] The pillars of *Bachsches System* were said to be four 'armies': a standing army of soldiers, a sitting army of office holders, a kneeling army of priests and a fawning army of sneaks.

He insisted that Dalmatia was "the cradle of the Croatian state" in which the Serbs were newcomers and guests, and concluded that the minority had to join the majority: "the country, the nation – that is indivisible." In 1869 he went a step further, asserting that the Croatian nation was "exclusively Croat." In 1877, on the eve of the occupation of Bosnia-Herzegovina by Austria-Hungary, Pavlinović went on to nationalist maximalism and argued that Bosnia-Herzegovina belonged to Croatia by historical right and that its natural border was on the Drina river.

The arch-irredentist claim of 'Croatia on the Drina' was audacious, and new at the time. Earlier in the century Matija Petar Katančić (1750-1825), a Roman Catholic priest who taught at the University of Buda, writing in Latin, noted that "the Croat identity has been propagated in Dalmatia, Bosnia and Serbia, but

 the Illyrian people of these parts never call themselves by that name." Katančić (l.) insisted that the Croats were distinct from Dalmatians "by language and fatherland" (*prefecto et hodie Croatas ab Dalmatis et patria, et laquendi ratione, distinctos bene novimus*).[50] A generation later another Catholic priest, Bosnian Franciscan Ivan Frano Jukić (1818-1857), noted that the Catholics of Bosnia and Herzegovina did not know the meaning of the word 'Croat.'

Hungarian resistance to Germanization, after the setback of 1849, was crowned almost two decades later – following Austria's defeat at Königratz – with the Compromise (*Ausgleich*) of 1867 which created Austria-Hungary. In the Dual Monarchy Hungary was effectively left to deal with its multiethnic, multilingual plurality as it deemed fit. The *Ausgleich* saved the Monarchy for five decades, but it made the position of non-Magyars in the Kingdom of St. Stephen more complex.

---

[50] Matija Petar Katančić, *De istro eiusque adcolis*. Buda, 1798, p. 107

The ensuing Croatian-Hungarian Agreement (*Nagodba*) of 1868 was a pact that governed Croatia's political status as a province of Hungary until the end of World War I. It recognized Croatia-Slavonia as a distinct political unit with its legislative *Sabor*. The Agreement granted internal autonomy to Croatia but also confirmed its subordination to Hungary. Its representation in the Hungarian parliament and its access to the central government institutions of the Dual Monarchy were restricted. Key elements of statehood, including taxation, budgetary issues, foreign and defense policy, remained beyond the reach of the authorities in Zagreb. It was seen as a defeat by many Croats.

Far from regarding the *Nagodba* as a recognition of Croatia's distinct statehood, the Hungarian political elite saw in it a carefully calibrated step on the road to Croatia's greater integration under the Crown of St. Stephen. On the other hand, the Croats wanted to see in the *Nagodba* a confirmation of the distinct legal and political personality of Croatia. After all, Article 59 asserted that "the Kingdoms of Croatia and Slavonia are made up of one single political nation." This seemed to contradict the 1867 Sabor declaration that the Serbian people in Croatia were "identical and equal" with the Croats.

In the light of Article 59 of the Agreement, the notion of the Serbs being *identical* acquired a new meaning. Constitutionally there were no Serbs *as such* in Croatia: they formed an integral part of the Croatian 'political nation' and in that sense were identical with it. Accordingly, in later years in various official statistics the Serbs were not identified as such but according to their religious confession ('Greco-Easterners'). The Serb name was omitted wherever possible. The Serbian Orthodox Church was described as 'Greco-Eastern' or 'Greco-non-Uniate' (*grčko-nesjedinjena crkva*) – an offensive term which implied the prospect of its eventual disappearance. Croatia thus displayed a distinctly Central European model of national integration, of clerical nationalism mixed with feudal traditions.

The ensuing attempt to Croatize the Serbs coincided with the end of the Military Border. As a reward for its loyalty to the

Crown in the suppression of the Hungarian insurrection in 1848, the Military Frontier was transformed in 1849 into a 'Crown Land.' But a decade later the writing was on the wall: the *Militärgrenze* was to be abolished. It no longer served any useful military purpose and it was becoming a social and political anachronism. The introduction of universal and compulsory military service (1868) was soon followed by the demilitarization of the Border, which was announced on June 8, 1871, and completed two years later.

For the Serbs, the Border's integration into Civil Croatia (*Banska Hrvatska*) was to bring economic, social and political turmoil. Many found it hard to become civilian tax-payers, as the authorities expected them to be, and even harder to give up their arms. The long agrarian crisis in southern Habsburg lands (1873-

1895) made many of them destitute, and forced thousands to emigrate. (The early Serbian diaspora in North America came mostly from the Krajina in the last quarter of the 19th century.) The peasant revolt of 1883 known as *Rakovička buna*, small-scale and disorganized, had an anti-Hungarian thrust: the traditional Grenzer loyalty to the Crown, and especially to the person of Emperor Francis Joseph I (l.), was not in doubt even though the Border had been abolished.

The final integration of the Military Frontier into Croatia-Slavonia (1881) led to a significant increase in the number of Serbs in the expanded *Banovina* and to the creation of a new center of political and economic gravity for the Serbian community in the Dual Monarchy, in addition to the existing one in southern Hungary (Vojvodina). It presented the Krajina Serbs with the task of articulating their political and cultural interests and aspirations as a distinct group.

The Serbs' strategic goal of seeking national recognition, religious equality and educational autonomy initially lacked suitable instruments, above all political parties, for its effective pursuit. The National-Church Congress was not regarded in Vienna as a representative body but merely as a corporate board of Orthodox subjects of the Crown. Before 1848 its primary function was to meet, with the approval of the Emperor, to elect the Metropolitan of Sremski Karlovci. It was nevertheless the only institution capable of exercising political leadership on behalf of the community as a whole, notably during the Hungarian Revolution. It was wholly inadequate to deal with the challenges and dilemmas facing the Serbs in Croatia, Slavonia and Dalmatia in the second half of the 19th century. The main challenge – to their very name and identity – was not to come from Vienna or Budapest, however, but from Zagreb.

Austria-Hungary, 1878-1908: Croatia and Slavonia (17) were part of the Kingdom of Hungary (16); Dalmatia (5) was an Austrian land. Bosnia and Herzegovina (18) were jointly administered by Vienna and Budapest

Ideology of State Rights

The historicist notion of Croatia's 'state rights,' based on the tradition supposedly harking back to the *Pacta Conventa*, inspired a radical form of Croatian nationalist ideology known as 'Rightism' (pravaštvo). Starting in the early 1850's, it was articulated by publicist and political activist Ante Starčević (1823-1896). Starčević's nationalism did not recognize the existence of Serbs – or, indeed, any other South Slavs west of Bulgaria – as distinct nations. To him they were all Croats, including not only Slovenes and Bosnian Muslims but also those people "mistakenly called *Serbs*" who should come to their senses and return to the Croat fold. Those "Croats of Orthodox faith" who obstinately refused to do so were *Slavo-Serbs* ultimately deserving of physical extermination. Starčević took as a model the Hungarian claim, launched at the end of the 18th century, that domicile in a particular polity rather than national culture defined nationhood, and that on the soil of Hungary there existed only one people. Starčević likewise proclaimed that in the territory of Croatia there was only one 'state-bearing' or 'political,' or, in modern parlance, *constitutive* nation: the Croatian nation.

Starčević's sentiments were soon expressed in the political arena. Following the end of Bach's absolutism in 1860, the Croatian political scene was dominated by the autonomist, implicitly pro-Austrian People's Party (Strossmayerists) and the pro-Magyar Unionist Party. The *Party of Rights* was founded in 1861 by Starčević and his leading follower Eugen Kvaternik with the slogan 'Neither Vienna nor Pest, but a free and self-governing Croatia.' It quickly became a key player in the political life of Croatia-Slavonia. The 'Rightists' allowed for the possibility of a personal union with the rest of the Monarchy, but only if such union was based on Croatia's full sovereignty. The arty attracted support mainly from the lower middle class which emerged from the ruins of the post-1848 feudal system.

Rightism may be connected in a direct line of development with the modern Croatian political mainstream. In addition to the clamoring for sovereign statehood, its defining trait was an extreme antagonism, bordering on obsession, towards the Serbs. The roots of this antagonism harked to the Serbs' special status as free, self-governed farmer-warriors who were not subjected to Croatian writ. They were successful in preserving their name, privileges, traditions, and religion under often trying conditions. By the time of the winding down of the Military Border they accounted for over a quarter of the population of today's Croatia and constituted a majority in a third of its territory. Most of them were farmers and soldiers, but in the final decades of the 19th century significant numbers were making inroads into the professions and commerce and competing with the young Croat bourgeoisie. If their presence and separate status had been an irritant to the Croatian-Hungarian feudal nobility and clergy in the 17th and 18th centuries, it was an even more acute thorn in the side of 19th century nationalists. They denied that those people were 'Serbs' in the first place.

With the emergence of the Party of Rights the social and political realignment of Croatian society in the second half of the 19th century was well under way. It reflected the maturing of the Croatian national identity, centered on the young bourgeoisie, and the associated demand for statehood as an essential expression of that identity. Starčević (shown in a 20th century monument in Zagreb, r.) and Kvaternik argued that the essence of Croatian nationhood was woven into the totality of the Croats' historical experience. Medieval institutions, reduced to the *Ancient Rights* and robbed of context and nuance, were to provide the political foundation.

The language, as restructured by the Illyrians, provided its cultural-emotional identity. Starčević treated the resulting Nation as a distinct, homogenous, organically structured personality. Members of the nation had to transcend the old, false identity based on the self, and perceive themselves as members of the corporate national entity. Any disagreement with this model was, to him, either an expression of 'deformity' caused by the long period of foreign rule, or else treason pure and simple. His messianic zeal led him to claim that only God was fit to judge his actions. 'God and the Croats' (*Bog i Hrvati*) was a Rightist slogan coined in the 1860s that has found resonance ever since. Starčević claimed that the Serbs did not exist, that they were 'a geographic term,' not a people.[51] He also proclaimed the Croatian separation not just from Serbs, but from Slavs as well:

> Who cannot see that the words Slav and Serb are the same in meaning, for both of those words can replace the word 'foreign'... The Croatian people view that Slavo-Serbian blood as foreign: the Croatian people will not stand by as these foreign people defile the holy land of Croats.

His followers wrote in the same vein. Fr. Mihovil Pavlinović, a deputy in the Dalmatian Diet (see pp. 66-67), argued that "in Croatia, whatever religion one wants to be, whatever name one calls himself, everyone is born a Croat," and ended his history of modern Dalmatia with a lament that "it is in truth only that the unfortunate name divides," and a plea that "we should all, regardless of names, be the builders of one single future; *regardless of any one of us regarding himself as a member of another nationality* [emphasis added], let us be conscious Croatian citizens."[52]

---

[51] Ferdo Šišić, "O stogodišnjici Ilirskog pokreta." *Ljetopis Jugoslavenske akademije*, Zagreb, Vol. 49-1936.

[52] Mihovio [Mihovil] Pavlinović: *Misao hrvatska i misao srbska u Dalmaciji, od godine 1848 do godine 1882.* Zadar, 1882.

Vjekoslav Klaić, leading nationalist historian at the turn of the century, held that 'the true national name' for all people between Istria and Bulgaria was *Croat*, while *Serb* was to him a 'tribal name': every Serb is a Croat, Klaić wrote, but a Croat is not a Serb.[53] Frano Supilo, a *Pravaš* politician who would eventually evolve into a proponent of South Slav unity, argued in the 1890s that Croats had to be clear about the "so-called" Serbian question: "Admittedly, there are Serbs, but in our lands there are no Serbs. Those in Croatia-Slavonia and Dalmatia who call themselves Serbs, are not Serbs but Orthodox Croats."[54] Having denied the Serbs' existence, the followers of Starčević advanced territorial and ethnic claims verging on the insane:

> The lands to which Croatia's state rights extended, in terms of history and nationality, stretch from Germany to Macedonia, from the Danube to the [Adriatic] sea. According to their separate provincial names, they are: Southern Styria, Carinthia, Carniola, Gorizia, Istria, Croatia, Slavonia, Krajina, Dalmatia, Upper Albania, Montenegro, Hercegovina, Bosnia, Rascia, Serbia; yet they all have one true name: the State of Croatia. The inhabitants of these lands number up to eight million people.[55]

An early Croat advocate of Yugoslavism, Imbro Ignjatijević Tkalac, commented a century and a half ago that a discourse of this kind was detrimental to Croats and Serbs alike. This may be "wishful thinking born of fiery patriotism," he wrote, but it is also "pure arrogance and ignorance of people's nature. Doomed to fail, it has merely increased the rift between the two most progressive and hardiest South Slav peoples, the Croats and the Serbs, and virtually turned it into national hatred."[56]

---

[53] Vjekoslav Klaić: „Hrvati i Srbi." *Vienac*, 1893, ch. 2, p. 25.

[54] *Crvena Hrvatska* (Dubrovnik), V, br. 26, 29. V. 1895.

[55] *Hervatska*, No. 6, 1871.

[56] Imbro Ignjatijević Tkalac, *Pitanje austrijsko: Kome i kada valja rešiti ga?* Paris 1866, pp. 77-78. Quoted by Krestić, op. cit. (1998), pp. 26-28.

Starčević's discourse, painfully 'modern' in its rhetoric and implications, was some decades ahead of his time. His opus provides a rare specifically *Croatian* contribution to the European history of ideas. The word 'genocide' was some 75 years from being invented when Starčević wrote that the Serbs are "the race of slaves, beasts worse than any other" and fit for extermination:

> There are three levels of perfection: that of the animal, that of comprehension, and that of reason. Slavo-Serbs have not quite reached the first level, and cannot rise above it. They have no conscience, they do not know how to read as humans, they are not teachable... Some call a magnitude of Croatia's populace 'Serbs' and a piece of Croat land 'Serbia' based on a name which they do not understand.[57]

Such language was novel in the European mainstream discourse of its time. Starčević's dehumanization of 'the Other,' the prerequisite of an eventual *final solution*, was unrestrained. "Give this beast breed a little bread, then strike it with an axe and skin it to the bone," was his final dictum on the Serb. Vladimir Dvorniković, renown Croatian anthropologist, remarked in 1939,

> Never before had a tribal, atavistic urge entered with such irrational force into the world of political formulae and programs as it did with Starčević's all-Croatness. At a time when two Serb states were already in existence, his notion of Croatizing South Slavs and his 'denying' of the Serbs and Slovenes was truly nonsensical.[58]

Starčević's opus has earned him, among the followers, the title of the 'Father of the Nation' – a designation approvingly revived in our time: there is hardly a town, in today's Croatia, without a street, a square, or an institution named after him.

---

[57] Ante Starčević, *Razgovori.* Djela, Vol 3. Zagreb 1894, p. 213.

[58] Vladimir Dvorniković. *Karakterologija Jugoslavena.* Beograd: Gregorić, 1939, p. 894.

Among the Serbs a parallel theme was developed by the linguistic reformer Vuk Stefanović Karadžić. He, too, subscribed to the popular 19th century dictum that nation was defined by language, and claimed that, therefore, all people who spoke Serbian (štokavian) were in fact Serbs, including Croats. Yet "Serbs, All and Everywhere" (*Srbi svi i svuda*), his famous article on this subject, did not have much impact on the Serbs' political discourse, in stark contrast to Starčević's impact on his audience. Had it been developed as a salient theme of Serbian politics and attitudes, the notion that all štokavian speakers were 'Serbs' would have justified the 'Greater-Serbian' accusation often directed against Belgrade in subsequent decades. In fact Karadžić's influence on Serbian culture was enormous but his impact on Serbian politics was not. Starčević mattered. His work ensured that, after the Austro-Hungarian *Ausgleich* of 1867 and the Nagodba of 1868, Serbs in Croatia-Slavonia proved reluctant to support the Croat cause of resisting Hungarian domination.

In Dalmatia, Croat identity was developed as an anti-Italian reflex before it turned on the Serbs. The coastal province was in a different position from Croatia-Slavonia. There were three nationalities to consider, and the language of administration had been Italian for centuries. But Dalmatia had been 'Hungarian' – and so at least indirectly 'Croatian' – long before the Ottomans came. Croatian claims to it were officially ignored and quietly resisted, until Vienna began to see anything Italian as treacherous. After the Italian provinces were lost in 1866, Vienna turned hostile and moved steadily towards Croatia's annexationist position. The use of Italian was restricted, to take one example, and schools told to use 'Slavic.' In the new climate some influential Dalmatian Serb leaders – notably Serbian Orthodox Bishop Nikodim Milaš (opp. p. r.) supported continued Dalmatian autonomy under Austria, rather than its unification with Croatia-Slavonia. The process led to further estrangement and the creation of Croat and Serb political parties with national programs and slogans. "We'll annihilate you," Rightist deputy

Ante Trumbić told the Italians in 1898.[59] He meant that their status as the defining population of Dalmatia would be erased, and indeed it was: by the turn of the century the Serb-Croat rivalry had taken the place of the old, Italian-Slav one. That rivalry escalated in the 1900s. Writing between the wars a Dubrovnik writer, Count Lujo Vojnović, protested wanton Croatization of his city's past:

> We are tired of this misuse of the name *Croat* and *Croatian*; this misuse does not come out of people's will, but out of certain elements which, with incredibly clever propaganda (a powerful hypnosis), are using the well-meaning Croat masses in order to turn them away from necessities of life, injecting their veins with poisonous frenzy, madness.[60]

Starčević's grand synthesis of the legal and political legacy of 'state rights' and the cultural claims based on alleged linguistic identity was not original. It was reminiscent of the Jacobin model elaborated in the aftermath of 1789, and replicated all over Europe (notably in Hungary) in the decades prior to 1848. It nevertheless secured Starčević's claim to local fame. He regarded the Party of Rights not as a mere competitor

for office but as a movement that institutionalized the yearning for the Croatian nation's self-fulfilment. Its formal program was made public only in 1894 after it had adopted the 'trialist' model of Croatia's constitutional future within the Monarchy.

The Party of Rights peaked at the triannual election in 1884, with 24 seats in the Diet (*Sabor*) of 112 deputies. Its support was wider than a fifth of the seats would indicate, however. The restrictive electoral law,

[59] Giuseppe Praga, *A History of Dalmatia.* Giardini, 1993, p. 268.

[60] *Vreme*, Belgrade, January 30, 1938.

under which fewer than two percent of the inhabitants of Croatia-Slavonia were entitled to vote, excluded many members of the Rightist constituency among the urban lower middle class and Catholic peasantry in the former Military Border.

One of Starčević's successors turned his vehement anti-Serbism into a central tenet of his 'ideology' and a determining feature of his 'Croatness.' This was the leader of the Pure Party of Rights (Čista stranka prava) Josip Frank, who split from the Rightist mainstream shortly after Starčević's death. He was memorably described by Croatian writer August Šenoa as the "infamous political louse" that "degrades and befouls all that is

Croatian, first to the benefit of the Magyars, and now of the Austrians."[61] Born in Osijek (Slavonia), Frank (l.) was a German-speaking Jewish convert to Catholicism who became a Croat in his adulthood. He defined his adopted identity in strictly terms of a crude Serbophobia. Unlike Starčević, who was a fervent believer in what he preached, Frank was an opportunist and an avid Austrophile. He tied his brand of chauvinism to the black-and-yellow mast of Habsburg loyalism. His *Pure Party of Rights* was an instigator of periodic anti-Serb riots, notably in 1895, 1899 and 1902, and the sworn opponent of the Croat-Serb Coalition in subsequent years.

Frank's unyielding position on the Serb question eventually made the Party of Pure Rights marginalized. It was left with only one political partner, small at the time but destined to become strong and important later. The agreement on joint political action of the Croatian People's Peasant Party (HPSS) and the 'pure Rightists,' drafted by the HPSS leader Stjepan Radić in August 1909, stated that both parties were imbued with Croatian

---

[61] Miroslav Krleža, ed. "FRANK, Josip." *Enciklopedija Jugoslavije*. Vol. III (1st ed.). Zagreb: Leksikografski zavod FNRJ, 1958, p. 387.

state law, "and will never depart from it even for the sake of the necessary and desirable popular accord with *that portion of our people who for various reasons call themselves Serbs.*" [emphasis added].[62] Frank's escalating Austrianism turned the legacy of the *Father of the Nation* on its head. His acceptance of an *administrative,* rather than constitutional solution for the proposed Croatian unit within the Monarchy caused a split even within the Pure Rightist ranks in 1907.

Frank's activists took the lead in various clandestine smear campaigns and overt propaganda directed against prominent Serbs and Coalition politicians, notably during the 'High Treason' trials of 1908-1909. After Frank's death in 1911 the Frankists (*Frankovci*) came to denote virulent nationalism characteristic of the shopkeepers of Zagreb's Vlaška Street and students at the School of Law, often subsidized village boys from the poor Dinaric regions of Lika, Zagora, and western Herzegovina.[63] Their numbers were modest but their zeal knew no bounds. The resulting atmosphere was summed up by a Croat *Rightist* historian in the aftermath of anti-Hungarian demontrations and parallel anti-Serb riots that accompanied Emperor Francis Joseph's visit to Zagreb in 1895. "Nowhere in Europe is there more animosity between peoples of different tongues," he wrote, "than in this country between those who speak the same language":

This animosity is lamentable but understandable. Croatian and Serbian ambitions are not leading them to fight each other arms in hand, for that would not be permitted by our present masters. Yet the struggle does exist, an under-handed, secret, dirty struggle ... without an end. So that we Croats may have an independent statelet like the Serbs and

[62] See Bogdan Krizman, *Korespondencija Stjepana Radića, 1885-1918* (Zagreb, 1972), vol. I, p. 471.

[63] Their favorite slogan in anti-Serb demonstrations in Zagreb in 1902 reflected the mindset: *Udri, udri in der štat, Slavo-Srbom štrik za vrat!* (loosely, "Go, go, gung-ho, hang the Serb by the neck!")

live free from fear, there would have to be a war between Croats and Serbs, a war bound to be very popular.[64]

Starčević died only months after these lines were written. The continuity of his life's work was assured.

Coat of arms of the Kingdom of Hungary, with Croatia (upper right), Dalmatia (Austrian province, upper left), and Slavonia (lower left)

---

[64] Pero Gavranić, *Politička povjest hrvatskog naroda od prvog početka do danas.* Zagreb 1895, pp. 325-326.

Serbs in the Political Arena

The dilemma of the Serbs in Croatia through the centuries may be reduced to the question "Who will grant us our rights in return for our loyalty?" From the time of Emperor Leopold I until the abolition of the Military Borderthe essence of the question had not changed. It was based on two assumptions: that 'we the Serbs' was a clear entity defined by religion, language and culture; and that its group rights were something to be granted – in the final instance by the Emperor – in the form of a charter or edict, on the basis of his authority and in consideration of a stated or implied *quid-pro-quo*. This attitude fit the pattern of politics all over the Monarchy, the pattern traditionally based on the competition of religious, territorial or feudal groups for imperial favor:

> The behavior of Serbs and Croats in the nineteenth century conformed completely to that model. Croatian (and Hungarian) state rights politics postulated the primordial existence of territorial units and aristocracies associated with them; those units and groups then acted as unitary entities in negotiations with the emperor.[65]

In the early 1880's, as old Grenzer privileges were being eroded under Ban Ivan Mažuranić (notably in the sphere of education), the answer to the Serb dilemma seemed clear. They decided to seek common ground with the Croat upper social and financial echelon, the stratum which, under Ban Karoly Khuen-Hedervary (l.) who succeeded Mažuranić in 1883,

---

[65] Nicholas J. Miller. *Between Nation and State: Serbian Politics in Croatia Before the First World War*. University of Pittsburgh Press, 1997, p. 45.

subordinated autonomist objectives to personal advancement and corporate gain. Khuen wanted to eliminate all opposition to Croatia's integration into the administrative, political and economic structure of Hungary. He had no political roots in Zagreb, however, at the time of his appointment by the government in Budapest. He developed a strategy which was in line with the time-honored Habsburg practice of distributing or withholding rewards and privileges among the competing national groups and provinces.

The Serbs, with a quarter of the population and a corresponding number of mandates in the *Sabor*, were a key element in Khuen's equation. In return for their support he gave them a stake in the system. To that end two important pieces of legislation were passed under Khuen, the legalization of the Serbian language and Cyrillic alphabet and the restitution of Serbian educational autonomy. In May 1887 Emperor-King signed them into law. Both measures were vehemently denounced by the Croat opposition. For the Serbs this in itself proved that working with Khuen was a matter of politics as the art of the possible. Many Croats, on the other hand, saw in their allegedly *mađaron* (Hungarian-serving) attitude nothing but additional evidence of the Serbs' inherent treachery. The circle was thus closed: Croat resentment of the Serbs' quest for rights and guarantees, first under the Austrian crown and now under Khuen, was turned by Starčević into malevolence towards the Serbs *as such.* Their reaction fed a self-fulfilling prophecy.

The Serbian Independent Party (*Srpska samostalna stranka,* SSS), the leading political institution representing the Serbs of Croatia, was founded in 1881 and played a key role in the political life of Croatia-Slavonia until the end of World War I. From the time of its founding until 1902 the party's leaders broadly accepted Khuen's framework. The fruits were tangible. After 1887 Serbian schools were self-governing and the Cyrillic script was not only legalized but its use was made mandatory in the municipal affairs of local authorities with a Serb majority. During this period the Serb enterpreneurial elite in Croatia was beginning to emerge as an economic and political factor in its own right. By the 1890s it came of age, as epitomized by the career of Vladimir Matijević (1854-1929). A self-made man born to the large family of a Grenzer officer, he founded the Serbian Bank in Zagreb (SBZ) in 1895 and soon turned it into one of the most successful financial institutions in the region. He was also the founder of the Serbian business association *Privrednik* ('Enterpreneur') two years later. In addition to providing networking to the Serbian business community, it was the leading provider of educational assistance to low-income Serb youths all over the Monarchy. The rising political and economic clout of the Serbs in Croatia was mainly due to their maintenance of pre-modern traditional institutions conducive to the community's internal cohesion, above all the continuity of ecclesiastical and educational autonomy.

The common goal of Serb politicians was to defend the religious identity and cultural integrity of their people. The  pursuit of that goal resulted in two diffeerent approaches. The Serbian Radical Party of Jaša Tomić (l.), which was especially strong in the Panonian region (Srem and eastern Slavonia), saw the Serbs as a beleaguered community threatened with assimilation and separate from Croatia's society and politics. The Radicals' focus was on political action through the National-Church Congress, the traditional corporate representative of the Serbs in Croatia in their direct dealings with the Crown.

In the early 1900's the Serbian Independent Party adopted a different course from the Radicals. It accepted the principle that its members should demand democracy and civic rights as citizens of Croatia, albeit citizens with a distinct identity. Several factors contributed to this change and made it politically possible.

In the late 1890's a new generation of activists started to emerge on both sides of the ethnic-confessional divide. They were known simply as 'the Youths' (*omladina*). Some of its members studied in Prague and came under the influence of Professor Tomaš Masaryk, an inveterate critic of the Czech variety of State Rights who also stressed the danger for the Slavs of a Germanic *Drang nach Osten*. He urged on his Serb and Croat students the need to overcome their differences in order to confront the danger common to both. Masaryk's seed fell on fertile soil. The discourse of the *Omladina*, at times articulated in joint publications, came to be characterized by the avoidance of old-style nationalist rhetoric, by political pragmatism and by heightened concern for social and economic issues. On the Croat side its members, subsequently known as the *Progressive Youth*, were about to discard the old Rightist denial of the Serbs' existence and identity. On the Serb side they were ready to accept the notion of Croatian statehood and civic identity as the framework for their people's political action. Both sides embraced the model of citizenship based on individual rights rather than collective privileges, and both allowed for the possibility of greater unity; although neither side expected the disappearance of one nation in favor of another.

This, in brief, was the formula that eventually produced the 'New Couse' in Croatian politics and gave rise to the Croat-Serb Coalition government. It was a radically new concept:

> The omladina introduced a truly revolutionary notion into Croatian politics. That notion, a century old in most of Europe, was that the individual, not the corporate entity (based on faith and/or territorial nobility) is the fundamental political actor. Their strong opposition to the politics of state right and their support for natural law as a guiding principle in politics marked them as political moderns.[66]

---

[66] Miller, op. cit. (1997), p. 51.

The overall crisis of dualism in the early years of the 20th century, coupled with the violence of the Frankist-led anti-Serb demonstrations in Zagreb in September 1902, had an electrifying impact across Croatia's political spectrum. The 'demonstrations' – riots is a more accurate term for those 'September events' in which Serb-owned shops were smashed and homes ransacked – were supposedly triggered off by an article, "Serbs and Croats," which was first published in a literary magazine in Belgrade and reprinted in Zagreb by the *Srbobran* ('Serb-Defender,' the Serbian Independent Party monthly journal).[67] Bonfires were lit with furniture and books looted from Serb properties. When the dust settled, however, politicians on both sides, including the Rightist mainstream, came to see the necessity of turning a new leaf. The Hungarian hegemony could not be resisted, many Croats realized, unless the Serbs were offered rights-for-loyalty.

The 'New Course' formula paved the way for the Croat-Serb Coalition, the leading political force in Croatia in the years before and during the Great War. It also created the intellectual and emotional climate for the rise of a modern, post-Illyrian Yugoslav sentiment. It was inspired by the notion of national unity or even national oneness (*narodno jedinstvo*) which sought to transcend the old zero-sum dilemma of identity.

The *volte-face* on the 'Serb problem'caused a split in nationalist ranks, leaving Stjepan Radić of the Croatian People's Peasant Party and Josip Frank's 'Pure Rightists' marginalized in

---

[67] Referring to Jelačić, the unsigned author (his name was Nikola Stojanović) quipped that a nation which reveres a servant of its foreign masters could not aspire to anything better than being a servant itself. He noted, with biting sarcasm, that Croat claims of pre-*Pacta Conventa* independent statehood were true, and all the sadder for that: "after all this time political identity has not developed into cultural identity." His key point was that there could be no truce between Serbs and Croats, but that the more likely destiny of the latter was to be assimilated by the former. The article was provocative and offensive to Croats, but certainly no more than the many far more vulgar outpourings of Starčević, Frank, and their followers had been to the Serbs.

their adherence to the principle that only one nation could legitimately exist in Croatia.

The Serbian Independent Party adopted the New Course and indicated its readiness to join the ranks of Khuen's opponents and to support Croatia's greater autonomy vis-à-vis Pest. The party was led until 1914 by the much-respected lawyer Bogdan Medaković, one of the wealthiest Serbs in the Monarchy, who presided over the Croatian Sabor from 1906 until the creation of Yugoslavia in 1918. The key man of ideas was Svetozar Pribićević (r.), SSS secretary and Medaković's eventual successor. He also edited the party journal *Srbobran* (known in 1902-1906 as *Novi srbobran*). Pribićević's approach to politics had two pillars. One was the principle that Serbs and Croats, for all their differences, have common interests and need to strive for unity because they were both part of the same South Slav  nation. The other was the reality of the political and constitutional institutions of the Monarchy. Short of a major European crisis, which was not on the horizon, this reality dictated pursuing the Serbs' collective interests and seeking a deal with the Croats within the framework of those institutions.

Pavle Jovanović, Pribićević's predecessor as *Srbobran's* editor, saw Orthodox Christianity as the defining trait of Serbdom. Pribićević epitomized the spirit of the New Course by rejecting both confessional determinism and integral, 'organic' nationalism and embracing liberalism. He saw language and culture as the essence of the national community, parliamentary democracy as the optimal framework for the expression of its interests, and social reform coupled with economic prosperity as the precondition of their successful fulfilment. This was an eminently modern paradigm. Interestingly, Pribićević was not *a priori* hostile to the notion of Croatia's 'state rights,' asserting that the 'political nation' was in principle a-national: a citizen's loyalty to a state was not to be predicated upon, let alone equated, with his membership of that state's majority nation.

This allowed for a more nuanced discourse on the issue of Serbo-Croat kinship than the clear-cut and effectively unbridgeable standard of confessional divide.

Pribićević's discourse was almost devoid of the invocations of Kosovo, St. Lazar and Serbia's glorious history. He insisted on the practical and pragmatic need to find common ground with the Croats, leaving the wider issue of South Slav unity for the distant future after that common ground had been established. By virtue of sharing the same lands, he claimed, Serbs in Croatia and Croats both shared the same interests, problems, and enemies. Greater autonomy for Croatia meant greater affirmation of Serbs within Croatia, Pribićević believed; by contrast, Croatia's absorption by Hungary would have reduced the Serbs in Croatia to just another non-Hungarian minority in the lands of the Crown of St. Stephen. But there was another, far greater threat, common to Hungarians and South Slavs: pan-Germanism. The Slavs' resistance to the Teutonic eastward march was, in Pribićević's view, the geopolitical imperative of the highest order. As a liberal, he regarded economic and social-cultural development as the key to success.

The New Course resonated with many Serbs tired of the old deadlock, especially the intelligentsia. The most famous Krajina Serb in history, scientist and inventor Nikola Tesla (l.), echoed Pribićević of the early 1900's when he declared in New York between the wars that he was "proud of my Serbian origin and of my Croatian homeland."[68]

In 1903-1905 the SSS establishment in Croatia-Slavonia and Dalmatia gradually adopted the New Course. In October

---

[68] Ironically, his statement was misused many decades later by Croatian nationalists to claim that Tesla – son of a Serbian Orthodox priest – was 'really' a Croat.

1905, at a joint meeting in Zadar, Serb deputies from both entities supported the *Rijeka Resolution* of Croatian representatives which demanded Dalmatia's unification with Croatia-Slavonia. By accepting this key Croatian demand the Serbs indicated they were ready for a deal. The resulting coalition accordingly treated the 'Triune' goal as its key pillar. In the dispute between Vienna and Budapest it opted for the perceived lesser evil – Hungary. It was expecting – vainly, as it turned out – the end of Magyarizing policies in return.

Electoral success came almost immediately, in 1906, propelling Frano Supilo (r.) to the position of leadership. Having started his political career as a 'Rightist,' Supilo had evolved by that time into a champion of South Slav unity. As a Germanophobe he tried to avoid disputes with the Hungarian authorities, but already in 1907 the hot-button issue of bilingual signs on the railways in Croatia-Slavonia  indicated that old habits died hard in Hungary. In October 1907 Vienna and Budapest reached an agreement to extend the Ausgleich for ten years and started laying plans for the annexation of Bosnia-Herzegovina which was effected a year later. The newly appointed Ban of Croatia, Paul Rauch, was given the task of neutralizing the Croat-Serb Coalition. That task proved difficult after the Coalition won another election in February 1908. Rauch refused to convene the Sabor, however, and started a campaign to discredit it. This campaign culminated in the farcical 'High Treason' trial of 53 Serbs, which opened in August 1908, and the closely connected Friedjung defamation trial in 1909, which exonerated Supilo from the Viennese accusation that he was in the pay of Belgrade. Both processes proved to be an acute embarrassment for the Monarchy, especially when it was established that the Habsburg foreign ministry planted forged documents to discredit the accused. The attempt to saw discord was nevertheless successful in the long run. Supilo left the Coalition in 1910, accusing the Serbs of being too willing to strike a deal with Rauch's successor, Ban Tomašić. The Coalition's honeymoon with Tomašić was brief, but its electoral appeal (reconfirmed in 1910 and 1913) proved to be enduring even without the charismatic Supilo at the helm. It remained in power until the momentous events in late 1918.

Croatia's political elite was able to devise a workable *modus vivendi* with the Serbs under Khuen in the 1880s, and – as it appeared – did so again, on a more solid basis, a generation later. The attempt hardly reflected the sentiment of the common people, however. Croatia's political scene under the Habsburgs, dynamic and diverse as it may have appeared to a casual observer, was limited to a narrow social base. The intelligentsia, lawyers, civil servants, merchants, and a small number of affluent farmers were entitled to vote under the system of limited franchise. Politically as well as socially, the vast majority of Croatia's population – its peasantry – did not yet participate in the province's political life. This exclusion from politics, coupled with archaic aspects of social structure and institutions, allowed the views of Croatia's peasants to be assumed rather than established. Croatia's political class, enterpreneurs and intelligentsia, did not know what 'the people' thought, but tended to express what, in their opinion, the people ought to think.[69] The Coalition's gradual loss of credibility in 1913, resulting from its inability to resist the pressure from Budapest, had its cause in its underlying lack of popular legitimacy.

There was, on the whole, less than met the eye in the appearance of co-operation created by the Croat-Serb Coalition. On the eve of the assassination in Sarajevo the traditions and aspirations of the two communities, so similar in appearance and language, were based on different sets of values, distinct political philosophies, and largely incompatible historical experiences.

---

[69] See Josip Horvat. *Živjeti u Hrvatskoj: Zapisi iz nepovrata.* Zagreb, 1983.

The Great War and Its Fruits

In the decades preceding the First World War Austria-Hungary was in a state of latent crisis. Its mosaic of nationalities could not be held together without radical constitutional reforms, but these were vehemently opposed – for different reasons – by the Hungarian land-owning nobility in the east and by the German nationalists in the west. The Monarchy tried to overcome home tensions through expansion in the Balkans, by occupying Bosnia-Herzegovina in 1878 and annexing it three decades later. In doing so, however, it turned Serbia from a client state of the Habsburgs – as it was in the 1880s under King Milan Obrenović – into an enemy under the rival Karadjordjevic dynasty, restored after the coup of May 1903. The Monarchy's attempts to subjugate Serbia by the means of a tariff war (1906-1911) proved ineffective and even counter-productive, by enhancing Belgrade's links with Paris and St. Petersburg.

The immediate trigger of the European war in 1914 was the desire of Austria-Hungary to settle accounts with Serbia once and for all, with Germany's backing and protection vis-à-vis Russia. The murder of Archduke Francis Ferdinand in Sarajevo (r.) was an opportunity to be snatched while it was available. This was the culmination of a conflict between Austria's Balkan expansionism and Serbia's  implicit *Piedmontism*. When Austria annexed Bosnia, the streets of Belgrade seethed with anger; and then, of course, Serbia did nothing.   Serbia's unexpected achievements in 1912-1913, however, inflamed the 'Yugoslav' sentiment in Habsburg lands. Vienna saw with consternation   the

triumph of Serbian arms against Turkey, then Bulgaria, and the doubling of its territory. It felt threatened; but the threat, real enough, was not *from* Serbia at all.

The war was not an 'accident.' For years before the assassination in Sarajevo on St. Vitus Day (June 28, 1914, old style) – the Serbs' hallowed *Vidovdan*, the anniversary of the Battle of Kosovo – Vienna had sought German support for a 'preventive' war against Serbia. It presented the forthcoming conflict as a test of strength with a wider continental significance. The shots fired by Gavrilo Princip were seen as an opportunity to settle the scores with a small but bothersome adversary. With a blank check hastily granted from Berlin, the Monarchy presented Serbia with an ultimatum with extravagant demands. It was not meant to be accepted: Austria-Hungary *willed* the war, and rushed into it, fuelled by a heady brew of crude Serbophobia that blended outright racism and a peculiarly Danubian brand of Orthodoxo-phobia. The popular jingle of August 1914, *Serbien muss sterbien*, suggested that the Frankist bile had been approved by the *Mitteleuropa*.

The consequences were dire for the Serbs of Croatia. Frankist-led rioters again took control of the streets of Zagreb, this time with the assistance of the police. Ivan Frank, their leader, later admitted that the Zagreb Chief of Police Mraović had urged him to murder several prominent local Serbs.[70] The

---

[70] *Obzor*, Zagreb, August 11, 1918.

atmosphere of pogrom was fuelled by the nationalist press, which, as a Croat deputy in the Austrian parliament recalled,

> published invented accounts of attempts made by Serbs to use bombs to wreck trains, railway lines, ships, and other means of communication, in order to justify the draconian measures adopted by the various authorities. All whose national sentiment was awake… were arrested, interned, cast into prison, ruined, condemned, executed; all who were too young or too old were doomed to die of hunger; and the rest were intimidated, demoralized, and outraged.[71]

"I'll never forget the horrible scene at the end of the first day of mobilization," another Croatian political leader recalled,

> "when a huge bonfire was burning at Jelačić Square fuelled by furniture and household items looted from the shops and homes of the Serbs of Zagreb. The bonfire was surrounded by a screaming Frankist mob, greeting with loud joy those bringing fresh items to feed the fire… and chanting 'Hang the Serb on a willow tree' [*Srbe na vrbe*]."[72]

The war against Serbia proved to be immensely popular among many Croats. Dr. Živko Prodanović, a Serb from Zagreb who was mobilized as a reserve medical corps lieutenant into the 26th Regiment in Karlovac, noted that "the entire city was filled with enthusiasm and joy: now was the moment to exterminate the *Vlachs* – down with Serbia!"[73] In his opinion, "the enthusiasm could not have been greater in Vienna or Budapest or Berlin. Some secret force intoxicated even the otherwise moderate Croats." Regimental officers were openly commenting that the war against Serbia was welcome "because a Greater

---

[71] Speech by Dalmatian deputy Ante Tresid-Pavičić in the parliament in Vienna, as quoted in *Novosti* (Zagreb), October 25, 1918.

[72] Dr. Ivan Ribar, *Iz moje političke suradnje, 1901-1965*. Zagreb: Naprijed, 1965, p. 133.

[73] Quoted by Vasa Kazimirović in *Srpsko nasledje*, No. 10 (October 1998).

Croatia can be built only on the ruins of Serbia, since there is no room for both." In Zagreb, "thousands of people poured into the streets, festive mood everywhere, Croatian flags flutter from every house, slogans praising our King, Francis Joseph, and demanding the destruction of Serbia."[74] The crowds in the streets of Croatian cities joined in singing the refrain of a new marching tune, calling for the punishment of Serbia.[75]

Lynchings of Serbs and lootings of Serb property were common throughout the months of July and August 1914; they were to continue, with lesser intensity, for the rest of the war. Persons marked in police dossiers as *P.V.* (politically unreliable) were fair game. Thousands of prominent Serbs were arrested and summarily deported, and dozens were killed, even before the war against Serbia was declared. As a Serb deputy stated during a debate at the Croatian Sabor in the summer of 1918, "When the war broke out, the prisons were filled to overflowing with Serbs from Zemun to Zrmanja. The cloud of suspicion fell upon them, Serb houses were ransacked and demolished, Serbs massacred and hanged without judge or judgment."[76]

A prominent victim of the pogrom-like atmosphere was Onisim Popović, a farmer from the area of Knin and a popular local mayor. In July 1914 he was mobilized. Within days he was arrested, brought up before a court-martial in Sinj on the strength of sworn affidavit laid against him, convicted of treason, and executed by firing squad in front of his regiment. Two years later, however, his accuser fell gravely ill and just before his death publicly confessed that he had falsely accused Popović.[77] Similar episodes were replicated all over Croatia-Slavonia and Dalmatia. The Serbs were saved from wholesale massacre thanks

---

[74] Isidor Kršnjavi in *Oesterreichische Rundschau*, October 1, 1914.

[75] "Oj hrvatski hrabri sine, prevezi me preko Drine!
Osvećena krv još nije Ferdinanda i Sofije!"

[76] Srgjan Budisavljević in the *Sabor*, August 1, 1918. *Novosti* (Zagreb daily), August 2, 1918.

[77] Onisim Popović was posthumously rehabilitated in 1917; shots were fired by a guard of honor above his grave; a military band intoned the Imperial anthem.

to the commendable *sang-froid* of the ruling Serb-Croat Coalition administration domestically and then to the sobering news of the Habsburg armies' military defeats externally.

Croatian soldiers fought with dogged determination in Serbia in the summer and fall of 1914. Unlike the mainly Czech soldiers of the Eight (Prague) Corps of the Habsburg army, who were surrendering to the Serbs *en masse* and often without firing a shot, units such as the 42nd Zagreb Regiment (known as *Vražja*, "Devil's Own") fought well. They acquired reputation for toughness in combat and for singular cruelty to the civilian population of occupied Serbian territories.[78] The bloodiest battle involving almost solely Serbs and Croats on both sides was at Gučevo, where the 13th Zagreb Corps was badly mauled. Losses were severe on the Serbian side too: 700 men of the Rudnik Detachment entered the fray, but only 50 remained fit to fight a week later. In December 1914, the 79th (Jelačić) Regiment, composed mostly of Croats, fought to the bitter end at Torlak, on the outskirts of Belgrade, while securing the rear of the retreating Austrian-Hungarian units.

Having suffered humiliating defeats in Serbia in 1914, Austria-Hungary focused its war effort on the Russian front. But after the Allied landings at Gallipoli in April 1915, Germany could no longer ignore Serbia and the Danubian link to Turkey any further; and after the fall of Russian Poland Germany was free to act. By October Serbia was doomed: Field Marshal August von Mackensen (r.) led the attack from the north while Bulgaria entered the war in support, and cut off Serbia's southern flank.[79] The campaign crushed Serbia but it did

---

[78] In the regiment's 10th company a sergeant was decorated for bravery on the Serbian front. Sergeant Josip Broz was later better known as Tito.

[79] After conquering Belgrade Mackensen erected a monument to the Serbian soldiers and declared, "We fought against an army that we have heard about only in fairy tales."

not destroy the Serbian army, which, though cut in half, marched across Albania to the coast. Allied ships kept the Austrian navy at bay, and 150,000 Serbian soldiers were evacuated. Following recuperation and complete rearmament by the French, these troops re-entered fighting on the Salonika Front where they won a decisive victory against Bulgaria in October 1918.

For the remaining three years of the war Austria-Hungary deployed its South Slav conscripts mainly on the Italian front.

Serbs, Croats and *Bosniaken* fought hard to prevent Italy from gaining the borders promised by Entente powers, which included most of Dalmatia. In an ironic twist, both Serbs and Croats fought the Italians under the Habsburg banner, although for different ends. They were ably commanded by Field Marshal Svetozar Borojević von Bojna (l.), son of a Serb *Grenzer* officer from the village of Umetići near Kostajnica and the highest-ranking South Slav in the history of the Habsburg army. Borojević is the second most prominent Krajina Serb in history, after Nikola Tesla.

As the war entered its decisive stage in the winter of 1917-1918, the future of the Monarchy was becoming uncertain. The Allies were prepared to see Serbia expand into Habsburg lands with large Serb populations, such as Bosnia and Vojvodina. Until the war's last year they did not envisage the creation of a *Yugoslavia*, let alone complete dismemberment of Austria-Hungary. President Wilson's Fourteen Points (January 1918) provided for 'autonomous development' for the Monarchy's nationalities, rather than sovereignty outside its framework.[80] Yet Wilson's espousal of self-determination was a revolutionary doctrine that could not be easily contained. It accelerated competing aspirations among the smaller nations of Central

---

[80] Ivo Lederer. *Yugoslavia at the Paris Peace Conference*. New Haven and London: Yale University Press, 1963, Chapters 1 and 2.

Europe and the Balkans that hastened the collapse of transnational empires and gave rise to ethnic conflicts and territorial disputes that remain unresolved.

President Wilson was an enthusiastic supporter of South Slav unity: the United States was the first great power to recognize the new state in January 1919. But the unification of Serbs, Croats and Slovenes came too late. When the powers rushed to defeat Russia in 1854-56, or to obstruct Russia in 1877-78 – the era of Germany's and Italy's own unification – it might have worked. Half a century later, the process of separate cultural development and formation of separate, and even competing, South Slav national identities had gone too far to be recalled. South Slav fusion would not happen merely because Allied strategists needed a big state in the Balkans to obstruct German influence in future, or because a handful of Allied scholars and journalists (such as R.W. Seton-Watson) thought they understood the Slav racial destiny better than their Viennese counterparts.

In chaotic times, when sound policy is most needed, it is pretty ideas and tempting concepts that rule, however good or bad. The supra-national, essentially cultural 'Yugoslav' model, founded on the ideas of the Enlightenment and mixed afterwards with the experiences of a romantic era, was already obsolete and anachronistic by the time it was applied:

> Adopted mainly by the liberal intelligentsia among the Serbs and Croats, the Yugoslav idea could not be implemented in the undeveloped, predominantly agrarian society, impregnated by various feudal traditions, religious intolerance, and often a xenophobic mentality. It was the example of an 'imagined community.' Both Serbs and Croats used linguistic nationalism in the form of a Yugoslav idea as and when needed, as an auxiliary device in respect of their own national integrations. Within the framework of their different political and socio-economic backgrounds,

the Serbs and the Croats used it with fundamentally different interpretations of its real content.[81]

Serbia was concerned with mere survival during the first months of the Austrian onslaught, but soon she articulated war aims that envisaged the "liberation and unification of all our brothers Serbs, Croats and Slovenes," as was officially stated in the temporary capital, Niš, in December 1914. The declaraation was made in the heady days after Serbia's early victories, when it may have seemed that the downfall of the Dual Monarchy was only a matter of time. Yet from a realist perspective, Serbia's adoption of a radical program of South Slav unity – at such an early stage of the war, and despite the evident enthusiasm with which some of those 'South Slav brothers' fought against Serbia – was an act of bravado, if not outright folly. It created

difficulties for the Serbs and their Allies even before Italy came into play in April 1915, by making the possibility of a separate peace with Austria-Hungary less likely.

The Serbian prime minister, Nikola Pašić (l.), acted as the Yugoslav project's strong supporter just before and during the war. He claimed that South Slav unity would bring peace and stability to the Balkans by creating "one national state, geographically sufficiently large, ethnically compact, politically strong, economically independent, and in harmony with European culture and progress." Pašić's estimate was wildly optimistic, yet he went out of his way to win over the Allies for the South Slav project. To that end in early 1915 a 'Yugoslav Committee' came into being, composed of Croat, Serb and Slovene political émigrés from Austria-Hungary who had made their way to Western Europe. They lobbied the Allies on the (often

---

[81] Dušan T. Bataković, "The National Integration of the Serbs and Croats: A Comparative Analysis." *Dialogue* (Paris), No. 7-8, September 1994.

exaggerated) plight of the South Slavs in the Dual Monarchy and propagated their unification with Serbia into a single state.

The creation of Yugoslavia was not the result of a wide Serbian grassroots movement. In Serbia, like in Croatia, the peasantry constituted the largest social stratum, but its role and status were different. As in Bulgaria and Greece, during the Ottoman rule the unity of *ethnos* and the Orthodox Church was legally ingrained in the administrative structure of the Empire based on the ethno-religious community, the *millet*:

> In a further development of the new, mostly secularized nation-states (Serbia, Greece, Bulgaria), the *millet* legacy was no obstacle to their liberal and democratic transformation. For the Orthodox nations in the Balkans the model of the *millet* proved itself to be a solid base for transition to the standard European type of national integration – the *nation-state* model, based on the experience of the French Revolution.[82]

The Serbian peasant fought for, lost, and regained independence in a series of bloody battles against the Turks (1804-1815). He fought under popularly acclaimed leaders whose autocratic tendencies were firmly resisted. He distrusted bureaucratic authority and titles, hated inherited privilege identified with alien rule, and took priestly sermons in his stride. By the mid-19th century Serbia, unlike Croatia, was characterized by considerable social mobility. By the end of the century the country's politicians were accountable to an electorate of all adult males. It was homogeneous, ethnically and socially. (This would change in 1912, with the incorporation of Kosovo and Macedonia.) After 1903 it had an established constitutional monarchy and a rapidly developing economy able to withstand Austria's 'Customs War.'

Serbia's considerable national dynamism in the early 20th century and its military efforts in 1912-1913 were chiefly

---

[82] ibid.

directed at liberating *Serbs* from foreign rule, and resulted in a doubling of the Kingdom's territory. The wider South Slav issue, in so far as it figured at all among common people, was perceived as an extension of that task. Ordinary Serbians did not feel any need for a wider South Slav context (Illyrianism, Yugoslavism) to protect and assert their identity. Having completed the process of emancipation from the Ottoman Empire (1878) and the parallel expulsion of the Turks and other Muslims, they no longer needed 'the Other' in order to define their identity and to articulate their objectives. The 'political nation' was one and the same as the nation itself.

Millions of Serbs in the devastated, occupied Serbia, and further hundreds of thousands in the Serbian Army overseas or in captivity, were fighting and praying for a resurrected and enlarged *Kingdom of Serbia*. They had no idea what their leaders were up to, and they were never going to be asked. Further millions of South Slavs living in Austria-Hungary had no idea that some 'Yugoslav Committee' existed in the first place, let alone that it presumed to negotiate political settlements of far-reaching significance on their behalf. The Committee was, in effect, asking to share power with the Serbian government:

> Pašić, of course, could not constitutionally share his or his cabinet's power. Nor could he speak for another Serb Allied combatant, Montenegro. But he was convinced that in dealing with the Allies, the South Slavs would be most effective if they spoke with one voice.[83]

The Corfu Resolution of 1917, eventually agreed between the government of Serbia and the Yugoslav Committee, proposed the creation of a "constitutional, democratic, and parliamentary monarchy headed by the house of Karadjordjević," to be called the Kingdom of the Serbs, Croats and Slovenes. Under its terms Serbia was not to be given any

---

[83] Alex N. Dragnich, *Serbs and Croats: The Struggle in Yugoslavia*. New York: Harcourt, Brace. 1992, p. 25.

privileged status or veto power in the new state, such as had been granted to Prussia in 1870. Both Serbia and Montenegro were supposed to cease existing as sovereign states. This outcome was a major political success for the Croats on the Committee. It reflected Pašić's weak position after the revolution in Russia (March 1917), an event that he rightly saw as adverse to Serbia's strategic interests and to his own political position.

The decision of the Serbs to reject the Treaty of London (map, below), sign the Declaration and to present it to the Allies as its official program – even though a 'greater Serbia' was in all likelihood readily available – was an act of folly, or conceit, or generosity; in some measure, it was all three. It prompted a delighted Ante Trumbić, the Croat chairman of the Yugoslav

Rene Albrecht-Carrie, Italy at the Paris Peace Conference. Archon, 1966

Committee, to declare that Serbia's sacrifices "for the union of our three-named people" gave her "the absolute right to be called the Yugoslav Piedmont." Britain and France would have preferred the 'small' solution, which would consist of a greatly enlarged Serbia united with Montenegro, Bosnia and Herzegovina, and the Adriatic coast south of Split. This solution could be accommodated with the Treaty of London, under which Italy was to get Dalmatia north of Split. Such an outcome would have left Croatia with a mere 'four counties' of its heartland around Zagreb. It would have been squeezed between two enlarged, victorious neighbours, Italy and Serbia. Without much coastline, bereft of friends or mentors, it would have had an uncertain future. The political class in Zagreb understood the danger and started looking beyond the Serb-Croat coalition. In the final year of the war, with the deteriorating internal situation in Austria-Hungary, the Yugoslav sentiment started gaining strength. The May 1917 Declaration (*Majska deklaracija*) of South Slav deputies in Vienna heralded the trend, by demanding the union of the provinces where Slovenes, Croats, and Serbs lived in a single state. The qualifier 'under the scepter of the House of Habsburg' was obligatory under the circumstances, but no longer seriously meant.

As the Dual Monarchy struggled to maintain the war effort, in early 1918 South Slav political representatives went a step further and urged the creation of a grouping of all forces aimed at the establishment of a 'democratically-based state of Slovenes, Croats and Serbs.' The new wave was driven by the fear of Italy's ambitions if the collapse of the Monarchy caught Croatia alone. The Yugoslav solution was seen as an obvious means of protecting Croatian interests. As the Monarchy crumbled in the autumn of 1918, the Croat-Serb Coalition was the driving force behind the founding in Zagreb of the National Council, an *ad hoc* body that proclaimed the 'State of Slovenes, Croats and Serbs' in the South Slav lands of the Monarchy. The vote in the Sabor to sever all links with Hungary and Austria (29 October

1918) came amidst a mix of -panic and euphoria.[84] When external military-political developments presented the unification of South Slavs as an immediate prospect, the decision-makers in Croatia could claim but a limited mandate for the fateful steps they were taking. The political enfranchisement of Croatia's peasantry took place only after 1918, in the Yugoslav state. That state might have had a happier start if things had not been rushed, but at the time of confusion and fear in the fall of 1918 Croatia's political leaders could see no alternative to an urgent union with Serbia on the basis of the Corfu Declaration.

The significant dissenting voice was that of Stjepan Radić, the leader of the small Croatian People's Peasant Party. He warned the delegates, as they were departing for Belgrade, that they had no mandate for what they were about to do: "You are roaming like geese in the fog!"[85] Radić's quip about *guske u magli* became famous, but at the time he was isolated and rebuked by other Council members for 'rabble rousing.' Their main concern was to get the Serbian army in, to keep the Italians out, and to keep the Reds down.

The delegates from Zagreb informed Regent Alexander Karadjordjević, on the last day of November, of the National Council's decision in favor of the unconditional union. On 1 December, 1918, the Regent accepted the offer of the National Council and proclaimed the establishment of the Kingdom of the Serbs, Croats and Slovenes. Yugoslavia was born.

---

[84] Cf. Bogdan Krizman. "Stvaranje Jugoslavije" in *Zbornik: Iz istorije Jugoslavije, 1918-1945*. Belgrade, 1958, pp. 147-164.

[85] Ferdo Šišić (1920), p. 279.

The Unhappy Yugoslav Experience

For most Serbs outside Serbia the creation of the Yugoslav state was greeted as a great and glorious event, an act of deliverance pure and simple. As the Serbian Army advanced into Habsburg provinces inhabited by Serbs, it was enthusiastically greeted as the harbinger of a new, expanded Serbian state. Patriotic speeches at assemblies that greeted the Serbian army in Knin, Petrinja, Otocac or Glina were filled with the imagery of Tsar Dušan, Kosovo and Karadjordje, of Serbia's sacrifice, resurrection and glory. There was no mention of 'Yugoslavia,' and little apparent awareness that it was an option about to become reality. The boundless enthusiasm of the long-suffering Serbs west of the Drina was natural and naïve. In the the two decades that followed it turned into disappointment with the Yugoslav experiment.

On the Croat side there was little enthusiasm outside the narrow circle of pro-Yugoslav intelligentsia and beyond the borders of Dalmatia threatened by Italian aspirations. To many common people the notion of Croatia's disappearance into what they assumed would be a Serb-dominated state was intolerable. The trouble started immediately. On 2 December 1918, the Frankists called for action against unification. Demonstrations broke out in Zagreb; several people died in the ensuing clashes with the National Council authorities. Within days Stjepan Radić started a campaign demanding plebiscite and the establishment of an independent Croatia. He sent messages to President Wilson and other Allied powers seeking help in the creation and recognition of a 'Croatian republic.' In subsequent years Radić appealed to, or attempted to involve, Lloyd George, the League of Nations, France, Austria, Italy, and even the Soviet Union, where he subsequently joined the 'Peasant International.' His attempts to internationalize the Croat problem, though invariably unsuccessful, aggravated the internal situation. The Serbs were dismayed: the state was formed, very much on the insistence of 'the Croats,' and 'they' were already trying to tear it apart.[86]

From the moment of its creation at the end of the Great War until its disintegration just over seven decades later, Yugoslavia was constantly beset by national problems. Those problems were dealt with in different ways and with different intentions, on average once every decade: from the centralism of the Vidovdan Constitution to King Alexander's imposition of Yugoslav integralism of 1929; from the quasi-federalism of the Serb-Croat Agreement of 1939 to the bloody Stalinist dictatorship of 1945; from quasi-federalism of the 1953 Federal People's Republic (FNRJ) Constitution to the confederal 'Amendments' of 1968; and finally, from the chaos of Tito's last period – embodied in the Constitution of 1974 – to the doomed attempt of his

successors to keep the clumsu edifice functional amidst the collapse of communism and the emergence of a unipolar world. The national problems which proved impossible to solve, in the first, royalist Yugoslavia (1918-1941) were no less difficult in the second, communist one (1945-1991). As Dr. Michael Stenton points out in his *Afterword* to this book, the Serbs were trapped into an appearance of responsibility for what was as much imposed on them as it was on others: "Yugoslavia was a country desired by the few, not the many." Structural deficiencies of each and every Yugoslavia, as a state and as a polity, were fundamental, and precluded the emergence of a viable political system. This was the root cause of its speedy and ignominious collapse in 1941, and its final, violent disintegration in 1991.

The issue of Serb-Croat relations was at the core of the Yugoslav problem. Those relations, already made delicate by the legacy of the Border, were poisoned by the creation of a common state. The circumstances surrounding the act of unification, and the decades that followed, drew a deep wedge between the two seemingly similar nations separated by one language. The collapse of Austria-Hungary presented the South Slavs with unification as a fact of practical politics that did not allow any delay. The leaders of the Croats insisted that the Serbian Army take immediate possession of Dalmatia and the Littoral, which they saw as the only effective insurance against Italy's well known ambitions. All parties were forced to improvise. This created a problematic legacy for the new state's internal development, just as its territorial disputes created the potential for conflict with its neighbors. Neither internal solutions, such as the centralist Constitution of St Vitus's Day (*Vidovdanski ustav*, 28 June 1921), nor external settlements, embodied in the Paris treaties, were effective in providing stability at home or security abroad.

The Croat nationalist response to the Yugoslav challenge, as represented by Stjepan Radić, was comparable to Jaša Tomić's response to the challenge of civic identity. After 1918, even more than before 1914, "Freud's narcissism of minor differences took over: if Serbs and Croats were really to be different peoples, then what little separated them had to be enhanced."[87] Serb-Croat relations would have remained ambivalent but tractable, had the two nations not been forced under the same roof. It is unlikely that they could have been any *worse* than they have been over the past century.

The results of the first election, held on November 28, 1920, displayed a sharp division between Serbs and Croats in the electoral districts of today's Republic of Croatia: eight counties (županije) in Croatia-Slavonia and two districts in Dalmatia. One member of parliament was to be elected by approximately 30,000 voters in each of the 56 constituencies on the basis of proportional representation: seats were allocated to party lists on the basis of their share of the vote. The Serbs' vote was divided between the Radical Party of Nikola Pašić, which was perceived as more supportive of specifically Serb interests, and to the newly-created Democratic Party of Svetozar Pribićević, which stood for the 'state-enhancing,' centralist Yugoslavism.

The Croats gave their votes *en masse* to the Croatian People's Peasant Party (*Hrvatska pučka seljačka stranka*, HPSS) of Stjepan Radić (r.), turning it into the undisputed political representative of the nation as a whole. Radić declared that his success was tantamount to a referendum in favor of the "neutral Croatian republic" that he advocated at the time, and changed the party's name to the Croatian Republican Peasant Party (HRSS). He continued to boycott the constituent assembly, insisting on a prior 'Croatian constitutional pact' that would lead to an agreement with Belgrade based on a confederal arrangement, taking account of the 'historical boundaries' of Croatia prior to December 1, 1918. The Radical-Democrat coalition, which

---

[87] Nicholas Miller, op. cit. (1997), p. 181.

formed the government after the election, rejected Radić's demand without ado and supported the unitary model. Both parties were opposed to the notion of "historical boundaries" as bound to cause divisions.

Prime Minister Pašić was reputed to hold the view that Serbia should not accept any solution that would fall short of the Serbs' unification within a single political entity. He was not *a priori* against the federal model, but insisted that it would have to be based on the principle of ethnicity:

> "Croats by themselves, Slovenes by themselves, Serbs by themselves, and then we can draw boundaries and make a federation... Splitting up the Serbs to facilitate the creation of Croatia... would be unjust to our people."[88]

In the course of debates in the Constituent Assembly deputies belonging to the Radical Party were specific in their rejection of Radić's demands. One deputy argued that "we can never accept that Serbs remain under non-Serb authority, even if it is under the fraternal Croatian authority."[89] Another pointed out that the principle of the will of the people had to be extended "to the Serb people of Srem, Lika, and Banija."[90] The Radicals, not enthusiastic about the unitary Yugoslav concept to start with, were prepared to talk about the borders; but they envisaged a plebiscite in the predominantly Serb-inhabited areas "so that those areas can be taken out and remain with the greater state community, while the reduced Croatia and Slavonia could include Medjumurje, northern Adriatic islands, and possibly Baranja."[91] Democratic Party leader Svetozar Pribićević saw

---

[88] In a letter to Milenko Vesnić. *Narodni glas*, April 29, 1926, 1-2.

[89] Miroslav Spalajković, in *Stenografske beleške Ustavotvorne skupštine* (Stenographic Notes of the Constituent Assembly), May 12, 1921.

[90] Quoted by Branislav Gligorijević, "Politički život na prostoru RSK (1918-1941)" in *Republika Srpska Krajina*, Belgrade 1996, p. 302.

[91] "Our Constituional Question": address by Lj. Jovanović at the Radical Party assembly, *Samouprava*, November 21, 1921, 1-5.

Radić's demands as a backhanded attempt to turn the Serbs in a future confederalized Croatia into a minority, and to achieve the long desired hegemony over them:

> He believed that this outcome could be prevented in a unitary state, without provincial boundaries, in which Serbs, Croats and Slovenes would rule "equally and with equal rights over the entire state." That position was embodied in the constitution, which was adopted by the Constituent Assembly with a simple majority of votes.[92]

Given Serbia's century of independence, its war record, and the Serbs' numbers, some degree of its predominance in the new state was not unexpected; but ineptly applied in the centralist framework, it appeared as hegemony to many non-Serbs. The Serbian political establishment failed to see that most Croats had accepted the new state out of necessity rather than conviction. With Radić's electoral success it became clear that they would have preferred a sovereign state of their own, just as most Serbs – had they been asked – would have preferred an expanded, strong and secure Serbia to the new amalgam that was forced upon them. By opting for the centralist concept the Serbian establishment erred by default. Challenges of nation building, of obtaining and defending recognized borders, of establishing a single currency, of regulating economic, educational and judicial systems, and above all of solving issues of multi-ethnicity, were immense. They were temporarily concealed behind the fiction of 'one nation with three names.' They demanded a departure from the well-established pre-war patterns of political action; but old habits and wishful thinking prevailed, on all sides, in the early years of the new state.

The legacy of different cultural, political and religious traditions – most obvious in the case of Serbia and Croatia – was underestimated. This legacy, coupled with uneven economic development and different aspirations of the three 'tribes' of the

---

[92] Gligorijević, op. cit. p. 302.

newly-promulgated 'nation,' could not be overcome by a centralist constitution and unitarist slogans. Such differences were at the root of the political conflict in the country, which appeared to revolve around the issue of centralism. Belgrade was inclined to view the new state as a continuation of pre-1914 Serbia, and advocated centralism on the premise of national, 'Yugoslav' unity. The Croats, in turn, knew historical rights and legal agreements, contracts, *Pacta Convaneta, Ausgleichen* and *Nagodbas*... devices based on a long tradition of seeking greater self-rule through corporate negotiation and in opposition to the centralist tendencies of external power centers.

Some Croats, too, were advocates of Yugoslav integralism, especially in Dalmatia, which was threatened by Italian irredentism, but their numbers and influence were small. To most ordinary people inhabiting the Krajina crescent – both Serbs and Croats – the slogans of 'national unity' did not make much sense. Serbs accepted them half-heartedly, Croats not at all. In preceding decades they had lived side by side or in mixed communities, mostly in peace, often uncomfortably; yet after 1848 at the latest they did not consider themselves one and the same people. Assimilationist claims by Starčević et al. only served to deepen the gap: they forced the Serbs to articulate and assert their goals. Likewise, after December 1918 centralism enhanced integration on the Croat side and bred opposition not only to the government in Belgrade but to the very concept of the new state. The opposition ranged from 'soft,' autonomist, to 'hard,' openly separatist.[93]

For most Serbs in today's Croatia the creation of Yugoslavia was seen as the solution to their problems, the fulfilment of their aspirations. The result was a 'national demobilization' on the Serb side, leaving it up to the state itself to take care of national interests. On the other side,

---

[93] For 'hard-soft' distinction cf. Ivo Banac. *The National Question in Yugoslavia: Origins, History, Politics*. Ithaca: Cornell University Press, 1984.

Croats were only beginning their national mobilization focused on the idea of the Croatian state within those boundaries that, allegedly, Austria-Hungary would have granted them, had there been a 'Yugoslav' unification under the Habsburg Monarchy. In 1922 Radić spelled out in his party program the basis of future order as a confederation … with the Serbs in a greater Croatia thus created reduced to the status of an ethnic minority, with … municipal autonomy in areas where they lived.[94]

The institution of French-style parliamentary democracy, well known to Serbia prior to 1914, did not provide an adequate venue to most Croat politicians groomed under the Habsburgs. They tended to assume an *us-and-them* posture in all dealings with the state authority, and Radić was the embodiment of such attitude. The inheritance of times past became apparent in an almost reflexive treatment of Belgrade as if it were Budapest. The Serbs' response was insistence on centralism. The result was a deadlock, sealed with the general election of 1923. The Serbian political establishment did not grasp the nature of the problem it faced. It continued to behave as if the Croat storm would somehow blow itself out, as if Radić were merely an opposition politician in pre-1914 Serbia. Both sides contributed to an almost permanent political crisis throughout the first decade of the Kingdom, even after Radić's apparent *volte-face* in 1925 when he accepted the legitimacy of the state and joined government. Even then, political parties and institutions proved incapable of developing a viable political system in a fundamentally flawed political entity. Its leadership after 1929, in the period of King Alexander's personal rule, brought neither stability nor happiness to his fourteen million subjects.

The new state's external challenges were acute. The most vexing problem concerned Italy. The Italians were unwilling to give up what had been promised to them in London in 1915 as a reward for their entry into the war on the side of the Allies:

---

[94] Gligorijević, op. cit. p. 303.

Dalmatia with its hinterland and most major Adriatic islands. To their dismay, in December 1918 the Italians found that this enemy territory became, by the act of unification, an 'Allied' land. Rome came to regard the Yugoslav state as an unwelcome successor to Austria in the eastern Adriatic, a rival and potential enemy, even though Mussolini regretted the ascendancy of Croat Italophobia over what the traditional Serb affection for Italy.[95]

The coalition between Radić and Pašić collapsed after a year, in April 1926. Radić accused his government colleagues of corruption, while Pašić complained of Radić's disloyalty and nationalist demagoguery. Pašić died only months later, while Radić, having gone into opposition, entered into another unlikely alliance in 1927, with none other than Svetozar Pribićević, the veteran leader of the Serbs in Croatia and an unyielding advocate of centralism in the early years after unification. By the late 1920s, however, he was in opposition both to the Radicals and to King Alexander. The efforts of these two odd allies ensured that parliamentary obstructionism would degenerate into virtual paralysis of the democratic process. Virulent recriminations and scenes of mayhem in the *Skupština* were a frequent spectacle thereafter. The tension culminated in June 1928, when a Radical Party deputy from Montenegro, Puniša Račić, shot five HSS deputies, including Radić. Two of them were killed on the spot,

among them Radić's nephew Pavle. The HSS leader was wounded and died two months later. His funeral (l.) offered his successors an opportunity for an impressive display of popular sentiment.

[95] *Documenti diplomatici italiani* (DDI), 7 ser. IV, No 59. Bodrero to Mussolini, 7 July 1925; No. 73; 24 July 1925.

The carnage caused shock in the country and abroad. By the end of the year a near-complete political paralysis had set in. The political system, less than a decade old, was not functioning. On 6 January 1929 King Alexander (r.) suspended the Constitution and assumed personal rule, thus acknowledging the failure of a decade-long attempt to devise a workable political system based on

the model of parliamentary democracy imported from Paris.

In subsequent years the Kingdom was run on authoritarian lines in an effort to develop from above a feeling of 'Yugoslav' unity. Organizations based on religion or nationality were banned or suppressed.The Croatian political leadership naturally opposed the King's course.[96] It resented the formal change of the name of the state to Yugoslavia and the introduction of the administrative system based on nine *banovinas*, units that bore no relation to historic provinces. Their boundaries cut across traditional and ethnic lines. This, and a renewed insistence on the concept of the 'Yugoslav nation' were seen as further steps away from federalism that would respect the individuality of Croatia.

---

[96] For a detailed study of the Croat inter-war policy cf. Ljubo Boban, *Maček i politika Hrvatske seljačke stranke, 1928-1941*. 2 Vols. Zagreb: Liber, 1974.

Yugoslavia In Crisis

King Alexander's attempt to enhance the unity of the Yugoslav state ended in a fiasco. His failure to nurture a degree of political consensus and the heavy-handedness of his personal rule proved profoundly important for Serbs and Croats alike. His actions disoriented the former and consolidated the latter. The collapse of the parliamentary system coincided with growing political radicalism throughout Europe and the beginning of a worldwide economic crisis. Yugoslavia nevertheless remained largely free of the totalitarian tendencies rampant in Europe at that time.

Following King Alexander's assassination in Marseilles in October 1934, the monolithic character of Croat opposition remained in sharp contrast to the disarray of Serb political parties. To Radić's successor Vladko Maček, the Croat question was the *alpha* and *omega* of all political activity. Every decision had to be examined through the prism of achieving national objectives. On the other hand, to the fragmented Serb opposition the re-establishment of democratic institutions and parliamentary life was a prerequisite of any long-term reform of the state. The Croatian opposition was always *national*, while the Serbian opposition remained *political*.

With the firm grip of the HSS on Croat loyalties, other political groups either ceased to exist as serious concerns, or else were forced to the margins of the political spectrum. The heirs to the tradition of Ante Starčević and Josip Frank felt frustrated by what they saw as Radić's inconsistency, manifest in his willingness in 1925 to accept the legitimacy of the state, the Crown and the constitution. This was anathema to them but they were powerless to challenge Radić's status as the undisputed national leader. With only two parliamentary deputies and a few thousand members (most of them in the city of Zagreb) the 'Rightists' could not hope to threaten HSS's political monopoly.

An option for 'hard' separatists was to abandon the constitutional process altogether and to engage in subversion and violence. This was the path chosen by one of the two Frankist deputies in Belgrade, lawyer Ante Pavelić, remembered as the founder of the Ustaša movement and the leader of the Croatian Quisling state during the Second World War. Pavelić's creation was to grow into a paradigmatic manifestation of 'native fascism' in South Slav lands: rabidly nationalist, racist, anti-democratic, and violent to the point of genocide.

Pavelić left Yugoslavia in 1929, shortly after King Alexander proclaimed his personal rule. In Austria and Hungary he established contact with anti-Yugoslav émigrés from Croatia who helped him obtain clandestine support of the Hungarian military. In Sofia he met the leaders of pro-Bulgarian separatists from Yugoslav Macedonia ('Internal Macedonian Revolutionary Organization,' VMRO). Soon thereafter he accepted an invitation to establish a permanent base in Italy. Once secure in his new abode, Pavelić defined the objective of his 'movement' as armed struggle for Croatian independence and invited all like-minded patriots to join him. First volunteers numbered about fifty and were recruited among Croat guest-workers in Belgium, France and Germany. They responded to Pavelić's fliers heralding an imminent anti-Serb uprising inside Croatia. In Italy they were promised board and lodging at a time when many were being laid off due to the great depression.

Pavelić established a 'headquarters' in the province of Brescia, where he promulgated the statute of the 'Ustaša, Croatian Revolutionary Organisation' (*Ustaša, hrvatska revolucionarna organizacija*, UHRO) in 1932 and the 'Principles' (*Načela Ustaškog pokreta*) a year later.[97] The key points of the *Principles* are assertion of continued statehood, claim on sovereignty over the entire 'ethnic and historical' territory, denial of legal and property rights to non-Croats in the future state, collectivism, and organic nationalism. The Statute

---

[97] *Hrvatska pošta*, Vol. 1, No. 1. A-VII, NDH, Kut. 85f and 290.

postulated complete blind obedience to the leader (*Poglavnik*): the *Fuehrerprinzip* applied only to him personally. The spirit of these documents, the rituals introduced by the putative Leader (a

secret oath before a crucifix, a bomb and a pistol), and the posturing of early volunteers (l.), were reminiscent of some secret nationalist societiy in the 19th century Balkan mould, rather than a 1930's movement seriously bent on taking power.

Pavelić's ideological grounding was provided by Ante Starčević. In the 1920s an updated treatment of 'the Serb problem' was given by Milan Sufflay, a historian and sociologist assassinated in 1931. Sufflay's main thesis was that there could be no accord between Croats and Serbs owing to the inherent biological and racial differences between them. Twelve centuries of divergent development had turned Croatia into a Western nation, by virtue of its religion, culture, and modes of thought, while Serbia leaned to the East, to Orthodoxy, and to Russia, as Byzantium's successor in world politics.[98] Sufflay claimed that such differences were genetically conditioned and therefore insurmountable. He also claimed to have established racial differences between the two, Croats being "a fair race with some Mongolian blood" and Serbs being "a darker race of paleo-Balkanic origin." Paradoxically, however, as soon as a Serb accepted Croat national consciousness, such differences no longer mattered to Sufflay: an act of will could override the genes. In a similar vein, half a century earlier Starčević included Serbs in the Croat nation, inviting them to return to the fold, and at the same time branded them an inferior race "lower than any breed of beasts."

---

[98] Milan Sufflay. *Hrvatska u svjetlu svjetske historije i politike.* Zagreb, 1928.

The Ustaša began to organize terrorist raids into Yugoslav territory from abroad, chiefly from Hungary, where they had a camp at Janka Puszta near Croatia's border. Following a failed attempt on the life of King Alexander by an Ustaša activist in Zagreb, Pavelić recruited an experienced VMRO assassin who murdered King Alexander and France's Foreign Minister, Louis Barthou in Marseilles in October 1934. Pavelić was placed under arrest by Mussolini but not extradited to France, where he was sentenced to death in absentia.

Pavelić postulated a thoroughly demonic concept of the Serb. The hatred of the 'Vlach' was the cornerstone of his followers' outlook, and above all the key defining trait of their Croatness. The Serb was a subhuman beast (Starčević), racially different from the Croat and genetically inferior to him (Sufflay), a 'scheming Byzantine oriental... an alien thorn in Croatia's very flesh' (Pavelić). Such views made a compromise impossible by definition.

By the late 1930's that compromise was not regarded as *a priori* unattainable by Croatia's political mainstream, still represented by the Peasant Party. It could not deal with a King determined to impose his utopian vision of integral Yugoslavism. After King Alexander's death his cousin Prince Paul took over the regency until young King Peter reached maturity – and he took the political initiative to resolve the country's crisis, however much he personally detested that task.

For several years the Prince (r.) relied on Milan Stojadinović, prime minister of Yugoslavia from 1935 until early 1939. He was a talented politician and financial expert with authoritarian tendencies. Initially, at the time of his appointment, Stojadinović made statements that indicated his readiness to resolve the Croat question. Maček was not ready,

however: he demanded that the Constitution of 1931 be abolished, and insisted that there had to be a clear understanding – in advance of any formal agreement – what exactly would be the territory and constitutional status of the future Croat unit within Yugoslavia. He expected the rising tension in Europe to work in his favor by making Belgrade readier to grant concessions.

Wooed by Germany, friendly with Italy, nominally allied with France and the Little Entente, Stojadinović believed he was building a strong external position and he was in no hurry. After he signed an agreement with Italy's foreign minister Ciano in 1937, all Ustaša activity was terminated and Pavelić's followers interned on the distant Lipari islands off Sicily. Many decided to return to Yugoslavia voluntarily, where they were promised amnesty. Stojadinović seemed unconcerned: the home branch of Pavelić's organization never numbered more than a thousand members. His authorities even tolerated the ultra-nationalist newspapers *Hrvatski narod* ('Croat People') and *Nezavisnost* ('Independence').[99]

Prince Paul decided to replace Stojadinović shortly after the election of December 1938. His decision was due to two factors. He was concerned that Stojadinović's policy of friendship with the Axis powers went too far. More importantly, in order to reach an agreement with Maček, which he regarded as urgently needed, Prince Paul knew he needed someone new at the helm. He selected Dragiša Cvetković, a government minister from Niš who was reputed to be in favor of an agreement with the Croats. Unfortunately for the Prince, the new government lacked credibility and a clear mandate among the Serbs.

Cvetković stated his intention to negotiate with Maček on March 10, 1939. He arrived in Zagreb three weeks later, not only as the Premier but also as Prince Paul's envoy. The talks proceeded smoothly, and by the end of April a tentative

---

[99] Arhiv vojnoistorijskog instituta, Beograd (A-VII), stenogram of interrogation of Mile Budak, I.O.9 4/3, 1-20

agreement was reached and sent to Prince Paul for approval. It was short and simple: an autonomous Croat province (*Banovina*) was to be created, embracing the Savska Banovina, the Primorska Banovina and the district of Dubrovnik (see map).

The new Banovina of Croatia would enjoy wide autonomy. A joint government would be formed to see the agreement (*Sporazum*) through. It was based on Article 116 of the 1931 Constitution, which provided for emergency measures in case of a threat to the country's security. After some additional talks the final version was signed by Prince Paul on 24 August 1939.

The Agreement opened with the statement that *Yugoslavia is the best guarantee of the independence and progress of Serbs, Croats and Slovenes*. This declaration of principle by the HSS reaffirmed its acceptance of the Yugoslav state. The Banovina of Croatia comprised more territory than envisaged in the provisional agreement of 27 April, by including several districts of Bosnia and Herzegovina inhabited by Croats. The central government, which the HSS joined as a coalition partner,

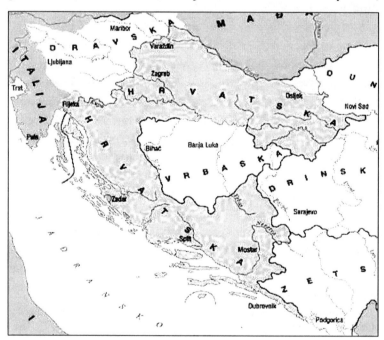

retained control over national security and defense, foreign affairs, and most financial issues. The first Ban became Ivan Šubašić (r.). known as a pro-Yugoslav HSS moderate. He was to be responsible to the Crown on the one hand, and to the *Sabor* of Croatia (yet to be elected) on the other. Laws pertaining to the Banovina of Croatia would be signed by the King and countersigned by the Ban.

As the only *Banovina* constituted on the principle of nationality and named after the nation which comprised a majority within it, the new unit came close to resembling a nation-state. The *Sporazum* that created it was similar in spirit to the Austro-Hungarian *Ausgleich* of 1867. It was the sort of deal that could have satisfied Radić two decades earlier. In the event, it was too little, too late to some Croats; too much, too soon to some Serbs. To the separatists the Agreement was a sellout, an act of treason. On the other side, many Serbs – notably the circle around Professor Slobodan Jovanović and the Serbian Cultural Club – thought that by 'solving' the Croatian question Prince Paul had helped exacerbate the Serbian one.

The Agreement was an emergency political measure meant to unify and strengthen the country on the eve of a new European war. For that it was too late. Far from strengthening Yugoslavia, King Alexander's dictatorship had disrupted political life and created disorientation among the Serbs, without breaking the Croats' striving for self-rule. The Serbs, as it turned out, were the only ones to fall for their own propaganda of 'one nation with three names.' The Yugoslav experiment had diminished their leaders' ability to pursue a commonly agreed Serb national interest. In contrast, throughout this period there had existed a consistent 'Croat line' embodied in the HSS. It was characterized by dual-track approach. Maček did not conceal his desire that the

Banovina jurisdiction and territory should be eventually increased, but he claimed to accept the Royal Yugoslav solution (embodied in the Banovina's coat of arms, r.) as the framework for the achievement of that objective. On the other hand, many HSS field activists and the party press talked of the Agreement as but a bare minimum, 'the first step,' and hinted that the final objective was nothing short of full independence. Such approach reflected  real differences of opinion within the HSS. The hard-liners attacked Maček for his failure to take advantage of the 'unique' situation, ally the Croat cause with the Axis, and work for an independent Croatia.[100]

The outbreak of war in September 1939 was immediately followed by Yugoslavia's declaration of neutrality. This was accepted by both belligerent camps. The Western allies accepted it since they knew that they could not expect more.[101] Germany's focus was elsewhere, and her supplies of food and raw materials needed for the war effort continued to arrive as before. Even though Belgrade was intimately sympathetic to Britain and especially France, Germany had little reason for concern. Her quick victory over Poland, while the Allies remained passive, created a deep impression.[102] Talking to Ciano on October 1, 1939 Hitler calmly remarked that "for the time being nothing new is going to happen in the Balkans." By the end of 1940, however, the geostrategic and political position of Yugoslavia suddenly grew precarious. The equation changed irreversibly

[100] Jere Jareb. *Pola stoljeća hrvatske politike, 1895-1945*. Buenos Aires: Knjižnica Hrvatske revije, 1960, p. 72.

[101] Cf. Shone to Halifax: PRO, F.O. 371, f-23885, R9975.

[102] *Documents on German Foreign Policy 1918-1945* (DGFP), D, 8, No 155, Heeren to the Foreign Ministry, 28 September 1939.

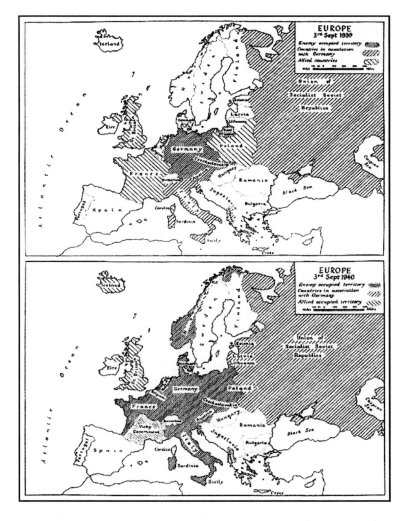

with Mussolini's attack on Greece. Subsequent Italian military setbacks and British involvement in the defense of Greece forced Germany not only to become more directly involved in the Southeast, but also to assume a more explicit final word in what was nominally Italy's zone of influence.

Increased German pressure on Yugoslavia initially took the form of vague demands that it should become more friendly to the Axis. Once its hand was forced by the Italian action in

121

Greece, Germany no longer wooed Belgrade; now was the time to bully it into submission.[103] The pressure was not only political, but also economic.[104] Prince Paul saw the writing on the wall.[105] His pessimism reflected the mood of shock which the rapid fall of France caused in Yugoslavia, especially among the traditionally Francophile Belgrade elite.

In early 1941 Germany's diplomatic and military pincer movement in the Balkans was in full swing. One by one, Yugoslavia's neighbors to the north and east were joining the Tripartite Pact and accepting German troops on their territory. The primary objective of Germany was to prepare the attack on the Soviet Union (Operation Barbarossa); the secondary was to reach Greece and attack it from the northeast. In the process, Belgrade found itself physically encircled. Most of Germany's new Balkan allies had actual or potential irredentist claims against Yugoslavia, which left the country vulnerable militarily and psychologically. In the Balkans, in the winter of 1940-1941, it was not easy to enjoy the distinction of being the very last 'Versailles creation' to have its 1919 frontiers still intact.

Prince Paul's policy of neutrality, pursued as long as possible, ended at the Belvedere on 25 March 1941. The signing of the Tripartite Pact was not an expression of the Prince's political will, but it was the best he could hope for: Hitler made several major concessions, including the pledge not to demand transit rights for German troops or supplies across Yugoslav territory. This was a diplomatic victory for the beleaguered government in Belgrade: "By dragging their feet for so long, they had shown unequalled courage in the face of a state so much stronger than themselves."[106] The leaders in Belgrade hoped that the watered-down version of the Pact, grudgingly

---

[103] DGFP, D, 9, No. 517. Heeren's report of 21 June 1940.

[104] Cf. e.g. DGFP, D, 9, No. 442. Policy Dept. to Heeren, 15 June 1940.

[105] DGFP, D, 10, No. 395. Heeren's report of 26 August 1940.

[106] Martin van Creveld. *Hitler's Strategy 1940-1941: The Balkan Clue*. Cambridge University Press 1973, p. 139

accepted by Hitler, would calm public opinion at home. It did not. The government of Cvetković and Maček, and Prince Paul personally, did not enjoy the confidence of the Serbian public necessary for the acceptance of a decision dictated by pragmatism but odious to common people's sentiment.

In the early hours of March 27, 1941, a group of officers led by Air Force generals Bora Mirković and Dušan Simović took power in an almost bloodless coup in Belgrade. It is still unclear what was their long-term plan, and whether they had one. The inability of the British to offer military assistance was already known in Yugoslav military circles. The strategic position of the country was hopeless. The apologists of the coup have claimed that, for all its awful consequences, it enabled Yugoslavia to avoid the allegedly inevitable further slide into the Axis war camp; but that argument is belied by the example of Bulgaria.

The sentiment prevailed and it was echoed in the streets of Belgrade (r.) and other Serbian cities in the slogan of 'Better grave than slave' (*Bolje grob nego rob*) and 'Better war than the Pact'  (*Bolje rat nego pakt*). The event is known in Serbia simply as 'the 27th of March.' It was an act of explicit rejection of political realism for unclear goals. The conspirators reflected a Serbian tradition harking back to the *hajduks* and the regicide of 1903. In 1941 the upholders of that tradition were disconnected from any notion of national interest rationally defined and prudently pursued. Its proponents sought legitimacy in the support of an excitable mob. Even their *a posteriori* claim that it contributed to victory over Nazism, allegedly by forcing Hitler to postpone his attack on Russia, was false. British intelligence was heavily involved, but its machinations would not have sufficed were it not for the Serbs' willingness to act rashly.

In Berlin the news caused shock. Hitler had an attack of fury and treated the coup as a personal blow. He decided to smash Yugoslavia.[107] He would do it with assistance from Italy, Bulgaria, and, a few days later, Hungary.[108] The German attack (see map) started on April 6, 1941, with a vengeful bombing of

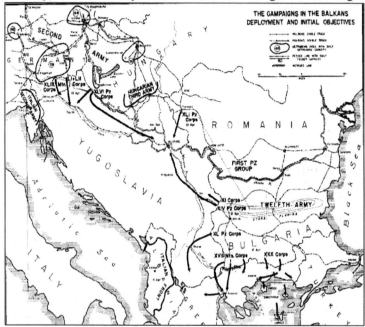

Belgrade. It ended in the military and political collapse ten days later. Unconsolidated Yugoslavia – or, rather, disoriented Serbia – may have "found its soul" (as Churchill claimed), but in doing so it headed straight for 'the Kingdom of Heaven' in the mythical tradition of Prince Lazar, martyred at Kosovo in 1389. The Serbs have not recovered since.

Hitler did not seek to break up Yugoslavia before the coup of March 27. He *did* want to break up the Little Entente and to exclude French influence from Central Europe. To that end, from

---

[107] Cf. DGFP, D, 12, No. 217. Conference Minutes, 27 March 1941.

[108] *The Confidential Papers of Admiral Horthy*. Budapest: Corvina Press, 1965, p. 176.

his earliest days in power, he sought to woo Yugoslavia rather than to seek its destruction. This was in contrast with his policy towards other 'Versailles creations,' Czechoslovakia and Poland. The theme of a strong Yugoslavia friendly to Germany as the key to Berlin's policy in the Balkans was a salient feature of German diplomatic documents in the 1930s.[109]

The main cause of the fall of Yugoslavia was the military superiority of the German Reich. Even if the country had been united in the will to resist, the defense would have been hopeless. In April 1941 there had been no military, economic, geo-political or psychological foundations for a sustained defense of the Yugoslav state.

The National Museum, Belgrade, after the bombing, April 1941

---

[109] Dušan Biber. "Ustaše i Treći Reich; Prilog problematici jugoslovensko-nemačkih odnosa." in *Jugoslovenski istorijski časopis*, No 2, p. 44.

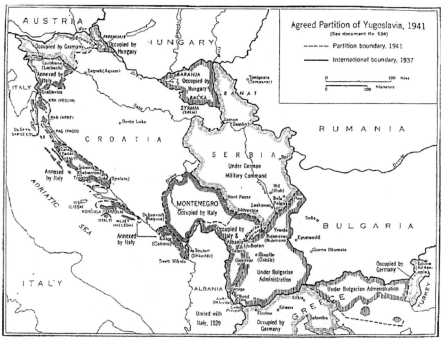

U.S. Department of State, *Documents on German Foreign Policy*. Series D (1937-1945), Vol. XII
Washington, DC: USGPO, 1962

YUGOSLAVIA AFTER AXIS CONQUEST, 1941-1945

Serbs Outlawed

The system of occupation in the former Yugoslavia, hastily created in April 1941, was an improvization presumably temporary in nature. Immediately following the successful completion of operations and the surrender of the royal army (17 April) Hitler paid scant attention to the newly conquered area. Initially, while planning the attack, he envisaged Croatia in some sort of union with Hungary, or as an autonomous rather than fully independent state, "probably under Hungarian influence."[110] A week later (12 April) the Wehrmacht Provisional Guidelines on the partition of Yugoslavia mentioned an "independent Croatian state," but with the specific exclusion of Bosnia-Herzegovina.

The proclamation of the 'Independent State of Croatia' on Zagreb's radio was made on April 10, 1941 by one of Pavelić's followers, former Austrian-Hungarian officer Slavko Kvaternik. This was not the Germans' favorite option, however. It was adopted in the absence of a better alternative following the entry of German troops into Croatia's capital earlier that day. In the preceding two weeks Vladko Maček had turned down repeated German offers of political power under their patronage. At the same time he annulled the potential moral capital of that refusal when he addressed the HSS rank and file over the radio immediately after Kvaternik and asked his followers to "extend sincere cooperation" to the new regime.

In the meantime the leader of the Ustaša movement and his two hundred followers were still in Italy. Until 27 March they were politically and militarily passive, dispersed all over the peninsula, and demoralized. The Italians insisted on their total inactivity, in view of the impending signing of the Tripartite Pact

---

[110] DGFP, D, 12, No 291. Unsigned memorandum initialled by Foreign Ministry officials Ritter and Woermann on 6 April 1941.

by the government of Cvetković and Maček.[111] But on 28 March, upon learning of Hitler's decision to attack Yugoslavia, Mussolini decided to reactivate Pavelić. Two meetings took place in the two weeks between the coup in Belgrade and Pavelić's departure for Zagreb. The first, on 29 March, was attended by acting foreign minister Anfuso, who was taking notes. Pavelic asserted his readiness to accept Italy's annexation of Dalmatia: "He confirms earlier obligations to Italy; he guarantees that he will carry them out; he disperses any doubts about his loyalty."[112] Anfuso's impression of Pavelić's talks with Mussolini was clear: "Of these two men of politics, who are discussing their national problems, one is fatally returning to his

home country as a traitor." Pavelić was well aware what effect the loss of Dalmatia would produce, but only wanted "to avoid the impression of being a renegade."

At his second meeting with Mussolini on April 11 Pavelić (r.) confirmed the agreement on Italy's right to annex Dalmatia reached two weeks earlier. [113] He left Rome for Trieste on the same day. On 12 April at 10 p.m., with his two hundred men in tow, he left Trieste in a convoy of municipal buses provided by the district military commander. They crossed the old Italian-Yugoslav border at Sušak shortly after 2 a.m. on 13 April. The group passed through the area of Gorski Kotar in jubilant mood. In the village of Srpske Moravice, the first settlement with a large Serb population (as its name implies), Pavelić's entourage halted and seized some two hundred inhabitants from their

---

[111] Eugen-Dido Kvaternik in *Hrvatska Revija* (1952), p. 209.

[112] Filippo Anfuso, *Roma Berlino Salo* (1936-1945). Milano: Edizione Garzanti, 1950, p. 186 and on.

[113] Anfuso, op. cit. pp. 189-190

homes. They were lined up at gunpoint, abused, threatened, and eventually set free. This was, after all, only the first day, but the writing was on the wall. The spectacle was repeated at Ogulin, where the local Roman Catholic parish priest, Fr. Ivan Mikan, addressed the captive Serbs and said "Now there will be some cleansing.... Scoot you dogs over the Drina." The terror started on the same day Pavelić arrived to take over his 'state.' On 15 April Pavelić arrived in Zagreb and entered the Ban's Palace in the Old City (Gornji Grad). The NDH had become the latest addition to the 'New European Order.' Thanks to Maček's endorsement of the new regime – contained in his radio call for *sincere co-operation* – Pavelić could rely on the administrative and paramilitary network of the HSS. Establishment of state

authority would have been much more difficult if the HSS rank-and-file had remained on the sidelines.

In the first weeks after 10 April there existed a degree of support for the new order among many Croats, reflected in the tremendous welcome given to German troops in Zagreb (l.). This early wave enabled Pavelić to consolidate himself in the initial period. Although he lacked the charismatic personality of a Hitler or a Mussolini, he was the undisputed leader of his initially small movement, and proceeded to equate 'Croat' and 'Ustaša.' This was the key feature of his propaganda throughout the war, coupled with the *Führerprinzip*. His mix of Nazi brutality and racism, fascist irrationality and reinvented primitivism soon turned Croatia into a pandemonium of anarchy and genocide.

The NDH never had a constitution; instead, on 16 April 1941 Pavelic swore an oath on the 'Ustaša Principles' and proclaimed them 'the supreme law' of the state. Numerous fiats introduced in the first weeks were not legislated through an assembly, because no such body existed. Legislation was reduced to a series of decrees and ordinances issued by Pavelić or on his orders. He had the sole right of appointing and dismissing ministers, secretaries of state and heads of state directorates (the 'Law' of 24 June 1941). All ministers were directly responsible to him; cabinet sessions were very rare and Pavelić dealt with his ministers one-on-one.

In addition, Pavelić established separate 'directorates' (*Ravnateljstva*) in charge of certain affairs that were taken away from the brief of the ministry originally responsible for them. The heads of such directorates were directly under his command, like ministers. A prominent example was that of the notorious Eugen-Dido Kvaternik, 'Marshal' Slavko's son, who became Director for Public Order and Security (*Ravnatelj za javni red i sigurnost*, RAVSIGUR), an institution separate from the interior ministry. In that post he unleashed an unprecedented reign of genocidal terror against Serbs, Jews, and any suspected or real opponents of the regime.

The state had no coherent program. The all-pervasive Serb-hatred and copycat Nazi antisemitism were coupled with the proclaimed goal to turn the NDH into an 'Ustaša-state' (*Ustaška država*). This meant Pavelić's unlimited personal power. In a speech on 21 May 1941 he said that he would bear responsibility "to the entire Croat people for all [government] acts, while all state organs, officials and employees will be responsible to me – and you know that I am not joking."[114] In practice this meant that he was not going to be accountable to anyone.

An elaborate apparatus of internal control was soon established. On 10 May the Ustaša movement constituted an armed militia (*Ustaška vojnica*) as its military muscle, and the Ustaša Supervisory Service (*Ustaška nadzorna sluzba*, UNS), the security service similar in structure and methods to the Gestapo in Germany. Independent of both stood Kvaternik-

---

[114] *Hrvatski narod*, 22 May 1941.

junior's dreaded Directorate for Public Security, with its own network of agents and armed units, and the Ustasa police (*Ustaško redarstvo*). The tools of terror were ready; the bloodbath could begin.

Germany's limited initial interest in Croatia was apparent in Hitler's instructions given to his newly-appointed plenipotentiary military representative in Zagreb, General Edmund Glaise von

Horstenau (l.). Suave and eloquent, a polished KuK officer with a solid reputation as a military historian earned between the wars, Glaise combined an intense nostalgia for the Habsburg Monarchy with Nazi sympathies.[115] On 14 April 1941 Glaise reported to Hitler at his special train in southern Austria to receive instructions. Knowing that Glaise was an inveterate Italophobe like most former Habsburg officers, Hitler warned him that Italy would have to be granted priority in the new state:

As for Croatia, the task is to get it swiftly consolidated so that German troops can withdraw. I will need the Second Army in another place soon, the Fuehrer remarked significantly, and he did not need to explain where that could be. This would be our political objective in Croatia; everything else the country would have to do by itself, while taking into account Italy and her aspirations.[116]

---

[115] Glaise's diary is an invaluable primary source on German policy in Croatia. Together with other papers from his tenure in Zagreb, it is kept in the War Archive in Vienna (KAW B/67). It was published in 1988 as the final volume of Broucek's trilogy: Peter Broucek (Hrsg.), *Ein General im Zwielicht. Die Erinnerungen Edmund Glaise von Horstenau*, 3 Bände, Wien: Böhlau 1980-88.

Similar instructions were given to the newly appointed German minister in Zagreb, *SA-Obergruppenführer* Siegfried Kasche. He was a newcomer to diplomacy, drafted by Ribbentrop into the Foreign Ministry to infuse it with the Nazi spirit.[117] Kasche was told on the eve of his departure for Zagreb that the Croats and Italians were not likely to get on well, and that the former would appeal to Kasche, hoping to turn him into an arbiter. As long as the war was going on, however, the German side was obliged to respect Italian sensibility without reserve. Any mediation would have to result in support for Italy, which would only alienate the Croats. Therefore, the German Minister should "stay aloof."

On 17 April Glaise came to see Hitler again and asked him if Germany had already accepted obligations regarding Italy's borders. Hitler said that no specific promises had been given but that Italian interests had to be given priority. He added that handing over Dalmatia to Italy could be useful because it would create "a permanent basis for conflicts between Italians and Croats, whereby Germany could always reserve the role of an arbiter." In addition to predicting Croat-Italian strife Hitler also envisaged the flaring up of internal conflicts between Serbs and Croats, which would prevent stabilization of the new state and result "in a permanent schism between nations which had been within one state until now." The effect on the future role of Germany would be the same: by creating discord between Croats and their neighbors, the Germans ensured their presence and enhanced their influence. Hitler was to repeat this formula often in later years, to the chagrin of German generals who regarded the Ustašas' anti-Serb policy as a major cause of permanent turmoil in the NDH. The policy of letting Italy make enemies of

---

[116] Glaise's diary, 14 April 1941. Hitler was alluding to the Barbarossa. Compare: Vasa Kazimirović, *NDH u svetlu nemačkih dokumenata i dnevnika Gleza fon Horstenau.* Belgrade: Narodna knjiga, 1987.

[117] Ladislaus Hory and Martin Broszat, *Der kroatische Ustascha-Staat, 1941-1945.* Stuttgart : Deutsche Verlags-Anstalt, 1965, pp. 60-61; Nachlass S. Kasche, PA, Nachlässe.

Croats and letting Croats make enemies of Serbs may have seemed a clever ploy to Hitler in April 1941. Ultimately Hitler's game of *divide et impera* turned into a major liability for Germany's position in southeast Europe.

The occasion to settle the partition of Yugoslavia (see map, below) and to coordinate Axis policy came in Vienna on 21-22 April 1941, at a meeting between Ciano and Ribbentrop arranged on German initiative. Ribbentrop indicated that the frontiers of the newly created state would be drawn "in accordance with Italian interests."[118] He said that the main goal of the new order in the Balkans was to prevent "once and for all" the repetition of a betrayal such as Serbia perpetrated in March 1941.[119]

Ciano responded by producing a map: the whole of Dalmatia and the rest of the Adriatic coast from Fiume to Cattaro [Kotor] would be annexed by Italy. Montenegro would be resurrected as a state in personal union with Italy, while parts of northwestern Macedonia and Kosovo would go to Albania. Croatia was likewise to be tied to Italy by a personal union.

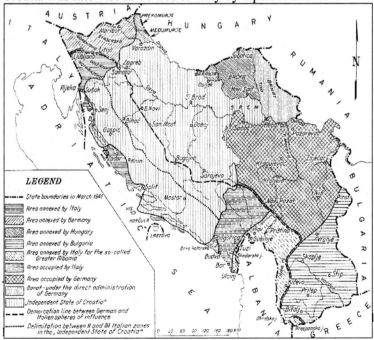

The Germans had no objection to the Italian annexation of Dalmatia.[120] The only surprise was their decision to maintain an occupation force "in a strip of Croatia running from north-west to south-east in order to safeguard the railroad communication with Serbia." Until that moment the Italians were made to believe that the whole of Croatia was their sphere of interest, but accepted the change without ado. The Axis position was thus fixed. The Vienna talks confirmed the nature of Hitler's strategy in the Balkans. Germany would let Italy enlarge itself on the eastern Adriatic shore, and Italy could do it only thanks to German acquiescence. Hitler was going to let Mussolini (r.) fall into a trap of his own making – and make Germany appear magnanimous for doing so.

The terms of Italy's annexation of Dalmatia were reached at a meeting between Ciano and Pavelić on 25 April 1941. (Ciano's diary entry says, "I see Pavelić, surrounded by his band of cutthroats.") The formal treaty to that effect, the *Rome Agreements*, was signed on May 18. Mussolini opted for an unnecessary and burdensome territorial expansion across the Adriatic. He allowed emotions to prevail over prudence; as Ciano noted on 1 May in his diary: "The Duce is aware of our real interest, but is stubborn about yielding on the question of Spalato." His insistence may have been due in part to the pressure of events in Africa, which were catastrophic for the Italian army. The morale-boosting effect of gains in Dalmatia were negligible, however. In the nineteenth and early 20th century Dalmatia was regarded as a legitimate national aspiration. In 1941, however, the Italian public at large was indifferent to it. The facts of geography and demography seemed irreversible: one in twenty inhabitants of Dalmatia regarded

---

[120] Ciano's summary of 22 April, ibid. Also: DGFP, D, 12, No 385.

himself as Italian. In the spring of 1941 most Italians were more worried about the food shortage, or the surrender of the Croatian King-designate's brother, the Duke of Aosta, to the British at Amba Aladji in northern Ethiopia.

The problem of Italy's relations with Croatia was formally solved, but it was only beginning. The marriage of convenience between Italian irredentism and Croat ultra-chauvinism was finally consummated. Dalmatia meant that they could not be permanently reconciled, but they needed each other to achieve their goals. Mussolini exacted his lump-sum payment in the form of an economically depressed and demographically alien territory but forfeited a permanent deed in the form of customs union and military control. Pavelić kept his side of the bargain. After that, there was little to keep the two parties together.

The surrender of Dalmatia marked an early erosion of the credibility of the new regime.[121] Three days after returning from Rome Pavelić attempted to rectify the effect by delivering a major speech in which he admitted that "we had to make some sacrifices."[122] He ended with grave threats against the Serbs, seeking to shift the focus away from the Rome Agreements onto the enemy within:

> We shall not allow enemies of the Croats to work against them, to poison them from within.[...] The times when the Croat people were but an object are over. The Croat nation is the master now, and everything else will be *its* object. These are clear indications of our intentions, which are being applied and will be carried out. I shall carry them out! And you know that I have fulfilled all my promises.

Pavelić was true to his word. The 'fulfilment' was to cost hundreds of thousands of lives.

---

[121] For immediate reaction of the people in Croatia, see Glaise's report to the OKW of 19 May: PA, Büro Staatssekretär, Kroatien, Bd 1.

[122] As reported by *Hrvatski narod*, Zagreb, 22 May 1941 (Vol. 3, No. 99).

After the coup of 27 March, Hitler was determined to impose a brutal, Carthaginian peace on the Serbs. Already the indiscriminate bombing of Belgrade on 6 April, and the instant decision to cut Serbia down to its pre-1912 size, indicated that they were singled out for special punishment. Hitler's vindictiveness was confirmed when Pavelić visited him on June 6, 1941, and received encouragement to start persecuting them.

During a preliminary meeting with foreign minister Joachim von Ribbentrop, the German asked Pavelić about his plans for solving the problem of the large Serb minority in the NDH. The Poglavnik replied that "there had been no Serb question" in Croatia until 70 years earlier, when the impact of Orthodoxy imbued those people with the "mistaken" feeling of Serb identity. [123] He said that they would be expelled.

Hitler welcomed Ante Pavelić later on the same day. [124] He said that the course of events in March 1941 had made him "an unwilling instrument of Croatia's liberation": he had not intended to act against Yugoslavia, but the Serbs forced his hand. The key part of the conversation concerned national policy. Picking up the theme mentioned by Ribbentrop, Hitler described plans to transfer Serbs from the NDH to Serbia and Slovenes from the Reich into Croatia as a 'momentarily painful' operation that was nevertheless preferable to constant suffering. [125] Then he added the key sentence:

> After all, if the Croatian state truly wishes to be strong, then a nationally intolerant policy must be pursued for the next fifty years, because too much tolerance on such issues can only do harm.

---

[123] PA, Büro RAM, Handakten Schmidt, Aufzeichnungen: 1941 (Teil II).

[124] DGFP, D, 12, Minutes of Hitler's talks with Paveli}, 6 June 1941.

[125] The Serbs in the NDH numbered two million, or one third of the population; for Ustaša estimate see *Hrvatski narod*, 19 May 1941.

With this statement Hitler explicitly endorsed the mass persecution of the Serbs in the NDH that had already started, but was to reach its climax in subsequent months. Hitler's encouragement to Pavelić at their first meeting (above) to pursue 'intolerance' was in line with his intention – stated to Glaise on 17 April – to encourage internal Serb-Croat conflict as "the guarantee of a permanent schism between nations which had been within one state until now." Using the formula of *divide et impera*, Hitler let the Italians make enemies of Croats; and he would let the Croats make enemies of Serbs. In the event, both Pavelić and Mussolini performed on cue.

Hitler's advocacy of 'intolerance' did not make any difference to the thousands of Serbs already slaughtered in the NDH before 6 June. The first recorded mass murder of Serbs occurred in Bjelovar on the night of 27-28 April 1941, when between 180 and 190 unarmed civilians of all ages were shot. Such instances were repeated in different areas throughout the month of May.[126] It is nevertheless unlikely that the wave of terror which engulfed the NDH in the summer of 1941 would have been so bloody had Hitler wanted to put a stop to it. His encouragement to Pavelić had a major long-term impact, not because it induced the *Poglavnik* to embark on genocide – the intent had been there all along – but because it gave him *carte blanche* to pursue his goal. In Berchtesgaden Hitler made Pavelić *feel authorized* to proceed with his attempted destruction of the Serbs, Jews (antisemitic Ustaša poster, r.), and Gypsies.

The Serb population in Croatia, Bosnia-Herzegovina and Srem was shocked by the speedy fall of the state they regarded as their own, and displayed mute acceptance of the new order. Some saw it as a re-enactment of Austria-Hungary – a state which, while not loved, was well respected. As they were to learn to their peril, in the NDH there was no rational correlation between a Serb's deeds and the state's attitude. Having a Serb identity was a political act in itself, tantamount to treason: "those who 'wanted to be Serbs' and

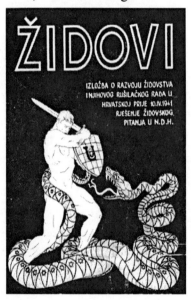

who 'insisted on being Serbs' should be punished for that."[127]

The quasi-legal instruments of punishment were developed with remarkable speed. Two days after arriving in Zagreb, on 17 April, Pavelić enacted a fiat called *The Law on the Protection of the People and the State*. It literally made it 'legal' for the regime to kill anyone. Capital punishment was made mandatory

---

[126] See Fikreta Jelić-Butić: *HSS*. Zagreb 1983, p. 47.

[127] Aleksa Djilas, unpublished PhD thesis, History Department, Harvard University, Cambridge, Mass., p. 245.

for all those who 'offended the honor and vital interests of the Croat people' and who 'in whatever way' threatened the NDH. There was no appeal, and each sentence had to be carried out within two hours. The 'law,' furthermore, had retroactive powers. 'Special popular courts' and mobile court-martials were immediately established with the discretionary powers of life or death. This 'law' was seldom invoked, however; when the killing started in earnest, even purely formal procedures were discarded as cumbersome and time-consuming.

On April 18, the first antisemitic racial law, on the *Aryanization of Jewish property*, was enacted. It enabled the regime to expropriate Jewish businesses and real estate and to distribute the spoils. Jewish-owned apartments were swiftly given to the emerging Ustaša *nomenklatura*.

Dozens of speeches by Ustaša officials at public meetings all over the NDH and countless propaganda articles published in May and June 1941 were preparing the ground for the pogrom. Pavelić's men were frank about the Serbs: "Destroy them wherever you see them, and our Poglavnik's blessing is certain," Viktor Gutic, district commander in Banja Luka, declared.[128] Pavelić's 'minister of justice' was equally clear:

This State, our country, is only for the Croats, and not for anyone else. There are no means which we will not be ready to use in order to make our country truly ours, and to cleanse it of all Serbs. All those who came into our country 300 years ago must disappear. We do not hide this is our intention. It is the policy of our State. In the course of its execution we shall simply follow the Ustaša principles.[129]

In a highly publicized speech in the town of Gospić (Lika) on 22 July 1941, Mile Budak, Pavelić's minister of education, announced to the roar of approval, "We have three million bullets for Serbs, Jews and Gypsies. We shall kill one third of all

---

[128] Kazimirović, p.111.

[129] From a speech by Dr. Milovan Žanić. *Novi list* (Zagreb daily), 3 June 1941.

Serbs. We shall deport another third, and the rest of them will be forced to become Catholic." The *so-called Serbs*, Budak (r.) added, are not any *Serbs* at all, but people brought by the Turks "as the plunderers

and refuse of the Balkans... They should know, and heed, our motto: *either submit, or get out!*"

Ustaša ideology evolved from three intertwined intellectual, social and emotional components: Ethnicity, religion, and violence.[130] In the tradition of Starčević, the Serbs' nationality was denied and the term *Vlachs* or 'Greek-Easterners' (*Grko-iztočnjaci*) applied instead. Paradoxically, however, they were also depicted as apostates and traitors, implicitly not of alien stock at all, but apostates who had betrayed 'their mother country' Croatia to foreign, Austrian, Hungarian, or Serbian interests. The implication was that they were Croats who had converted to Orthodoxy and thus accepted the Serb name by default. (This view was reflected in Pavelić's tragicomic 1942 experiment with the *Croatian Orthodox Church* under a Russian émigré bishop, Germogen.) Hermann Neubacher, Hitler's political expert for the Balkans, summed up the Ustaša intent: "One third must be converted to Catholicism, another third must be expelled, and the final third must die. The last part of the program has been carried out."[131]

Another German observer noted the wide circulation, as soon as the new regime took over, of slogans such as "Hang the Serbs on willow trees" (*Srbe na vrbe*), "there will be blood up to the knee," or "we shall tear their babies out of their mothers'

---

[130] Jonathan Gumz, "German Counterinsurgency Policy in Independent Croatia, 1941-1944." *The Historian*, Vol. 61 (1998), pp. 33-51.

[131] Hermann Neubacher. *Sonderaufrag Südost 1940-1945. Bericht eines fliegenden Diplomaten.* Goettingen: Muster-Schmidt-Verlag, 1957, p. 18.

wombs!"[132] The religious component was prominent. The old notion that Serbs were 'Orthodox Croats' was replaced by the demand for outright conversion or death. The Croatian Catholic press wrote gloatingly about what was in store for the 'schismatics' and other enemies of the New Order:

> When in the past God spoke through papal encyclicals, they closed their ears. Now God uses other means. He will set up missions ... upheld not by priests but by army commanders, led by Hitler. Their sermons will be heard thanks to guns, tanks and bombers.[133]

The German security service (SD) expert for the Southeast, Dr. Wilhelm Hoettl, noted that forced conversions from Orthodoxy to Catholicism figured prominently on the Ustaša agenda:

> Since being Croat was equivalent to confessing to the Catholic faith, and being Serb followed the profession of Orthodoxy, they now began to convert the Orthodox to Roman Catholicism under duress. Forced conversions were actually a method of Croatization."[134]

The Roman Catholic hierarchy in Croatia, aligned with the Habsburg cause until 1918, saw the creation of Yugoslavia as an unwelcome episode. After the *Sporazum* of 1939 its publications felt emboldened to publish articles calling for full independence. After April 10 part of the hierarchy became *de facto* accomplices, as did a majority of the clergy. The leading NDH racial 'theorist' was a clergyman, Dr. Ivo Guberina, whose writings sought to reconcile religious 'purification' and 'racial hygiene.' He urged Croatia's 'cleansing of foreign elements' by any means. His views were echoed by the influential head of the Ustaša Central Propaganda Office, Fr. Grga Peinović. When the

---

[132] Dr. Josef Matl in *Iskra* (Munich), March 20, 1959.

[133] *Katolički Tjednik*, Zagreb, 31 August 1941.

[134] Walter Hagen. *The Secret Front: the Story of Nazi Political Espionage.* London: Weidenfeld and Nicholson, 1953, p. 238. 'Hagen' was Hoettl.

anti-Serb and anti-Jewish racial laws of April and May 1941 were enacted the Catholic press welcomed them as vital for "the survival and development of the Croatian nation."[135] On the subject of those laws the Archbishop of Sarajevo Ivan Šarić (r.) declared that "there are limits to love."[136]   The head of the Croatian Catholic Church, Archbishop Alojzije Stepinac, was careful with his early public statements; Saric was less circumspect: "It is stupid and unworthy of Christ's disciples to think that the struggle against evil could be waged in a noble way and with gloves on."

Within weeks of April 10, 1941, all gloves were off.

Coat of arms of the Ustaša Croatia

---

[135] *Hrvatska Straža*, May 11, 1941

[136] Šarić published a poem in the Christmas 1941 issue of *Katolicki tjednik*: "Dr Ante Pavelić! the dear name! Croatia has therein a treasure from Heaven. May the King of Heaven accompany thee, our Golden Leader!"

The Bloodbath

The Ustaša terror unleashed in the summer of 1941 was without precedent in the history of Southeastern Europe, a region known for its violent past. It was also, if only by a few weeks, the first attempted genocide in the Second World War. The goal of the Pavelić regime in making that attempt was not in doubt to its Axis mentors: "From the start the main Ustaša objective was to annihilate the Orthodox, to butcher hundreds of thousands of persons, women and children."[137] Some German sources saw this annihilation as the goal not limited to the Ustaša regime but shared by the non-Serb population at large: "There is no doubt at all that the Croats are endeavoring to destroy the entire Serb population."[138]

The application of the Ustaša program meant that, in the words of German historian Ernst Nolte, "Croatia became during the war a giant slaughterhouse." In late spring and summer of 1941 dozens of towns and villages throughout the NDH were subjected to a wave of terrorist operations. It was unprecedented, far bloodier than anything seen in the Balkans until that time. Hundreds of of thousands of Serbs, as well as tens of thousands of Jews and Gypsies, were murdered on the spot or led away to camps to be killed. As an officer and a gentleman of the old school, General Glaise von Horstenau was horrified by the 'barbaric' methods used against the Serbs. He noted the fact that they were "fundamentally placed outside the law, outlawed" (*vogelfrei*).[139] Even the hardened Nazis were shocked by what they witnessed: according to a Gestapo report prepared for

---

[137] SS *Obergruppenführer* Arthur Phleps, *Tagesbuch*. Nr.Ia/545, 44 J.G.

[138] General Bader, quoted in Karl Hlinicka. *Das Ende auf dem Balkan 1944/45: Die Militärische Räumung Jugoslawiens durch die Deutsche Wehrmacht.* Goettingen: Musterscheudt, 1970, p. 187.

[139] Gert Fricke. *Kroatien 1941-1944: Die "Unabhängige Staat" in der Sicht des Deutschen Bevollmächtigen Generals in Agram, Glaise v. Horstenau.* Freiburg: Rombach Verlag, 1972, p. 39.

Himmler, "The Ustašas committed their bestial crimes not only against males of military age, but especially against helpless old people, women and children."[140]

The number of victims will never be known; it is still a politically charged issue. Holocaust historians estimate that half a million, and perhaps as many as 530,000 Serbs were killed.[141] Yad Vashem center in Jerusalem quotes a similar figure:

> More than 500,000 Serbs were murdered in horribly sadistic ways (mostly in the summer of 1941), 250,000 were expelled, and another 200,000 were forced to convert to Catholicism... [S]ome 30,000 of Croatia's Jews died ... 80 percent of the country's Jewish population.[142]

Given that, in April 1941, the Serbs constituted about one third of the total NDH population of six million, this level of casualties makes them the second hardest hit population in Hitler's Europe, right after the Jews.[143]

Estimates made by several high-ranking German and Italian officials during the war were even higher.

In a report to Heinrich Himmler, SS General Ernst Frick thus estimated that "600 to 700,000 victims were butchered in the Balkan fashion."[144]

Hitler's political envoy to the Balkans Hermann Neubacher was of the opinion that as many as 750,000 Serbs were killed.[145]

---

[140] PA, Büro RAM, Kroatien, 1941-42, 442-449. IV/D/4.

[141] Jonathan Steinberg, "Types of Genocide: Croatians, Serbs, and Jews, 1941-1945," in David Cesarani, *The Final Solution: Origins and Implementation.* Routledge 1996, p. 175

[142] "Croatia," in *Shoah Resource Center.* Jerusalem: The International School for Holocaust Studies at Yad Vashem, 2005.

[143] For a demographic study using statistical methods of calculating demographic losses, see Bogoljub Kočović. *Žrtve drugog svetskog rata u Jugoslaviji.* Belgrade 2005.

[144] Hlinicka, op. cit. p. 292.

[145] Neubacher, op. cit..

General Lothar Rendulic, commanding German forces in the western Balkans in 1943-1944, estimated the number of Ustaša victims to be 500,000:

> When I objected to a high official who was close to Pavelić that, in spite of the accumulated hatred, I failed to comprehend the murder of half a million Orthodox, the answer I received was characteristic of the mentality that prevailed there: "Half a million, that's too much – there weren't more than 200,000!"[146]

The NDH needed no quasi-legislation for the slaughter to begin. With all power in the hands of Pavelić, and some 30,000 armed Ustaša volunteers at his disposal by June 1941, he and his henchmen on the ground felt they could do literally as they pleased. They would pick up a Serb village or town, as they did in Glina in August 1941, have it surrounded, order all inhabitants to gather in the local Orthodox church, tie them and kill them on the spot. They could throw them down a nearby karst pit – as they did at Golubinka near Medjugorje, in Herzegovina – or send them to a death camp such as Jadovno, which operated in June-August 1941. Throughout the summer of 1941 one of these scenarios was unfolding on daily basis. The method of killing, in the camps and villages alike, was typically a slit throat or a blow with a heavy club in the back of the head. More piquant

---

[146] Lothar Rendulic. *Gekaempft, gesiegt, geschlagen.* Welsermühl Verlag, Wels und Heidelberg, 1952, p.161.

methods, such as sawing off the head of the victim (l.), were too time consuming and therefore rare. The hardest hit areas were in Herzegovina and the Krajina.

The Ustaša regime introduced the methods of terror and extermination soon adopted by the *Einsatzgruppen*: mobile detachments of hardened killers roamed the countryside, destroying entire communities regardless of age or gender solely on the basis of their ethnicity and religion. This parallel was not incidental. It reflected a key similarity between the Ustasa regime and the Nazis, their essential nihilism. Just as the military goals of Barbarossa were incidental to the objective of killing Jews and enslaving Slavs, so the enlistment of Croatia into the Nazi-sponsored New Europe was incidental to the Ustašas' central purpose: eliminating Serbs.

Terror and genocide were to be pursued even if this endangered vital state interests, e.g. by causing mass uprisings of Serbs or by fanning insurgency in previously peaceful areas. Far from helping the war effort the terror undermined it, but the Ustaša and Nazi leaders considered genocide *a fundamental duty* that transcended the victory in war itself.

The commitment to genocide as an existential good-in-itself distinguishes Hitler's and Pavelić's bloodbaths from other despotic regimes in history. Some Ustaša leaders freely acknowledged their priorities. In late 1942, shortly before he was removed from his post as the head of *Ravsigur*, Eugen-Dido Kvaternik told his old classmate, HSS activist Branko Pešelj, that he allowed for the possibility that Germany could lose the war and conceded the danger that in that case the NDH would cease to exist. However, he added, "regardless of the outcome of the war there will be no more Serbs in Croatia." This "reality of any post-war situation," Kvaternik said, would be a *fait accompli* for whoever turned out to be the victor.[147]

Between May and August 1941 over a dozen camps were established to handle huge numbers of Serbian and Jewish

---

[147] Branko Pešelj to the author, Washington D.C., May 12, 1988.

deportees from all over the NDH (Danica, Caprag, Kerestinec, Pag, Kruščica, Tenj, Loborgrad, Gornja Rijeka, Djakovo, Sisak, Jastrebarsko, Jadovno, Lepoglava...). The system of hastily constructed and rudimentally organized facilities, of which the one at Jasenovac was the most prominent, turned the NDH into 'a land of concentration camps.'[148] Some establishments (e.g. Jadovno on the Velebit mountain, situated next to a deep limestone pit) were death camps in their own right from the outset, with no accommodation facilities: a primitive precursor to Treblinka. From others, many inmates were moved on for killing to Jasenovac. A major difference between Ustaša and Nazi terror emerges from the accounts of the conditions at Jasenovac given by a handful of survivors.[149]

A notorious massacre took place in August 1941 in the town of Glina. It was one of the largest single acts of mass murder to occur in Yugoslavia during the Second World War. In the weeks preceding this event some 500 Serbs from Glina and the surrounding villages were killed, prompting many Serbs to go into hiding in the region's forests. The Ustaša district command in Glina responded by announcing an 'amnesty' and a guarantee of safety to those Serbs who returned to their homes and agreed to be converted to Roman Catholicism. Several hundred Serbs, mainly old and families with small children, accepted the offer and turned up at the Serbian Orthodox church for the conversion ceremony. The exact numbers are disputed, ranging from at least three hundred (cited at Nuremberg in 1946) to 1,200.[150] The Serbs were herded into the church, the doors of which were locked shut after the last had entered. Only one of the victims, a Serb named Ljubo Jadnak, survived after playing dead and later described what had happened:

[148] Cf. Croatian historian Antun Miletić in *Koncentracioni logor Jasenovac 1941-1945.* Beograd: Narodna knjiga, 1986.

[149] *Izveštaj Državne komisije za utvrđivanje ratnih zločina okupatora i njihovih pomagača* (1948). Arhiv Jugoslavije (AJ), 110-1.

[150] The latter figure is quoted by Tim Judah in *The Serbs: History, Myth and the Destruction of Yugoslavia.* Yale University Press, 2000, p. 127.

They started with one huge husky peasant who began singing an old heroic song of the Serbs. They put his head on the table and, as he continued to sing, they slit his throat; then the next squad moved in to smash his skull. I was paralyzed. "This is what you are getting," an Ustaša screamed. They surrounded us. There was absolutely no escape. Then the slaughter began. One group stabbed with knives, the other followed, smashing heads to make certain everyone was dead. Within minutes there was a lake of blood. Screams and wails, bodies dropping right and left.[151]

The bodies were taken by trucks to a large pit, prepared in advance, from where Jadnak was able to make his escape. The church was destroyed by the Ustaše shortly after the massacre; it was never rebuilt, and some of the construction material was used after the Second World War to make a nearby hydroelectric dam. According to one of the killers, Hilmija Berberović (a Muslim from Bosanski Novi), the killing was carried out by flashlight in seven or eight shifts, with about a hundred victims liquidated in each.[152]

Whereas the Nazi Holocaust adopted the style and methods of a developed industrial state (complex equipment, intricate administrative network), Ustaša terror was 'primitive' and 'traditional.'[153] Nazi system included plans, reports, lists of victims, statistics; Ustaša orders were mostly oral and the apparatus of terror functioned in an arbitrary manner and with a random selection of targets and methods of killing. Nazi terror was for most part *depersonalized and bureaucratic*, it was *cold, abstract, objective* – just like Nazi hatred; the Ustašas were *direct and personal*. Some aspects of Nazi terror – with its somber discipline and bureaucratic pedantry – were 'puritanical,'

---

[151] Gerhard Falk, *Murder: An Analysis of Its Forms, Conditions and Causes*, McFarland, 1990, p. 67.

[152] *Vjesnik*, Zagreb, 29 July 1969.

[153] Cf. A. Djilas PhD Thesis, op. cit.

whereas the Ustašas engaged in orgies of sadistic violence, against children (l.) and adults alike. The commander of the (Italian) Sassari division reported that "population in some places was completely exterminated, after having been tortured and tormented":

> The horrors that the Ustasi have committed over the Serbian small girls is beyond all words. There are hundreds of photographs confirming these deeds ... pulling of tongues and teeth, nails and breast tips (all this having been done after they were raped). The few survivors were taken in by our officers and transported to Italian hospitals where these documents and facts were gathered."[154]

In July 1941 transports of prisoners started arriving in Jasenovac in railroad cars, in trucks, and some on foot. They stopped in front of the Camp Administration, where guards escorting the transports delivered them to the commander or one of his deputies. Even while in transit prisoners were starved and tortured. Max Luburić, Ljubo Miloš, or Matijević, the chief commandants in the camp, personally performed the inspection of victims. Luburić gave a 'speech' to every group full of insults and curses, during which a whip or a truncheon was used to beat them. Then they would be robbed of their possessions, stripped naked and clothed in old rags. Prisoners who were brought to Jasenovac merely to be killed were kept apart, naked and barefoot, for hours and sometimes for days, either in the main warehouse or out in the open. Eventually they would be taken to

---

[154] *Il Tempo*, Turin, September 10, 1953.

Gradina, on the Bosnian side of the Sava, and executed by most brutal methods imaginable.

The Jasenovac guards designed a special handle-less knife, the 'Serb-cutter' or *kukičar* ('hooker,' r.), for speedier slitting of throats. Epidemics, too, ravaged the camp, especially typhus. Hardly any prisoners who contracted the disease survived. The food was inedible and grotesquely insufficient. The quarters were cold, infested by bugs and lice, and dirty. The inmates were forced to build barracks and dikes to protect the camp from floods. While they were working, the Ustaše beat them with truncheons and rifle butts, forced them to dig faster and run at all times. If an individual collapsed from exhaustion, he would be finished off on the spot.

Whenever the camp was full, the Ustaše would carry out mass executions of prisoners to release capacity. Sometimes they would stage 'public performances.' Assembled prisoners would be invited to sign up to go to work in Germany, or to a hospital, or some other camp. The Ustaše considered this amusing, laughing at the people signing up for death. Large groups of prisoners were executed at the Granik or near the villages of Gradina and Uštica, on the Bosnian side of the Sava. Witness Jovan Živković described liquidations on the Granik:

> Sometimes it lasted all night. Victims would wait in the Main Warehouse, or some other building, or out in the open. Before leaving the Ustaše would strip them naked, tie their hands behind their backs, and herd them one by one to the Granik. A victim would be forced to his knees. They would hit him with a mallet, a sledgehammer, or with the dull side of an axe on the head. They would often rip their stomachs open and dump them into the Sava.

Some prisoners would first have to dig long and deep pits. The Ustaše would strip them naked, kill them, and extract the gold fillings out of their mouths with pliers and knives. Witness Egon Berger described these killings:

> We buried about 200 to 300 victims daily. Pits were three to eight square meters in size. While we were digging graves, Ustaše headed by Lieutenant Mujica were killing victims tied up with wire. They were hitting them on the temple, or killing them by an axe blow across the neck, or by driving wooden stakes into victim's mouths with axes; the stake would surface at the top of the head. Sometimes they asked victims if they had any relatives, and when they established that they did, they would force them to kill each other. ... They would look over every victim, and when they saw that a victim had gold fillings in his teeth, they would pry them out with their knives.

Torture and death by starvation were commonplace. All inmates of Camp III-C were literally starved to death. A 'Bell Warehouse' was a special torture chamber specifically designed for that purpose. It was a small barrack without windows but with a glass door, so that from outside it was possible to view everything. The Ustaše locked victims inside, keeping them there without food or water for days on end. From the barracks desperate screams resounded: "Take us away! Kill us!"

While in Germany the "final solution" was mainly carried out far away in the East, initially by a small number of *Einsatzgruppen* and later by specially selected camp staff, Ustaša terror was open and explicit. It was designed to involve as many Croat and Muslim civilians as possible by making them beneficiaries of the distribution of Serb land and property. Protests were rare.[155] While many Germans could plausibly claim

---

[155] An exception was a petition sent by prominent Muslims of Banja Luka to two Muslims in Pavelić's government (Džafer Kulenović and Hamdija Bešlagić) on November 12, 1941, protesting the treatment of their 'Serb neighbors.' A-VII, no number, 12 novembar 1941.

ignorance of what was being done to the deported Jews in Poland, few Croats or Muslims could have harbored such doubt as entire Serb communities were brutally slaughtered. Moreover, the Croats had lived in a non-totalitarian society until April 1941. There had already been a marked right-wing radicalization in Croatia, even in the Peasant Party. The Jewish Question in Germany – however alleged, debated and defined before 1941 – was a far smaller concern for ordinary Germans than the 'Serbian Question' for ordinary Croats.

By making their terror public in wide areas, and especially in the Dinaric regions of the Krajina and Bosnia-Herzegovina, the Ustašas sought to make inter-communal breach irreversible. Their goal was to eliminate all Serbs; their inability to do it on a truly industrial scale was the only factor hindering its achievment.

'The Struggle of Europe in the East' – 1942 Ustaša poster

Uprising

The wave of anti-Serb terror caused a series of Serb uprisings all over the Independent State of Croatia, which eventually turned into a major guerrilla war with international ramifications. Uprisings also occurred in the summer of 1941 in Serbia and Montenegro, but their motivation was resistance rather than survival. The political and social context were different, which was reflected in the response to German pressure. By the end of 1941 both had been pacified, and remained so – in the case of Serbia – for almost three years, until the arrival of the Red Army in late September 1944. No such pacification could be effected in the NDH. The constant threat of Ustaša massacres gave the Serbs an unmatched incentive for immediate and sustained resistance. It was at first an exclusively anti-Ustaša resistance.

The degree of insurgent activity in the NDH was almost invariably in direct proportion to the intensity of anti-Serb terror in any given area. The Ustaša were not very numerous – about 30,000 in 1941 – and could not be everywhere at once. The conscripts in the Home Guard (*Domobranstvo*) were often unwilling to fight. In eastern Herzegovina a spontaneous Serb uprising occurred as early as June 1941, in response to a wave of savage slaughters the Ustašas carried out in the area of Bileća, Gacko, Nevesinje and Trebinje.[156] The regions of western Bosnia, Lika, Kordun, and northern Dalmatia, which were also the scene of savage mass slaughters, were up in arms by late July. At the same time, other areas with a Serb majority or plurality – Srem, Semberija, parts of Slavonija and Podravina – remained relatively quiet for as long as they were less brutally affected by terror. Srem, for instance, became a hotbed of insurgency only after a savage Ustaša 'cleansing action' in 1942.

---

[156] This event, long ignored under Tito, belied the official myth that the uprising throughout Yugoslavia was organized and led by the CPY.

The initial form of self-defense in many Serb villages was to establish village guards, to set up observation posts and patrols on the surrounding roads and to warn their inhabitants if an Ustaša column was approaching. When alerted of danger people escaped into the surrounding countryside. Rudimentary sanctuaries (*zbegovi*) were organized in remote spots, such as caves and hidden crevices, to accommodate women, children and the infirm. Village committees organizing such evacuations were usually led by men with some prior military experience, typically reserve officers or gendarmes. The next task was to provide these emerging groups with weapons. They were for the most

part hunting rifles and farm tools; a military rifle was a highly prized rarity in the early days.

Orthodox priests and other prominent local leaders were the first targets of Ustaša slaughters. One priest narrowly evaded them: Fr. Momčilo Djujić, parish priest in Strmica near Knin (r.), who would soon play a leading role in the resistance movement. Many of his parishioners were not so lucky: in two months before the uprising over 500 Serbs were killed in Knin and its surroundings. The slaughter was directed by Juco Rukavina, a senior Ustaša officer sent from Zagreb. One of his aides, Marko Rosa, instructed his men only to avoid violent acts in the presence of Italian soldiers.

The first shots of organized resistance were fired in the city of Drvar, in western Bosnia, on July 26, 1941. Within days the entire Tromedja region was up in arms. Platoon and company sized local Ustaša garrisons could not handle what they had provoked and quickly lost control of the situation. They were, on the whole, not competent soldiers and unable to cope with lightly armed but desperate Serb peasants fighting for survival. When unable to stem the tide, retreating Ustaša units went looking for the mountain sanctuaries in which Serb non-combatants were hiding. After an insurgent attack on Divoselo in Lika on August 5, 1941, the Ustaša withdrew into the nearby Velebit mountain. They stumbled upon, and killed, all 565 women and children hiding there while their menfolk were fighting.

Thousands of Serb civilians sought shelter in the areas annexed by Italy along the Dalmatian coast and in the hinterland. The Italian army and civilian authorities provided them with food, medicine and clothing. Local Italian commanders were aware of the atrocities, deplored them, and feared for the stability of the region even before the flare-up of insurrection.

Prominent Serbs, refugees from Lika and western Bosnia, appealed in May 1941 on the Italians to extend their occupation zone.[157] The Italians proved responsive, especially after they established the nature of the regime they helped install. As early as May 21 the commander of the Italian Sassari division in Knin learnt of the Ustaša plans when three Croat dignitaries visited him, led by the Franciscan friar Vjekoslav Simić. According to the Italian record, they declared that they had been designated by the Zagreb government to take over the civil administration in the Knin region.

> The Italian general asked them what was the intent of their policy. Fr. Simić replied, "To kill all the Serbs as soon as possible." The division commander did not believe his own ears. He made him repeat the statement, which Simić did: "To kill all the Serbs, that is our program." "I am aghast," the Italian commander replied, "that such a heinious project is promoted by a man of the cloth, a Franciscan at that!"[158]

---

[157] T-821, roll 232, frame 6: 6th Corps Command to 2. Army Command, 10 May 1941; frames 8-9: 11 May 1941; frame 27: 17 May 1941.

[158] *Il Tempo*, No. 250, September 9, 1953.

The Italian army chief of general staff, General Mario Roatta (r., described by Count Ciano as "the most intelligent general I know"), decided that his troops would not assist what he saw as the Ustaša campaign of "wholesale extermination of the Serbian Orthodox populace."[159] He found the Ustaša acts deplorable: "Their campaign was characterized by the  slaughter of tens of thousands of persons, including the aged, women, and children, while other tens of thousands, confined in so-called concentration camps (consisting of stretches of desolate land, bereft of shelter, surrounded by barbed wire and cordons of guards) were left to perish of exhaustion or torture. The Italian troops could not remain indifferent to these excesses, Roatta went on, and therefore "they immediately intervened wherever they were located… and thus saved the lives of much of the Serbian-Orthodox population," earning the "grateful recognition and gratitude of the Serbian Orthodox population of Croatia." He continued the same policy when he became senior Italian commander in the former Yugoslavia in 1942-1943.

The Ustaša authorities berated the Italians for their lack of willingness to assist them in the 'cleansing operations.' Their inactivity, or even alleged help to the insurgents, was blamed for the speedy loss of control over large areas of the Tromedja region, including the towns of Drvar, Grahovo, and Donji Lapac. Having been installed in power by Hitler and Mussolini, they expected to be assisted in their campaign of genocide. The success of the insurgency in its early months was due to the desperate insurrection of the Serbs, to the inability of the Ustaša regime to complete the gruesome job by itself, and to the

---

[159] Mario Roatta's *The Battle of the Balkans and Its Consequences* (Ch. 8, p. 170), as quoted in Lazo M. Kostich, *Holocaust in the Independent State of Croatia.* Chicago: Liberty, 1981, p. 155.

unwillingness of their Axis partners to help them or even (in the Italian case) to let them proceed with it unhindered.

In the upheaval that followed the first wave of pogroms no ideological foundation was needed for Serb resistance: it was in the early phase a struggle to preserve their very lives. Its leaders saw that the Italians were sympathetic and repeatedly assured local Italian commanders that their quarrel was only with the

Ustaša bands. At a meeting in Benkovac on July 23, the Serbs asked that the area around Knin – awarded to Pavelić under the Rome Treaties –be annexed to Italy. On July 29, Governor of Dalmatia Giuseppe Bastianini (l.) informed Rome that insurgent activities were not directed against the Italian army and that many Serbs would welcome extension of Italian control.[160] The tacit understanding between Serb leaders and Italian officers was severely tested in the aftermath of the German attack on the USSR and the arrival in insurgent areas of Communist activists from the cities. Before Barbarossa some leading Croatian Communists – such as Andrija Hebrang – had not intended to resist the new Ustaša regime and contemplated seeking legalization as the 'Communist Party of the Independent State of Croatia.' The passivity of the Communist Party in the early months of the NDH was not surprising. Until the mid-1930s the CPY opposed the very existence of the Yugoslav state, to the point of expressing support for the Ustaša movement and trying to woo its members into the Communist fold. The official Party organ hailed the Ustaša-instigated 1932 'Lika Uprising': "The Communist Party salutes the Ustaša movement of the Lika

---

[160] In 2003 Bastianini, who died in 1961, was honoured – along with several other Italian diplomats and military personnel – by Israel for his part in saving thousands of Croatian Jews by sheltering them in Dalmatia, issuing false documents, and helping some get to Switzerland.

peasants and fully backs them. It is the duty of all Communist organizations and of every Communist to help this movement, organize it and lead it."[161]

Just as the CPY hoped "to organize and to lead" the Ustašas in the early 1930s, it sought "to organize and to lead" the leaderless victims of those same Ustašas a decade later. In this latter venture the Party scored far greater success. The Serb peasantry of the Krajina had been favorable to Yugoslavia, although that loyalty was submerged in anti-Croatian bitterness. They did not grasp that the CPY had only belatedly been instructed to turn 'pro-Yugoslav.'

After 22 June 1941, the credit unexpectedly secured for the Communist Party by the emergence of the Russian factor enabled its activists to preach 'brotherhood and unity' of Serbs and Croats among the survivors of freshly burnt Serb villages (r.). Contrary to common sense and to the villagers' instinct for self-preservation, they could also advocate incessant armed struggle against *all* occupiers, even if that meant attacking Italian soldiers who were often protecting those same Serb villages from Ustaša pogroms. In the name of its long-term political objectives, the CPY demanded rejection of a pragmatism conducive to Serb survival.

In the initial stage the uprising was a purely Serb affair, and on the whole remained so for over two years, until after the fall

---

[161] "Ustaški pokret u hrvatskim zemljama" (unsigned). *Proleter*, No. 28, December 1932.

of Italy. In 1941-1942 Croats were extremely rare among the insurgents outside the area of annexed Dalmatia. They could be found among the small but disciplined core of Party cadres sent by the CPY into the field immediately after the attack on the USSR. Those activists were in an awkward position, however. For years they had been indoctrinated in the spirit of extreme antagonism to 'greater Serbian hegemony,' and internalized the Party rhetoric on Yugoslavia as a 'prison house of nationalities.' The line between anti-greater-Serbianism of the commissars and plain anti-Serbianism was fine and often blurred.

The invasion of Russia suddenly provided the Communist

Party of Yugoslavia with an argument to present itself as a viable national force by appealing to the latent Russophile sentiment of the Serbs. Its invocation of the image of 'Mother Russia' was a cynical ploy, but it worked wonders for the small band of Party cadres who needed to deliver a strong pitch to their early recruits (above). In the Krajina those CPY activists were mainly Croats.[162] They were indoctrinated by the standard Party line, that Yugoslavia was an artificial creation lorded over by the 'greater Serbian bourgeoisie.' While initially concealing their true colors, in many places they managed to impose themselves on a leaderless and desperate peasantry. Like the SS in Poland, the Ustaša always attacked the local Serbian establishment, with

---

[162] Notable Croatian communists active in trying to impose their leadership on the insurgents in the Krajina were Marko Orešković, Jakov Blažević, Stipe Ugarković-Palenta, Većeslav Holjevac, Dr. Ivo Marinković, Šime Balen, Grga Rupčić, Karlo Mrazović, and Ivan Rukavina.

teachers, priests, merchants, prosperous farmers and educated people in general always the first target. This created political opportunities: it opened the way for the Communists to gain an early foothold in the insurgent ranks.

In the summer months of 1941 many beleaguered Krajina Serbs looked east for deliverance. Traditional trust in 'Mother Russia' transcended all ideological reservations and offered a ray of hope in the nightmare of Pavelić's state intent on destroying them. This almost religious veneration of the great Slav ally was common both to the majority of Serbs who were traditional in their outlook and to the minority of activists who were fanatically loyal to 'the first country of Socialism.' Initially the insurgents hoped that these two groups would form a common front, united by the Ustašas. Political distinctions did not matter to an uprooted population, blinded by grief, that took to the hills in the summer of 1941. The red-blue-white Serbian tricolor and the Communist red banner often flew side by side, and the five-pointed red star could be seen alongside the traditional cockade on caps and hats.

The Communist Party accepted this ambiguity temporarily but it did not want it to last. The leaders mandated resistance for revolutionary ends, and they did so to an extent that for a time disturbed even Moscow. Its activists knew that where they could find a leaderless peasantry they would lead fighters. Even when condemning Ustaša atrocities the Party leaders knew that social collapse caused by the slaughter offered them an opportunity to pursue revolutionary goals. The Ustašas had driven to their ranks young men of exceptional motivation drawn from families with a strong military tradition, the *Grenzer* tradition of Lika, Kordun and Banija. Once they had joined, these men were in an 'army' with strict discipline and a fighting ethos. By destroying the pillars of the old order, Croatian *Einsatzgruppen* cleared the ground for the agents of the Comintern.

Within the insurgent movement the Communist Party urged that Russia's predicament entailed fighting all occupiers, immediately and regardless of consequences for the civilian population already threatened by physical extinction. They did not need to say that to forego Italian protection was to intensify the social dislocation that accompanies mass murder, and so secure revolutionary objectives. This strategy was functional for the leaders of a small, ideologically-driven conspiracy as hot-headed and millenarian as the Ustaša themselves. Party members seem to have believed quite genuinely that the Red Army would in a matter of weeks grind the Wehrmacht to pieces and ride to the rescue. What was exceptional about them was their sense of excitement and belief in the possibility of conquering power, a lust for revolution. Nothing, save Stalin's direct orders, was likely to restrain them. To local Serb leaders primarily motivated by saving their families and villages from destruction, their struggle appeared utterly dysfunctional. 'Revolutionary realism' of the Communist Party inevitably clashed with the existential realism of the non-communist resistance movement.

By the end of 1941, the non-communist resistance groups all over the Krajina came to be known as *Četniks* (below), their name harking back to the Serbian guerrilla tradition in the Ottoman-ruled southern Serbian lands before 1912. Their leaders came to realize, often reluctantly, that co-existence with the

Communists was no longer possible. They sensed that behind Communist militancy was an indifference to Serb survival that was perversely linked to the Ustaša program. The communists retorted that the Četniks must be eliminated: they were blind reactionaries and monarchists rejecting the true path of Serb heroes because they were afraid of freedom and the equality of Yugoslav peoples. Then they fought.

The ensuing multicornered war was brutal, merciless, and deadly. It had no precedent and no parallel, not even in the collective tragedy of Europe in 1941.

German 1942 poster threatening retaliation against civilians in case of Četnik attacks

Bekanntmachung

Es häufen sich die Fälle, dass Tschetniks, in grosser Überzahl auftretend, einzelne Angehörige deutscher Organisationen entwaffnen und versuchen, Lastkraftwagen unbrauchbar zu machen.

Die Geduld der Kreiskommandantur ist nunmehr erschöpft. In Zukunft werden in jedem Dorf, welches dem Tatort am nächsten liegt,

FÜR JEDEN FALL EINES ÜBERGRIFFS, BIS 20 HÄUSER NIEDERGEBRANNT WERDEN.

Die betroffene Bevölkerung mag sich hierfür bei den Tschetniks bedanken.

Der Kreiskommandant.

ОГЛАС

Чести су случајеви, да четници, наступајући у великом броју, разоружају појединe припаднике немачких организација и покушавају да онеспособе теретна кола.

Стрпљење Крајскоман-дантуре је исцрпљено. У будуће, у сваком селу, које је најближе месту препада, биће у случају сваког напада до 20 кућа до темеља спаљено. Погођено становништво има за ово да захвали четницима:

Крајскомандант.

German and Italian Responses to the Slaughter

There were far fewer Wehrmacht troops in the German zone of the NDH than Italian forces in theirs, and their ability to document Ustaša behavior on the ground was accordingly more limited. By the end of June 1941, however, German field commands were well aware that a major bloodbath was under way. The first official report on "the increasing anti-Serb Ustaša terror" reached Berlin on 2 July 1941. Its author was Edmund Veesenmayer, the special representative of the German Foreign Ministry in Zagreb. He stated that "authoritative representatives of the regime" looked on the Serbs in Croatia as a problem "which is under the exclusive competence of Ustaša police and court-martials."[163]

General Edmund Glaise von Horstenau was the first high-ranking German in Croatia to realize that Pavelić wanted to kill or otherwise eliminate *all Serbs*. As soon as he arrived in Zagreb Glaise started developing an efficient intelligence network. It provided him with detailed information on Ustaša atrocities. Glaise's chief information gatherer was Captain Häffner, his assistant, who had lived in Zagreb for many years before the war, spoke the language fluently, and had good contacts throughout Croatia. His reports contained graphic eyewitness accounts of the slaughters. According to his tally, which was subsequently proved to be surprisingly accurate the number of Serbs "who have fallen as victims of animal instincts fanned by Ustaša leaders" exceeded 200,000 by early August 1941.[164] As the terror grew, so did Häffner's disdain for its perpetrators. He wrote of "the strong inferiority complex of Ustaša leaders and their flock vis-à-vis the Serbs, who are more numerous and superior in life energy."

---

[163] PA, Büro Staatssekretär, Kroatien, Bd. 1, No. 290. Veesenmayer to the Foreign Ministry, 2 July 1941.

[164] Kazimirović, op. cit. pp. 112-117.

Glaise collected such reports in a special file and repeatedly raised the issue of atrocities with Pavelić, Slavko Kvaternik, and other NDH officials. As a decent officer of the old school he was horrified by what was going on. He was concerned that the Serbs would take up arm to defend themselves. He was especially alarmed to hear that the Germans were being blamed for Ustaša crimes. In a report dated 18 July 1941 Häffner warned Glaise that German troops were seen as being supportive of the regime's excesses:

> The Ustašas promote the impression that they act not only *in agreement* with German instances, but actually *on their orders*. There is a deep mistrust of Germany because it is supporting a regime that has no moral or political right to exist... [regime] of robbers who do more evil in one day than the Serbian regime had done in twenty years.[165]

In early July, Glaise took advantage of the temporary absence from Zagreb of the pro-Ustaša German minister, Siegfried Kasche, to raise alarm in Berlin. He found an ally in Heribert Troll-Obergfell, a former Austrian diplomat and counselor at the German legation in Zagreb. They alerted their superiors on two fronts. On 10 July 1941 Troll-Obergfell sent a report to the Foreign Ministry and warned that Ustaša crimes were creating "an explosive situation wherever Serbs lived," which could soon erupt into hotbeds of unrest which would be hard to quell.[166] On the same day Glaise sent his report to the High Command (OKW). He objected that "our troops have to be mute witnesses to such events... [which] does not reflect well on their otherwise high reputation":

> I am frequently told by our military, as well as by some Croat circles, that German troops would finally have to intervene against Ustaša crimes. ... [But] even if we

---

[165] Häffner's report dated 18 July 1941, ibid. p. 113.

[166] PA, Büro Staatssekretär, Kroatien, Bd.1, No.307. 10 July 1941

overlook that Croatia is an independent state, also that it is in the Italian sphere, our occupation forces – only six infantry battalions – are too weak to assume adequate police control. Ad hoc intervention in individual cases could make the German Army look responsible for countless crimes which it could not prevent in the past.[167]

Troll-Obergfell also spoke on 11 July to the newly appointed NDH foreign minister Mladen Lorković and raised the reports of Ustaša excesses. His statement was supported by photographs of massacred victims taken by German soldiers.[168] Troll demanded resolute measures to stop any "tendentious rumours" that anti-Serb actions were being carried out with German approval. These early reports tended to express concern about the effect Ustaša crimes would have on "the reputation of the German army and the Reich." German officers, whatever they knew or heard about mass murder in Russia, had a useful pragmatic argument which they used to the full. It was their job to secure occupied territories with as few troops and as little trouble as possible. The Ustaša were making this task impossible. The Germans knew that harmless civilians were subject to slaughter because they were *Serbs*, not because they lived in areas where resistance groups appeared to thrive – which would be considered by the Wehrmacht a legitimate cause for killing them:

> Most Wehrmacht officers recognized that Ustaša violence emanated from a strategic framework different from the Wehrmacht's and therefore rejected Ustaša violence. The simplest form of recognition consisted in the realization that Serbs, however determined, were the main targets of Ustaša violence. Captain Konopatzki [714th Division intelligence officer] maintained that 'Serbs,' not Partisans, not Četniks, not enemies, were the object of Ustaša attacks. Major C.

---

[167] BA/MAF, No. 178/41 Glaise to OKW/Ausland, 10 July 1941.

[168] PA, Büro Staatssekretär, Kroatien, Bd. 1, No. 726, 11 July 1941.

Geim, General Bader's intelligence officer, argued that the Ustaša attacked Serbs with the objective of "exterminating the Serbian portion of the population in Croatia."[169]

In contrast the Wehrmacht rarely targeted specific ethnic groups as part of anti-partisan operations in the NDH. In fact, some Wehrmacht units based in the NDH, such as the 714th Division, demanded from the troops "not to distinguish between members of different nationalities" when trying to determine who is the enemy.

Glaise raised the issue of atrocities with Pavelić's *Vojskovodja* ('Marshal') Slavko Kvaternik (r.) on several occasions during July. As a fellow veteran from the Habsburg army, Kvaternik appeared amenable to open discussion.[170] On one occasion Glaise told Kvaternik that "the Croat revolution was by far the bloodiest and most awful... in Europe since 1917."[171] On another Glaise convinced Kvaternik that they should go to Pavelić together and press on him the need to stop the slaughter of Serbs. Once they were with Pavelić, however, Kvaternik changed his tune completely and "talked in such radical tones" that Glaise grew irritated and commented "Dear Slavko, I am happy that you are at least letting me stay alive!" Pavelić listened politely to Glaise and did nothing.[172] He realized that he could afford to ignore Glaise's appeals for as long as Hitler supported 'intolerance.' With the one single but important

---

[169] Jonathan Gumz, op. cit.

[170] Hungarian minister in Berlin Döme Sztojay described Kvaternik (whom he knew well in his younger years at the military academy) as *ein Mordskerl* – a common murderer. Cf. Hory and Broszat, op. cit. p. 75.

[171] BA/MAF, No. 207/41. Glaise's report to the OKW, 19 July 1941

[172] BA/MAF, No. 192/41. Glaise's telex to the OKW, 12 July 1941.

exception of Siegfried Kasche, German officials in the NDH had no doubt that there was a link between the Ustaša crimes and the spreading Serb resistance. Legation Counselor Troll reported to the Foreign Ministry on August 10, 1941,

> Contrary to Croatian claims that responsibility for the rebellion is exclusively due to Serbian influences, the German military commands and sober Croatian circles are of the opinion that responsibility for the outbreak of rebellion is attributable to the uncontrollable and bloody acts of the Ustaša.[173]

Demands for intervention to stop Ustaša massacres soon started pouring in from many German quarters, including the Commander South-East Wilhelm List (l.) and the leaders of the *Volksdeutsche* community in Croatia.[174] Rudolf Epting, the Nazi Party *Auslandsorganisation* (foreign branch) chief in the NDH, shared their concern and, in a report to Hitler, named the Ustašas the main culprits.[175] Walter Schellenberg of the Reich Security Service (RSHA) foreign department also held that the slaughters caused the rebellion: "Without recruits from the Serb population which was terrorized by the Ustašas, this Četnik warfare would have been nipped in the bud."[176] The RSHA had an extensive network in the NDH and was thorough in its reports of Ustaša atrocities and the effect they had on the unrest. Its agents sent literally hundreds of such reports. The summary was presented to the Reichsfuehrer SS, Heinrich Himmler, in a detailed report: "Increased activity of the

[173] PA, Buro Staatssekretaer, Kroatien, Bd. 2, No. 24, 10 August 1941.

[174] Gert Fricke, op. cit. pp. 39-40.

[175] Hory and Broszat, op. cit. pp. 129-130.

[176] Ibid, p. 151.

bands is chiefly due to atrocities carried out by Ustaša units in Croatia against the Orthodox population."[177] According to Wehrmacht eyewitnesses, the Ustaša 'slaughtered' the villagers and 'plundered' their property in acts of pure terror.[178] German reports of Ustaša violence described it as "uncontrolled and transgressing all boundaries":

> The same terms, 'plundering,' 'excesses' and 'atrocities,' also described acts which Wehrmacht commanders explicitly prohibited their troops from participating in and therefore further reinforced the terms' criminal connotations when used in reference to Ustaša violence... as "in defiance of all the laws of civilization ... A Wehrmacht regimental commander in Bosnia, Lt.Col. von Wedel, who commanded a regiment in *Kampfgruppe Westbosnien*, complained to Glaise of an Ustaša's company massacre of Serb women and children. According to von Wedel, the Ustaša killed them "like cattle" in a series of "bestial executions."[179]

General Walter Kuntze, commander of Wehrmacht forces in Southeastern Europe through August 1942, characterized the NDH as the 'problem child' of the region. His successor, General Alexander v. Löhr, also objected to the Ustaša bands' rekindling of unrest, which placed into serious question all the previous German efforts at pacification. The view was replicated down the command chain: Ustaša violence produced the 'general insecurity' and the 'renewal of bands' in areas of the country the Wehrmacht had 'mopped up.'[180] The intelligence staff of the commanding general in Serbia warned that the "boundless and undisciplined efforts of the Ustaša are the main reasons for the

---

[177] PA, Buero RAM, Kroatien, 1941-42, 442-449. IV/D/4 RSHA to Himmler, 17 February 1942

[178] 714. Division, Operations Staff, "Activity Report: Recent Fighting," NA, T-315, translated and quoted by Jonathan Gumz, op. cit.

[179] ibid.

[180] 714 Division, Operations Staff, T-315/2258/887.

further development of anarchic conditions."[181] Ustaša violence provided the Germans with a general explanation for the failure to subdue the insurgency in the Independent State of Croatia. They also applied deadly violence against the civilian population in their own areas of operation, but this was done in the name of military necessity.

The Italian approach was different. During the first Serb uprising, in eastern Herzegovina in June 1941, armed local groups made it clear to the Italians that their quarrel was only

with the Ustašas. Serb village heads approached Italian garrisons to request food and protection.[182] As Italian units moved into the area of unrest to secure the lines of communication between the corps command at Dubrovnik and its hinterland, they stumbled upon horrendous scenes of carnage in the Serb villages of eastern Herzegovina (l.). At the same time they encountered no opposition from the insurgents. Both sides had a common interest: restoration of order and peace. If this objective demanded the removal of the cause of unrest – the Ustaša armed bands and the remnants of Pavelić's civil administration – the Italians had no qualms about doing it.

With considerable political and diplomatic skill Italian commanders proceeded to achieve their primary objective, overall pacification. General Dalmazzo, the commander of the Sixth Army Corps in the region of Dubrovnik, which included the rebellious eastern Herzegovina, asserted that the Ustašas and

[181] Kommandierender General und Befehlshaber in Serbien, Intelligence Staff, "Situation Report" quoted by J. Gumz (op. cit.)

[182] See e.g. reports by the Sixth Corps to 2. Army: T-821, roll 232, frame 78 (31 May 1941); frame 116 (9 June 1941) and frame 120 (11 June 1941).

local pro-Ustaša Muslims were guilty of causing the uprising. The Second Army headquarters gave him a free hand in restoring order.[183] The Italians disarmed the remaining Ustaša garrison in Trebinje and armed Serbs entered the town on 1 August 1941 without incident.[184] They undertook not to attack Italian troop movements by road or rail provided that transports carried no Croat soldiers or officials. The victims of Ustaša massacres were exhumed from mass graves and buried with proper Orthodox Church rites allowed once again by the Italians. Normality had returned, for the moment, at no cost in lives or treasure to the Italians. The model seemed well worth replicating elsewhere.

In the summer of 1941 Italian officers in the NDH faced a challenge more serious than their German counterparts. The slaughter on their side of the Demarcation Line was worse and the Serbs' reaction to it more violent. The German commanders, with few troops and no political orders, did not have much of a dilemma: Berlin denied them a free hand. Italian officers enjoyed greater autonomy of action. By acting in a conciliatory manner with non-Communist Serb insurgents, the Italians made less effective and plausible the Communist advocacy of total war against 'all enemies,' as instructed by their center in Moscow and the CPY leadership.

---

[183] T-821. roll 232, frame 163. Sixth Corps to the 2. Army, 19 June 1941. Same roll, frame 279: Sixth Corps to the 2. Army Command, 10 July 1941.

[184] Cf. reports to that effect from the Sixth Corps to the 2. Army Command, eg. of 3, 10 and 18 August 1941. T-821, roll 232, frames 414, 454, 502.

The Serbs' Civil War

The sophisticated approach adopted by key Italian generals split the Serb insurgent ranks. This gave local Italian commanders a clear picture of where they stood with the local insurgent leaders. In Northern Dalmatia the process of intra-Serb differentiation resulted in the permanent expulsion of the radical, pro-Communist minority from the area. Non-Communist groups became the Četniks, and accept the formal command of General Dragoljub-Draža Mihailović and his Yugoslav Army in the Homeland.

Yet Yugoslavia was not a single place. Different Četnik groups faced very different regional challenges, in central Serbia, say, or Montenegro, or Dalmatia. Those in Serbia, under Mihailović's direct control, had fought both Germans and Communists in the fall of 1941. Local Serb groups in the NDH were left to their own devices, sought a truce with the Italians, and had no contact with Mihailović until a regular radio link was established in 1942.

The Italians knew that Mihailović was an enemy of the Axis (German 1941 *Wanted* poster, l.). His men avoided conflict with the Italians, but that would be likely to change if the times changed. In Serbia the lull was not the result of his acceptance of the occupation system, it was entirely due to German reprisals. Insurgents had attacked German forces and civilians, and paid a dreadful price: in the city of Kragujevac at least 2,300 were shot on 20 October 1941. Similar events in Kraljevo, Šabac, and Belgrade itself, were based on the ratio of a hundred Serbs for one dead German. Mihailović's unwillingness to stage major operations against the Germans reflected the concern for civilian lives rather than any readiness for collaboration, as his Communist enemies were claiming. In the west, too, there remained many problems in the relationship between Četniks and Italians:

> Under pressure from Rome, the Italian commanders felt obliged to accord their Croatian 'ally' formal respect and weapons deliveries. Rather than fighting Partisans, the Croats lost no time in training their acquired Italian guns on Serbs... Četnik leaders concluded... that every agreement with Italian military commanders would be tenuous.[185]

Nevertheless, wherever they were free from Communist influence, Serb insurgents refused to fight the only party that offered them protection. In northern Dalmatia four commanders of local units became prominent during the summer of 1941: Momčilo Djujić, Pajo Popović, Momir Prijić, and Obrad Bojanić.[186] Their 'Command of Guerrilla Units' was under pressure from Communist forces based in Drvar and led at that time by Vladimir Ćetković, a member of the CPY Central Committee. He insisted that "all occupiers and their domestic servants" should be treated as equally odious mortal enemies. The emerging split was reflected in the change of name of the insurgents, on August 12, into the 'Command of Guerrilla and Četnik Units for the Krajina of Knin.' This was the first time the

---

[185] H. James Burgwyn, *Empire on the Adriatic: Mussolini's Conquest of Yugoslavia 1941-1943*, Enigma Books (2005), op. cit. p. 140-141.

[186] Djujić combined military talent with political acumen and personal charisma. Born in 1907, impressive looking and a gifted orator, he was known locally as 'Father Fire' (*pop vatra*) for his sermons, and especially for his support of striking local workers in the late 1930s.

Četnik name was formally introduced into the designation of insurgents. At a meeting in Padjene on August 25, 1941, its leaders agreed the terms of a truce with the local Italian command, which in turn pledged to guarantee physical safety to the Serbs, and freedom of religion and education. Military and civilian authority was assumed by the Italian army; while a civilian Croatian 'commissar' with no executive powers would be attached to the Italian staff.

At a meeting in Drvar Communist leader Ćetković insisted on initiating attacks on the Italians, but this was rejected by those local commanders who were becoming identified as Četniks. As Djujić, one of the participants at this meeting, travelled back to his stronghold at Strumica, he narrowly escaped an ambush set up by Communists. The split within insurgent ranks was becoming irreversible. Momčilo Djujić, who emerged as the leader in the area of *Tromedja* ('Tri-Boundary' of Lika, Dalmatia and Bosnia) established a strong and effective fighting force that made the local Serb population secure from the Ustašas and at the same time obstructed Communist attempts to push them into a self-defeating fight with the Italians.

In early fall 1941 political contacts were established in Split between the VI. Corps commander Dalmazzo and two senior Serb representatives, Dobrosav Jevdjević (l.) and Ilija Trifunović-Birčanin, a seasoned veteran who headed the Serbian National Defense in Belgrade before the war.[187] Dalmazzo reported that both had told him they were primarily interested in saving Serb lives and that, accordingly, they advocated a policy of coexistence with the Italians.

[187] V.I.I. *Zbornik*, XIII/2, pp. 51-52. Report dated January 17, 1942.

They were not in radio contact with General Mihailović at that time and acted of their own accord in establishing the Committee for Refugee Assistance (*Odbor za pomoć izbeglicama*), which soon evolved into the Serb National Committee (*Srpski nacionalni komitet*).

In the medium term, Birčanin wanted to unify all Četnik groups in the Italian zone and bring them under Draža Mihailović's command. Most leading Četnik commanders in the Tromedja region responded favorably, including commanders of the early territorial regiments in the area of Knin (r.). The response was not favorable in Lika, however, where Communist activists had been able to  impose themselves as leaders in the aftermath of the slaughters of July and August 1941. By the end of 1941 they established specially trained 'Flying Squads' to carry out a series of murders of real or potential nationalist opponents.

The internal Serb civil war was taking shape, caused by the incompatible strategic objectives of the Communist Party and other Serb leaders. It was sealed after a firefight at Tiškovac in March 1942. This process was unsurprisingly supported by the NDH authorities. The nominal Croatian governor of the district of Knin (*veliki župan*) David Sinčić, who had no real power after the Italian re-occupation of the region, thus told his superiors in Zagreb that "the gap between Četniks and Partisans is indescribable and irreparable. In fact this is the schism among the Serbs themselves, who are destroying each other. We need to support this struggle and prevent their reconciliation."

Djujić took off his priestly cassock for good in early 1942 and created a single regional command structure. The result was the establishment of the Dinara Četnik Division command staff

on February 15, 1942.[188] Its commander stated, "We are under the command of Draža Mihailović. We are King Peter's soldiers and the guarantee of our people's freedom."[189] The stated objective was the establishment of a Serb national state under King Peter II. The NDH was the implacable enemy. The Italians were to be treated in accordance with the principle "don't touch me if I don't touch you." The Germans were the enemy, but distant and therefore not relevant to the local challenges.[190] The new formation introduced regular insignia of rank. Its flags (above) and its emblem (r.) were based on the symbols of the Četnik organization in Serbia before World War I. The territory under the Division's control had all attributes of *de facto* statehood, including collection of taxes, administration of justice, and municipal bodies. Forced into the paradoxical position of owing his allegiance to the King and his government in London, but at the same time establishing *modus vivendi* with one of the Axis, Djujić refused to sign agreements with the Italians, but made understandings with their field commanders. As he recalled years later,

---

[188] Momčilo Diklić, *Srpsko pitanje u Hrvatskoj, 1941-1950*. Beograd: Zora, 2004, p. 89.

[189] A-V.I.I. Zbornik, XIV/1, p. 143.

[190] Diklić, op. cit. pp. 365-366.

Yes, we let them stay in peace in their barracks. We also got them to feed six thousand Serb refugees from the villages destroyed by the Ustaše all over western Bosnia, Lika and Dalmatia. And yes, they supplied us with weapons: on one occasion we received five hundred brand new cavalry carbines. When Ustaše attacked Vrlika, in the Cetina region, I persuaded them to open artillery fire and chase the Croats away. I don't see that as any kind of treason or collaboration, but as nifty diplomacy. We were completely cut off from other Serb lands, and short of everything. My goal was to save as many Serb lives as possible, to preserve as many Serb homes as I could, not to kill Italian soldiers who were saving my people.[191]

Djujić's role-model, he said, was Prince Miloš of Serbia, who had to make various accommodations with the Ottoman authorities while consolidating the semi-autonomous principality in the 1820s and 1830s: "Had he tried to fight the Turks when Serbia was weak, there would have been no independent state a generation later!" Djujić also pointed out that the Italians were not carrying out reprisals against the Serbs in the area under his command and were never involved in pillage or violence. His own summary of the policy he pursued was simple: "This was the only way to survive!"

During the summer and early fall of 1941, while Italian commanders were bringing some semblance of normality back to Herzegovina, Dalmatia and western Bosnia, in many areas Ustaša terror was continuing. Mostar, Glamoč, Gospić and Duvno are but some locations southeast of the German-Italian line of demarcation where many thousands of Serb civilians were killed in July and August. The Italian Second Army command at Sušak concluded that nothing less than the complete elimination of Ustaša influence throughout the area would bring lasting stability. Greatly expanding the Italian occupation zone

---

[191] Statement to the author, 22 May 1988.

was also seen as the key to pacifying the Serb rebel movement.[192] Last but not least, an extension of the occupation zone would serve the additional purpose of consolidating the Italian strategic position in the heart of the Balkans vis-à-vis their German partners, whose assurances of the lack of interest in the region were never fully taken at face value.

By the middle of August of 1941 the disdain and contempt of Italian officers and common soldiers for the Ustasa regime and its henchmen in the field turned into an articulate anti-Ustaša stand of the Italian Army as a whole. It was indicative of the relative independence of the Italian army from Fascist ideology and politics. Mussolini had never brought his officer corps to heel as Hitler had done in the late 1930s. The Italian army was a political factor in its own right, and on the issue of Croatia it had a clear position. Mussolini accepted it and approved the removal of the Ustasas, politically and militarily, from the entire coastal area of the NDH (Zone II).

The NDH government in Zagreb was notified of the Italian decision on 16 August 1941.[193] The head of the Italian military mission in Zagreb, General Oxilia, supported the action and was so hostile to Pavelić that he positively gloated at the prospect of delivering the news.[194] Mussolini's instructions did not allow for any consultations, let alone negotiations, with Pavelić or any other Croatian instances. The Italian High Command (*Comando Supremo*) had already issued its orders to the Second Army to reoccupy the Demilitarized Zone on 15 August, one day *before* Pavelić was to be given the news. The NDH civilian and military authorities had to transfer all authority to the Italians. The Second Army commander, General Vittorio Ambrosio, proceeded with gusto to "undo the legacy of four months of

---

[192] Cf. Srdja Trifkovic. *Ustaša: Croatian Separatism and European Politics.* London: The Lord Byron Foundation, 1998, pp. 153-155.

[193] V.I.I., *Zbornik,* 12/1, No.118, p.312. Roatta to 2. Army, 15 August 1941

[194] V.I.I. *Zbornik,* 13/1, No. 128, pp. 335-342. Oxilia to Comando Supremo, 23 August 1941.

Ustaša misrule."[195] All 'irregular' Ustaša units, guilty of many atrocities against the Serbs, were disarmed and disbanded. The rest were given until 1 September 1941 to leave the Second Zone. Only token Home Guards (*Domobrani*) and civilian staff could remain.

The impact of Ambrosio's (r.) measures on the 'sovereignty' of Pavelić's state was clear from his proclamation to the people of the Second Zone on 7 September 1941, which stated that he was "assuming all military and civilian authority in the area." The Italians promulgated a series of administrative and legal measures aimed at restoring Serbs' rights. In areas with a Serb majority they were reinstated to local administrative posts, while Serb property confiscated by the NDH was returned to its original owners. Orthodox churches were reopened and contact established with local leaders of insurgent groups.

One of Ambrosio's objectives had been to isolate the Communist-controlled wing of the insurgent movement. His strategy appeared to be working in northern Dalmatia and in Herzegovina. In a few places (notably around Drvar) Communist-dominated groups strengthened their position at the expense of the 'nationalists,' but this was an exception rather than the rule in the Italian zone.[196] For most Četniks the dominant motive was to exact revenge on the Ustašas and their supporters, which occasionally resulted in their revenge killings of non-combatants, and to prevent their return.[197] A few Croatian

---

[195] VI.I., *Zbornik*, 13/1, No. 130, pp. 345-353. Also T-821, roll 474, frame 535. 2. Army, "Occupazione zona demilitarizzata," 30 August 1941.

[196] T-821, roll 232, frames 691 and 735. 6th Corps to 2. Army Command, 16 and 22 September 1941.

[197] T-821, roll 232, frs. 635-639. 6th Corps to 2. Army, 8 September 1941.

units were still present within the Second Zone, however, including Ustašas pretending to be Home Guards. This was sufficient to convince the Serbs that they should stick to their guns regardless of subsequent Italian attempts to disarm or control them.[198]

If the Italian attempt at pacification was to be permanent, it became necessary to rid the area southwest of the German-Italian demarcation line of *all* Partisans and Ustašas. This demanded a major extension of the Italian mission by filling the vacuum between Zone Two and the demarcation line, an area that was turning into a haven for both. Ambrosio therefore argued that his design needed to be completed by the reoccupation of Zone Three, about a fifth of the NDH territory, including some of the wildest mountain landscape in the Balkans. His suggestion was approved in Rome. By mid-October 1941 the Italian occupation was extended all the way to the demarcation line. It covered a half of Pavelić's 'state,' dividing it into two economic, administrative, military, and political halves. In the Italian zone Croatian sovereignty was purely notional.

The extended occupation area created many new problems for the Italians. It was an area where topography and climate would have represented obstacles to effective control even

without the presence of various armed groups. In view of the security situation Italian commanders tended to confine their units to the fortified towns and expended great effort merely to keep the roads open and railways functioning. In addition, the political powers in Rome were wavering. Hard pressed by Berlin, in early 1942 Mussolini told the army chief of supreme command, Marshal Ugo Cavallero (l.), to end pro-Četnik

---

[198] T-821, roll 232, fr. 684. 6th Corps to 2. Army, 15 September 1941.

policy and to warn the military against maintaining its "openly pro-Serb posture":

> [T]he Italians were at all costs to avoid creating the impression that they favored the Orthodox population. Frustrated by continuing disorders, Cavallero wavered between giving Ambrosio full powers to suppress the revolt militarily by declaring the whole area a zone of war, and the defensive strategy of pulling the Italian troops to the cities and along the major lines of communication.[199]

Another, more serious problem was in the making: In the winter of 1941-1942 numerous Communist units, having been driven out of Serbia and Montenegro, infiltrated the Italian zone of the NDH just south of the Demarcation Line and challenged Ambrosio's precarious balance. The Germans were facing a major crisis of their own in Russia; the Ustašas were the cause of disorder in the first place; in the end the Četniks were pro-Allied royalists and therefore unreliable from the Italian viewpoint. The only party likely to profit from the murky times ahead were Tito's Communists.

By early 1942 the Četnik-Partisan split was open and violent. The breaking point was the Communist-led attack on the Italian garrison in Korenica (Lika) in December 1941, and the killing of several Četnik leaders by Communist flying squads in the winter of 1941-1942. What ostensibnly started as a tactical disagreement on the deployment of insurgent units reflected the two sides' fundamentally incompatible political and military objectives. Četnik peasant-warriors wanted to survive, to save their families, to protect their communities, and to take revenge. Partisan leaders wanted to use the Serbs – who comprised more than nine-tenths of their rank and file in 1941-42 – as cannon fodder in the long-term strategy of taking power at the end of the war. The Italian occupation policy in turn was twofold: support

---

[199] Matteo J. Milazzo, *The Chetnik movement and the Yugoslav resistance.* Baltimore: Johns Hopkins University Press, 1975, p. 60.

for the local Serb population in resisting Ustaša onslaughts, and tolerance of their armed groups, but only for as long as they excluded Communists.

Deeply hostile to the Ustaša regime, distrustful of the Germans, and threatened by the intransigent Communists, Italian commanders did not have many options. They treated the Serb nationalist movement not as a trusted partner but as the least of all evils.[200] Hitler, on the other hand, held that the insurgency in the NDH was an uprising (*Aufstand*) caused by Serb nationalists and communists, both of whom were equally dangerous. He rejected the view of many German officers – and most

prominently Glaise – that a rational solution to the Serb problem was the *political prerequisite* without which no military success was possible.[201]

General Alexander von Loehr (l.), who became Wehrmacht Commander South-East in the summer of 1942, shared Glaise's views on the problem created by Ustaša pogroms.[202] Six weeks after taking his new post in Salonika, Loehr reported to Hitler that "Croatian troops are disintegrating," while "the Ustaša government itself is on the verge of chaos."[203] Loehr added that the attitude to Pavelić needed re-examination, since Ustaša anti-Serb crimes enabled the rebels to grow strong. Hitler dismissed Loehr's arguments

---

[200] While Mihailović avoided direct links with the Italians, the British were encouraging him to establish contact. Cf. Peter Boughey, Yugoslav Section, SOE London, quoted in Nora Beloff (1985), p. 78.

[201] E.g. Glaise's talk with Loehr, 17 September 1942. T-501, roll 264.

[202] KAW, B/521, No. 1484. Loehr's personal letter to Diakow.

[203] OKW War Diary, quoted by Kazimirovic, op. cit. p. 237.

with a wave of the hand, however, and cynically told him that the Ustašas should be allowed "to let their steam off" with the Serbs.

Pavelić flew to Vinnica in the Ukraine and visited Hitler at his headquarters there on 23 September.[204] Hitler said that Germany wanted a stable regime in Croatia as the best guarantee against the resurgence of "young Serb fanatics." Yet again Pavelić felt encouraged: he could afford to overlook pressures from other German quarters. He took the opportunity to complain to Hitler that General Roatta had not disarmed "his" Četniks. Hitler was indignant. He had always insisted on the designation of all insurgents as "rebels" and "bandits." His hatred of Četniks reflected a deep anti-Serb sentiment that was shared by many Germans and, in particular, Austrians who were former Habsburg Army officers. One of them, General Franz Böhme, was guided by the spirit of 1914 when he issued his draconian orders for the suppression of the insurgency in Serbia in October 1941.

On Hitler's orders the OKW chief, Field Marshal Wilhelm Keitel, demanded from his Italian counterpart, Marshal Ugo Cavallero, "unified and energetic measures" against the Četniks in order "finally to break the backbone" of the insurgent movement.[205] In his view, "the prerequisites for arriving at an amicable agreement with the enemy do not exist." At the same time Mussolini was pressed from Berlin to replace General Ambrosio, seen as a chief advocate of pro-Četnik policy. But Ambrosio's replacement, General Mario Roatta, continued his predecessor's policy, however. He told the Germans he favored joint action to destroy the centers of revolt.[206] At the same time

---

[204] ADAP, E, III, p. 530-538. Minutes of the talks between Hitler and Pavelić, 23 September 1942.

[205] German Liaison Staff with the Italian Second Army No. 153/42 of 26 January 1942. Cf. Paul Hehn, *The German struggle against Yugoslav guerrillas in World War II: German counter-insurgency in Yugoslavia, 1941-1943*. Boulder : East European Quarterly, 1979, pp. 100-101.

[206] Milazzo, op. cit. pp. 70-72.

he suggested an *even more extensive cooperation* with the Serbs, if necessary at the expense of the Croatian state. Zagreb would seek to obstruct such policy, he added, but it was a mistake to create an independent Croatia. His statement, made so soon after he had assumed command at Sušak, indicates that by early 1942 a distinct Italian Army position on of the Serb-Croat problem was firmly in place. The Germans were trying in vain to force Italian generals to disarm the Četniks.[207] Roatta was not interested in shedding the blood of his men unless he could be assured of *political* gains.[208]

The Germans were in for a new surprise in June and July 1942, when Roatta suddenly withdrew Italian forces from most of Zone 3 and even from some parts of Zone 2. He ordered his field commanders to execute the withdrawal swiftly, and in doing so he created a power vacuum in a large corridor from Bosanska Krajina in the northwest to the Sanjak in the southeast. With the war in Russia and North Africa entering the decisive phase, Roatta wanted to have his forces near the coast, rather than continue the endless, bloody game of hide-and-seek in the Dinaric wilderness. Pavelić was pleased to regain a foothold southwest of the demarcation line.[209] In return he had to swallow the bitter pill of condoning legalization of Četnik units under Italian patronage and under the label of 'Anti-Communist Voluntary Militia' (*Milizia Volontaria Anti-Comunista* MVAC), the model of coopting anticommunist forces that was already applied in southwestern Slovenia. Local Italian commands could veto all actions by the NDH forces.

The Germans were concerned that, since the Croats in their view were not equal either to the Četniks ('national Serbs') or to the Communists, the area evacuated by the Italians would

---

[207] Wehrmachtbefehlshaber Südost Ia, No. 845/42 of 30 March 1942.

[208] The Italian Supreme Command on 9 May 1942 changed the name of the Second Army to *Comando Superiore Forze Armate Slovenia - Dalmazia*, abbreviated *Supersloda*.

[209] T-120, roll 208, No. 1470. Kasche to Foreign Ministry, 20 June 1942.

become "a continuous insurgent center."[210] Indeed, in many places (Bihać, Ključ, Drvar, Glamoč, Kupres, Livno, Prozor…) the Italian withdrawal enabled Tito's forces to move in unopposed. With increasing alarm the Germans registered the steady advance of Tito's 'proletarian brigades,' by now battle-hardened shock units, along the vacated corridor just south of (and parallel to) the demarcation line.[211] The alarm was justified: the long march gave a new impetus to Partisan activity in the evacuated area. It enabled Tito, in the second half of 1942, to establish a large 'liberated territory' under his control. The Partisans surged in the direction of least resistance. As they advanced, they were focused on the party they regarded as their main enemy – the Četniks – and mostly avoided clashes with the Germans, Italians, or Croats.

As the crisis in Russia reached its climax, Hitler decided in December 1942 to pacify the western Balkans.[212] His Instruction 47 stated that there was increased danger of Allied attack which would be supported by insurgents. He entrusted Loehr, who had under his command Army Group E, to pacify the rear and "destroy bands of all kinds" – and to do it in co-operation with the Italians. For the duration of military operations in Croatia, however, all authority would pass to the commander of the German forces.[213]

The operation known as *Plan Weiss* was the most determined and ambitious anti-insurgency drive in the former Yugoslavia during World War II. In a preliminary round of talks with foreign minister Ciano, Hitler said that under the circumstances there was no alternative to destroying all Četniks and dealing with 'the bands' with the utmost brutality.[214] It is noteworthy that Hitler mentioned *only* the Četniks. According to

---

[210] T-120, roll 380, No. 1864. SD to Luther, 8 July 1942.

[211] E.g. T-120, roll 380, No. 1864. Helm to SD, Zagreb, 23 July 1942.

[212] V.I.I., *Zbornik*, XII/2, pp. 961-965.

[213] T-120, roll 212, no number. OKW to Ritter, 3 January 1943.

[214] ADAP, E, 4, pp. 538-555, 562-564, 582-585.

Glaise, for a long time he remained convinced that there was no great difference between the rival movements, above all because both were composed of Serbs. Ribbentrop spoke in the same vein at the meeting: the real enemy were the Serb nationalists, not the Communists. He also insisted that Roatta's unacceptable co-operation with the Četniks had to stop.[215]

The Italians were not convinced, and the misgivings of the military were shared by political leaders.[216] The generals suspected that much and acted accordingly. On 11 January 1943 Roatta issued his final instructions to Italian commanders and said that 'MVAC units' (Italian euphemism for national Serbs) should be actively used against Tito.[217] Apparently unaware of Roatta's schemes, however, Loehr outlined his plan to the Italians: Weiss I called for the encirclement and destruction of Partisans in western Bosnia and Lika. Weiss II would push those Partisan forces that managed to escape encirclement into the trap further south, towards the Neretva river, where they would be destroyed. Simultaneously, Weiss III in the Italian zone had for its objective the complete disarmament of all Četniks. Roatta did not say so openly, but he was not going to play along.[218] The Četniks were in the way of the main body of Tito's battle-hardened shock troops and Roatta expected them to bear the brunt of the fighting, which would save his own men.

What followed was the heaviest fighting seen in the Balkans that far in the war. By the beginning of February 1943 the Partisans – in full retreat and battered but not beaten – escaped across the demolished, and then partly repaired, bridge across the Neretva river (above). Yet in Berlin the Četniks were still seen as more dangerous. The Germans feared an Allied landing in the Balkans which would revive the Četniks, giving them a decisive

---

[215] T-821, roll 21, fr. 975. CS, *Argomenti militari...* 19 December 1942.

[216] Ciano, *Diary*, 6 January 1943.

[217] V.I.I. *Zbornik*, IV/9, No. 211. Roatta to V Corps, 11 January 1943.

[218] V.I.I. *Zbornik*, IV/9, No. 218. Comando Supremo to 2. Armata, 15 I. 1943.

advantage over Tito. In a letter to Mussolini on 25 February 1943, Hitler therefore refused to prioritize:

> If we do not succeed in disarming the Communists and Četniks in the same measure, and in pacifying the land completely – then at the moment of invasion disorder will break out, all links with the Peloponnese cut off or interrupted, the few German divisions will be busy fighting the Communists and Četniks, and Italian troops will no longer be able to halt the invasion."[219]

Hitler was right: both movements were inimical to his goals, while the Četniks' understanding with the Italians was tactical and therefore unreliable. That understanding was based on necessity, not choice, and it was bound to end with the landing of the first Allied contingent in Dalmatia.

As for the Italian army, its policy of support for the Četniks continued even to the point of defying Mussolini's explicit orders. It made solid strategic sense on the assumption that Italy needed to diversify her options since the war was lost for the Axis. After Stalingrad and El Alamein this was evidently the case. Therefore, if Italy was to get off Hitler's doomed bandwagon, the generals felt they needed to cultivate those who could facilitate such a transition. The military governor of Montenegro, General Alessandro Pirzio-Biroli, thus sent a message to Mihailovic in late 1942, saying that he supported a separate peace with the British. This message was passed to London, but Eden subsequently noted, "I have decided against pursuing any of these contacts."[220]

The lack of Italian commitment or cooperation made it impossible to carry out Hitler's orders in practice. Italian commanders warned the Cetniks of the Germans' advance, and sometimes evacuated them under the Germans' noses. Berlin accordingly instructed its commands in the NDH to prepare a

---

[219] ADAP, E, 5, pp. 171-172. Hitler to Mussolini, 16 February 1942.

[220] PRO, FO 371, R8802/3700/22, Eden to Churchill, 2 December 1942.

new action, strictly on their own, code-named Schwarz: "In view of the close links between the Četniks and the Italians, the Führer attaches great importance to the strictest concealment of both the intention and the preparations."[221] Unknown to the Germans, however, the Partisans had entered the area of northwest Montenegro and southeast Herzegovina – the Sutjeska river valley – where the brunt of the German attack was to come. After a month of desperate fighting in late spring 1943, the Germans failed – yet again – to capture or deal a decisive blow to either Tito or Mihailović.

Hard pressed Partisans established contact with the Germans in early March 1943, ostensibly in order to arrange an exchange of prisoners, including German Major Arthur Strecker (l.). As early as November 1942 Tito put out feelers to find out if the Germans would let him concentrate all his forces against the Četniks. In return he offered a truce south of the Sava and a suspension of all Partisan attacks on the key Zagreb-Belgrade railroad north of the river.[222] That idea could not be pursued, however, because at that very time Hitler decided to deal a mortal blow to all insurgents with his *Directive 47*.

Unaware of Hitler's position, at the height of *Weiss II* three high-ranking Partisan officers went to the 717th German division headquarters to negotiate an exchange of prisoners. They were Koča Popović, Milovan Djilas and Vladimir Velebit. The first two were Tito's generals, and Djilas was a member of the CPY Politbureau. They initially said that they demanded recognition

---

[221] *Kriegstagebuch des Oberkommandos der Wehrmacht* (KTB), III, p. 255

[222] Cf. Walter Roberts *Tito, Mihailović, and the Allies, 1941-1945*. Duke University Press, 1987; Krizman (1983), p. 540.

as belligerents. Then they went further and stated that they did not want to fight against the NDH forces, and certainly not against the Germans, but only against the Četniks.[223] They also indicated that, if their proposals were accepted, they would fight the British together with the Germans if they were to land on the Adriatic Coast.

On 11 March Glaise was informed of the Partisans' offer and realized the possibilities for saving German lives through political fine-tuning. He phoned his friend Wilhelm Hoettl at the RSHA.[224] Hoettl immediately contacted the RSHA chief of foreign intelligence, Walter Schellenberg, who then passed the information to Ribbentrop. When Ribbentrop approached Hitler with the news, however, the Fuehrer cut the whole business short by saying that "one does not negotiate with the rebels, one shoots them." Unaware of Hitler's rigid stand, Kasche eagerly reported on March 17, 1943, that negotiations with Tito's envoys had opened the possibility that the Partisans would halt all combat against Germans, Italians, and Croats, and deal exclusively with the Četniks.[225] Kasche stressed the Partisans' readiness to accept 'pacification' of the NDH. Three days later he added that "in the context of the Partisans' earlier statements" their ongoing and promised actions against Četnik forces were "quite useful" to the Germans.[226]

The Partisans, too, did not realize that Hitler had rejected their schemes. Milovan Djilas therefore went to Zagreb once again. This time he offered the Germans an open-ended truce. In return the Partisans asked to be left alone so as to devote all their energies to fighting their main enemy, Draža Mihailović.[227] The offer of a truce to open up a showdown with Mihailović was approved by Tito. The Germans asked the Partisans, as a token

---

[223] T-501, roll 267, No. 15. Report by Colonel Pfaffenroth, 11 March 1943.

[224] Walter Hagen, op. cit., Ch. 4.

[225] T-120, roll 212, No. 1174, 17 March 1941; ADAP, E, V, pp. 416-417.

[226] T-120, roll 212, No. 1271. Kasche to foreign ministry, 23 March 1943.

[227] T-120, roll 212, No. 1303. Kasche to foreign ministry, 26 March 1943.

of good will and a basis for eventual negotiations, to stop all attacks on the key railroad connecting Belgrade and Zagreb.[228] The Partisans agreed and all attacks were unilaterally halted. They were renewed only some months later, when Tito realized that the Germans would not play along.

The common ground that the Germans had with the Partisans in the spring of 1943 – their animosity to Mihailović (l.) and the Četniks – had given Tito great hopes. Even without waiting for the outcome of talks in Zagreb he issued orders that all activity against German, Italian and Croatian forces should be stopped; this was reiterated even after Djilas and Velebit returned from Zagreb with discouraging news.[229] He sent couriers (sometimes under German protection) to local Partisan units with the message that "the most important task right now is the destruction of the Četniks of Draža Mihailović."[230] He also ordered his commanders to shoot all captured Četnik officers 'without mercy' and 'on the spot,' while other ranks were to be either drafted or liquidated if they did not join the Partisans.[231]

A month earlier General Mihailović had made some off-the-cuff remarks at a baptismal celebration in Montenegro to the effect that his Communist enemies were worse than the occupiers. It was reported immediately to London and caused him much damage with the Allies. The Partisans thought the same of him, and acted accordingly, but they were more prudent

---

[228] Krizman (1983), p. 543; Kazimirović, op. cit. p. 182f.

[229] Djuretić, op. cit., Vol. I, p. 248.

[230] V.I.I. *Zbornik* II/8, p. 392. Tito et al. to Iso Jovanović, 29 April 1943.

[231] A-VII, Box 7, Reg. No. 2-2; also in Djuretić, op. cit. Vol. I, p. 249.

in their public statements. Furthermore, an important segment of Tito's British support came from outright Communist agents who systematically altered the incoming intelligence to make it look like the partisans were doing all of the fighting and the Četniks were collaborating.

In reality the Partisans, with a view toward post-war politics, fought most of their battles against the Serb nationalists, not the Axis occupation troops. Throughout the war years the Partisans deliberately and routinely provoked retaliatory strikes on peaceful villages, by sneaking into an area, killing a few Axis soldiers, and then running away. Villages "liberated" by Tito's zealots often endured a reign of terror; yet Churchill, who reveled in the dramatic, eagerly boosted Tito's reputation as a resistance leader.

The Soviet-inspired coat of arms of Tito's Yugoslavia featured six torches burning together as one flame, symbolizing the country's six federal republics. The date is the 'Republic Day,' the second AVNOJ session at Jajce

Communists Victorious

Winston Churchill was a leader who had been badly wrong about Gallipoli in 1915 and just as wrong about Greece in 1941. He had an enduring obsession with finding strategic opportunities in the Balkans which left him open to the suggestion that the Partisans, who could certainly fight well, were far more effective than was plausible. He accordingly tried to commit the United States to Adriatic operations by claiming that the Partisan forces along or near the Dalmatian coast were a major strategic factor. Washington did not agree, and Yugoslavia's post-war fate was thus sealed.

If Churchill was misled about Tito's strength or intentions, he helped along his own deception by intervening capriciously in the intelligence chain. As Prime Minster, he briefed British agents himself and dropped broad hints about the recommendations they would make. Sometimes he interviewed them again when they returned to London.

There were several Communist double agents in British intelligence who were in a position to pass upwards what the Prime Minister seemed to want to hear. Two are directly relevant. One was John Cairncross at Bletchley Park, who worked on German Army intelligence related to the Balkans.[232] The other was James Klugmann, the Special Operations desk officer in Cairo who doctored agents' reports from the Balkans on a daily basis to favor Tito. (Klugman was deemed so reliable a Communist that after the war he was entrusted with the task of writing the official history of the Communist Party of Great Britain.)

---

[232] *The Independent*, 28 June 1997, quoted an ex-employee at GCHQ Bletchley Park (Section 3L) who prepared a weekly summary of the Yugoslav situation for Churchill: "At the time I wasn't particularly suspicious that our information didn't seem to be acted upon, but have become so since. I now wonder if many of our reports were sent to the section where people like Philby were working."

The conspirators worked, from two geographically and operationally different centers, to reinforce Churchill's growing conviction that the Partisans, and hence *not* the Četniks, were tying down unlikely numbers of Axis 'divisions.'[233] The signals sent by Klugmann, who was an intimate of the traitors Anthony Blunt, Kim Philby, and Guy Burgess at Cambridge in the late 1930's, became public in 1997 and for the first time confirmed earlier claims that Klugmann was principally responsible for the massive wartime sabotage of the Mihailović supply operation and for keeping from London information about the impressive activities of his forces in the fight against the Germans.[234]

Hitler was unaware that the *strategic* threat from the Yugoslav insurgencies was largely Communist. He remained adamant that both resistance movements in Yugoslavia were equally hostile and needed to be destroyed simultaneously. The ambiguous course and results of Operation *Weiss* appear to have contributed to Hitler's intransigence, which was on full display during Pavelić's third visit on 27 April 1943 at Klessheim near Salzburg.[235] Responding to Pavelić's remark that all Serbs, regardless of political orientation, were enemies of Croatian statehood, Hitler described them as "old troublemakers." The only immediate effect of Pavelić's visit – to the chagrin of the Wehrmacht commanders – was a fresh increase in the incidence of Ustaša anti-Serb terror.[236]

In early May 1943 Tito finally realized that the Germans would not change their minds. He sent a message to his units to resume the acts of sabotage, suspended in late March. Once again, however, the Četniks were named as his chief enemy. The lull in fighting in April, coupled with Tito's hopes of a deal with the Germans, slackened his guard and contributed to the

[233] For a shrewd judgment of British exaggeration of Partisan record, see Vane Ivanović, *Memoirs of a Yugoslav*. London: Harcourt Brace Jovanovich, 1977

[234] Cf. Andrew Boyle, *The Climate of Treason*. Hutchinson, 1979.

[235] ADAP, E, V, pp. 713-714. Talks between Hitler and Pavelić, 27 March 1943.

[236] T-501, roll 267. Lüters to Glaise, 6 June 1943.

confusion in his ranks when Operation *Schwarz* – initially intended to destroy both Četniks and Partisans simultaenously – hit his forces in mid-May. Also known as the Battle of Sutjeska, 'Schwarz' achieved near total surprise. It was fought south of Foča between the Piva and Tara Rivers in extremely challenging mountainous terrain. Led by the commander of German troops in Croatia General Rudolf Lüters, the attacking force surrounded and sealed off the Partisans and then slowly tightened the noose between 15 and 20 May. In the end Tito's depleted main force was able to cross the Sutjeska River on an extremely narrow front and advance into East Bosnia. Although Tito managed to escape with half his men after a month of intense fighting, his losses were nevertheless catastrophic.

On the plus side for the Communists, following the surrender of German and Italian forces in North Africa – also in May 1943 – the morale of the Italians reached a new low. Glaise reported that, with regard to Italy's collapse, "the question is not 'if' but only 'when'..."[237] Mussolini's demoralization was evident when he met Hitler on 19 July 1943. By that time the atmosphere in Croatia was on the verge of panic, as Glaise reported on 16 July.[238] Italy may collapse, he wrote, yet "the Croatian army cannot be counted upon." While many Ustašas would be only too happy to see the Italians go, the Germans knew that their departure would create scope for increased resistance activity.[239]

After Mussolini fell from power and was interned, the Germans received Marshal Badoglio's assurances that Italy would fight on, but they did not believe him. Loehr assumed that Italy would drop out of the war.[240] Hitler signed his *Directive No. 48* on the disposition of German forces in the Balkans if

---

[237] Krizman (1983), p. 569.

[238] T-501, roll 264. Glaise to Förtsch (for Loehr), 16 July 1943.

[239] T-120, roll 212, Unterstaatssekretär Pol. No. 395, 16 July 1943.

[240] See Loehr's order to Lüters of 25 July 1943, in V.I.I. *Zbornik*, XII/3, p. 464.

Italy collapsed.[241] He also issued an order on the "Increase of Croatian fighting strength" on 7 September 1943,[242] demanding their "energetic and positive co-operation," under German guidance, in enhancing German war effort. But General Lothar Rendulic, the newly-appointed senior commander of German forces in the NDH, did not believe that any such cooperation was possible. He was transferred from Russia to the Balkans in August 1943, and soon concluded that Pavelić and the Ustašas were an obstacle to his brief from Hitler: to pacify and control the area with as few German troops as possible. Rendulic wanted the NDH government replaced by a German military administration, "with but a pretense of regard for the Ustaša state."[243]

Rendulic's assessment was shared by Hermann Neubacher (r.), who was appointed special political envoy in the southeast in August 1943. His task was to "politically organize national forces and guide them in their struggle against Communist bands." No German official in the Balkans enjoyed such wide powers as Neubacher, who quickly joined the ranks of Pavelić's enemies. He prepared a plan for comprehensive pacification of the area which was, as he readily admitted, "aimed against the continued existence of Pavelić's regime." That regime regarded him, in his own words, "as the main Enemy of the State."[244] This view from Zagreb was hardly surprising, since Neubacher also proposed the creation of a

[241] Ibid, pp. 472-477.

[242] KTB, Band III, Zweite Halbband, pp. 1456-1459.

[243] PA, Büro Staatssekretär, Kroatien, Bd. 6, No. 162771.

[244] Neubacher, op. cit. p. 155.

"greater-Serbian federation" that would include eastern Bosnia, Montenegro, and an outlet to the Adriatic. By modifying the territorial penalties imposed on the Serbs in 1941 and belatedly offering them a place under the German 'New Order,' Neubacher hoped to drive a wedge in the Communist 'zip' (*Reisverschluss*) that was tearing the Balkans apart.

Neubacher's main problem was the lack of Hitler's support for such plans. In Hitler's words Germany should not allow a nation with "the sense of political mission" to become predominant in the Balkans, "and the Serbs are one such nation. They have shown that they possess great state-creating energy, so I have serious reasons not to encourage this nation in its ambitions."[245] Hitler's stand was dutifully echoed by Ribbentrop: "Germany waged the war in the Balkans in order to destroy, once for all, the Serbian hotbed of unrest... We have no interest in re-igniting the greater-Serbian spirit..."[246]

The Četnik stronghold in the Dinara-Tromedja region faced a serious challenge at the time of Italy's capitulation (l.) in

September 1943. On British orders – transmitted by Marshal Badoglio to the troops in the Balkans – most of Italian weapons and stores went to Tito's forces. The Četniks were dismayed by such an outcome. Nevertheless they expected an Allied landing sooner or later, and they cut off the strategic railway that connected Split and Knin with Zagreb and established a foothold on the Adriatic coast between Šibenik and Karlobag. At the same time, along the eastern edge of their

---

[245] ibid. p. 160.

[246] ADAP, E, VII, p. 374. Ribbentrop to Neubacher, 29 January 1944.

territory they were under constant pressure from the Partisan stronghold in Drvar. As scarce German units rushed to the Adriatic coast, large areas of Bosnia and continental Croatia – cleared of Partisans in the first half of 1943 – came under Tito's control yet again.

The vital issue to the Serbs was to prevent the return of Ustasa units to the coastal hinterland. That issue was decided in Berlin. Pavelić wanted to annex Italian Dalmatia to the NDH, but he was rebuffed. Ribbentrop wrote,

> The Croatian government is not allowed in any way to make any demands of us, or to make its desires known to us, even if they are justified... [It] must be satisfied with whatever it gets, as even that will be entirely thanks to the force of German arms.[247]

The Četnik strategy in the Krajina region was to avoid open clashes with the Germans for as long as they did not allow the Ustaša menace back, to keep any contacts with the Wehrmacht purely informal, and at the same time to conserve and position forces for a possible Allied landing. In line with his political instructions Field Marshal Maximilian von Weichs, Loehr's replacement as commander in the Balkans, decided neither to attack the Četniks nor to cultivate them.

The Četnik primary objective was still to save lives and to preserve their fighting strength. The Partisans had lost the least fear of German reprisals – or, as before, welcomed them as a recruiting tool. Unconcerned with such intricacies, Winston Churchill remained interested only in which side was 'killing more Germans.'[248] That was the reason why in 1942 Mihailović enjoyed the public support of the Western Allies, and that is why in early 1943 the mood in London shifted towards supporting Tito.

---

[247] ADAP, E, VI, pp. 579-582. Ribbentrop to Kasche, 23 September 1943.

[248] See David Martin, *The Web of Disinformation: Churchill's Yugoslav Blunder*. San Diego and New York: Harcourt, Brace, Jovanovich, 1990.

Before the end of the year a dramatic switch in policy had occurred, in no small part due to the impact of William Deakin's rapport with Tito (l.) and his subsequent two-hour personal report to Churchill. From that point on Mihailović was cut off from further British support. London and Moscow were, somewhat paradoxically, unanimous in their backing of Tito's Partisans. Such outcome was due to three factors: British Communist infiltration of the intelligence apparatus, causing disinformation and deception in various British institutions; Tito's fighting capacity (eminently visible to Deakin at the time of the battle of Sutjeska); and Mihailović's lack of political acumen and experience.

With the acquisition of Italian arms and stocks at home and the rising support of Allied powers abroad, Tito's fortunes took a lasting turn for the better in September 1943. By late November he felt confident enough to convene the 'Anti-Fascist Council of National Liberation' (AVNOJ) in Jajce, in northwestern Bosnia. It was a quasi-legislative body, under Communist control, which was supposed to provide a pseudo-legal cover for Tito's intended take-over of post-war Yugoslavia.

Assured not only of Soviet but also of British support, which was unaffected by the Četniks' epic rescue of over 500 Allied airmen in the summer and early fall of 1944 (opp. p., top), Tito thought that he could finally give up his tactic of constant movement. He set up his headquarters at Drvar, in western Bosnia, where he felt secure from sudden intrusion amidst the gorges and passes of the Dinaric Alps (and where he was almost captured by German paratroopers on May 25, 1944).

In the fall of 1943 the Partisan movement started attracting, for the first time, large numbers of Croats. They were tempted to join the side that increasingly looked like winning. The

Communist leadership was keen to attract them and diversify the ethnic mix of the Partisan rank-and-file. It often overlooked the fact that some of these new recruits were former Ustašas, including officers, guilty of horrendous crimes against the Serb civilian population. Such a lenient attitude was justified by the Party's urgent need for non-Serb cadres. Ideologically, the switch was possible because both had a common enemy: the Četnik movement.[249] The villages known for Četnik sympathies were doomed to suffer from both.

By mid-1944 the Allies were so firmly committed to Tito that they engineered his 'coalition' with the Yugoslav government-in-exile, in the person of Ban Šubašić. It was only a temporary ruse, designed to give the Communist takeover a veneer of legality. It was nevertheless effective as a British tool to pressure young King Peter into disavowing Mihailović and calling on his followers to join Tito. An Anglo-American landing on the eastern Adriatic coast remained the only hope of non-Communist groups in Yugoslavia – yet no such action was planned at a time when Normandy demanded the concentration of Allied force and effort.

In southern Krajina, in the meantime, the Četnik mini-state continued to function in 1943 and most of 1944 as if Pavelić's government did not exist. The NDH authorities could only take note of the fact that "all Orthodox businesses are paying taxes

[249] Cf. Slovene author Aleksandar Bajt, quoted by Diklić, op. cit., p. 135.

 levied by the Četnik Division, and they are forbidden to pay anything to the Independent State of Croatia, which they do not recognize."[250] At the same time the leaders of the western Serbs were running out of strategic and political options. The destiny of the Četnik forces was being decided by battles and events that were developing completely beyond their control.

The entry of the Red Army into Serbia in late September 1944 and the Soviet taking of Belgrade on 20 October (above) had a decisive effect on the outcome of the civil war: Tito was the winner. He would have been the leading contender for post-war power in any event, but the Red Army decided the strategic issue. With the loss of Romania and Bulgaria in August, and the arrival of the Soviets in the Pannonian Plain in September, the Wehrmacht was forced to evacuate large tracts of territory in the Balkans in late 1944. In occupied Yugoslavia those areas were taken over by Tito's Partisans, from Vojvodina and Šumadija in the northeast to Herzegovina and Dalmatia in the southwest.

Having received additional infusion of fresh recruits by accepting Domobran and Ustaša deserters, Tito's commanders started to move major forces into the region around Knin and the Tri-Boundary (*Tromedja*) region of Bosnia, Lika and Dalmatia. By the end of November 1944, the Četnik stronghold of southern Krajina was threatened by a rapid advance of Tito's well armed and supplied forces. Their left flank was pushing northwest along the Adriatic coast while the right flank was sweeping through western Bosnia. By the end of November this steady

---

[250] A-V.I.I. NDH, 267-43/1

pincer movement exposed Djujić's forces around Knin to the peril of encirclement. The Četniks could not contemplate a pitched battle on their home ground, however, as they were short of supplies, especially ammunition. Evacuation of their still intact fighting force, including those civilians who were at risk from Communist terror, emerged as the only real alternative to a futile last stand. Djujić rejected suggestions from Mihailović to head east, into central Bosnia, as logistically impossible and militarily untenable.

The leader of the Dinara Division thought that the best option would be for all Serb nationalist forces to gather in Slovenia and develop a foothold inside the country in advance of the anticipated arrival of the Allies from the west.Dobrosav Jevdjević supported this option, too. In an urgent radio message he warned that "withdrawing into Bosnia is certain death" and insisted that the only option was to march from the Knin area due north and then northwest, through Lika towards Rijeka and southwestern Slovenia.[251] This was the final plan of action.

The first task of the Četnik command was to break out of the looming encirclement, known in Partisan historiography as the Knin Operation. After a fierce battle at the village of Padjeni on December 3-4 1944, the Dinara Division broke through and started its long withdrawal. It suffered 800 casualties in that single engagement, but the road north was at least temporarily open.[252] After the march through Lika to southwestern Slovenia the Division reached its winter quarters along the old Yugoslav-Italian frontier as a compact and battle ready unit. Within weeks its officers (pictured in Slovenia, r. overleaf) could report that the unit was yet again battle-ready.

The first months of 1945 saw failed attempts to establish a common front among various anti-Communist forces in Slovenia. The problem was that they belonged to different military commands and subscribed to diverse, or even

---

[251] Nikola Plećaš-Nitonja, *Požar u Krajini*. Chicago 1975, P. 437.

[252] *Spomenica Dinarske četničke divizije 1941-1945*, p. 532.

incompatible ideologies. Djujić's Četniks, Ljotić's 'Volunteers,' Slovenian 'White Guards' and a few hundred stragglers from other formations could not be forged into a coherent body of men at a short notice, especially when the political unity was absent at the top.

Not even the arrival in Slovenia of Patriarch Gavrilo and the much revered Bishop Nikolaj (Velimirović), just released from German captivity in Dachau, could help overcome the atmosphere of mistrust. The military situation, in the meantime, was going from bad to worse. In March 1945 came the news of the annihilation of Pavle Djurišić's retreating column of Montenegrin Četniks, which was ambushed by heavily armed Ustaša forces at Lijevča Polje in northwestern Bosnia. More disheartening still was the loss of hope that General Mihailović might come to Slovenia, after all, and provide the backbone to anticommunist resistance in the westernmost part of Yugoslavia's territory.

On April 30 1945, after a final clash with Tito's forces just outside Gorizia, the Dinara division crossed the Isonzo into Italy. The Serbs' civil war was over. A mix of internal and foreign factors, mostly beyond control of the local actors, ensured that Tito's Communists were the winners.

A week later the Četniks had to surrender their weapons to the British in the camp at Palmanova (above). The wartime exploits of the Krajina Četniks were over. The arduous life of enforced exile was about to begin.

The British authorities treated all Serbs, regardless of uniform and command, as 'surrendered enemy personnel.' That designation, besides being factually wrong, was to prove fatal to seven thousand Četniks and members of other anti-Communist formations who reached southern Austria in early May 1945. At the summit at Yalta in February 1945, Stalin demanded the return of all Soviet citizens that may find themselves in the Allied zone. This was agreed to by Churchill and Roosevelt. Accordingly, hundreds of thousands of Soviet POWs liberated by the Allies were sent east, regardless of what Stalin had in store for them. In addition, in May 1945 thousands of refugees from Yugoslavia – anticommunist resistance fighters and assorted collaborationists – were rounded up by the British in southern Austria, and forcibly delivered to Tito. Most of them were summarily executed in the natural crags and rocky pits of the Slovenian Alps. Forced repatriations were known as *Operation Keelhaul* — the 'last secret' of World War II, as Alexander Solzhenitsyn called it. Serbian royalists were supposedly exempt from the deportation order, but key officials in the British chain of command surreptitiously included them.

There was panic in the camps around Klagenfurt when the men realized what was going on. The British told them that they were to be taken to Italy; if the subterfuge did not work, the guards used rifle butts and bayonets as prods. Some refugees committed suicide by sawing their throats with barbed wire. In mid-June 1945 the original policy of screening would-be deportees was reinstated, but it was too late. Most of them were already dead, including refugees not covered at Yalta (above). The key figure in the affair was Harold Macmillan, Minister Resident in the Mediterranean and later prime minister, who believed that Stalin had to be appeased.[253]

Some 14,000 Serbs who withdrew into Italy, and who were eventually transferred to a large camp at Eboli near Naples, were more fortunate. The living conditions were tolerable and in 1945-1946 they hoped a favorable shift in global events would open up the possibility of their return to the fatherland. They did not see the Communist triumph as final and irreversible.

In Yugoslavia, on the other hand, Tito's authorities were not reconciled to the fact that thousands of their sworn enemies were out of their reach. They wanted to deal with them the way they had dealt with all other 'enemies': by execution or long imprisonment. The model was established in the fall of 1944 and in the first half of 1945, when all over Serbia tens of thousands of people were summarily executed as 'enemies of the people,' 'collaborationists,' or 'traitors,' and applied again in Slovenia in May. Tito's authorities were encouraged by the precedent of the British 5th Corps in Klagenfurt. They expected that a mix of propaganda and political pressure would coerce Western allies to

---

[253] British historian Count Nikolai Tolstoy has written three books on the subject, as more suppressed information came to light: *Victims of Yalta* (1977), *Stalin's Secret War* (1981), and *The Minister and the Massacres* (1986).

repeat this exercise in Italy. In late 1945 the Communist regime in Belgrade started a wide-ranging campaign to have all of the 'traitors' and 'collaborators' extradited to Yugoslavia.

It was fortunate for the exiled Serbs that, among the Western allies, there had been no unanimity on this issue. Unlike the British, American military and political authorities refused in principle to extradite exiled Serbs to Tito from the territories under their control. In Washington the position of President Truman (unlike that of FDR) was marked by disdain for Communists of all hues. The Americans were not burdened, vis-à-vis Belgrade, by the pro-Partisan bias of Tito's British admirers such as William Deakin and Fitzroy MacLean (soon to become the author of a best-selling book, r., promoting the Tito myth on a grand scale).

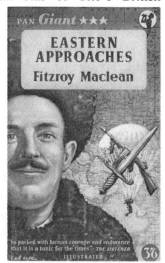

In July 1947 the exiles were finally set free. With the opening of the camp gates one problem was being resolved, but another problem was only beginning. Thousands of young Krajina Serbs, of whom many had not yet reached the age of thirty, had to decide what to do with their lives. They became a small segment of the deluge of DPs, 'Displaced Persons' from all over Eastern and Central Europe trying to start a new life in a new country. They ended up dispersed all over the world, from the United States and Great Britain to Canada and Australia.

Krajina Under Tito And His Successors

The anti-Serb tenor of the Comintern's pre-war slogans about royal Yugoslavia were reflected in the assumptions on which the second, Communist Yugoslavia was based. The Montenegrins, Macedonians and Slovenes had their own republics. Kosovo-Metohija and Vojvodina were granted autonomy within Serbia, but the Serbs of the Krajina did not even merit an autonomous area within Croatia. Indeed, the historical Krajina had now vanished altogether. Not only Dalmatia but also the newly-gained Istria, Fiume (Rijeka) and the Quarnero, by contrast, were confirmed – for the first time in history – as integral parts of Croatia.

Internal boundaries between Yugoslav federal units were arbitrarily established by the Partisan leadership at the end of 1943, at a meeting of the Communist-controlled provisional legislature (AVNOJ) organized by Tito. The decision was presented to this forum in a ready-made form, not open to questions and debate. It received its final touches in 1945 in an equally undemocratic manner. Those boundaries are still in force today, as internationally recognized state frontiers.

The national Communist parties of Croatia and Slovenia were represented at the 1943 AVNOJ assembly; the Serbs fighting on Tito's side – the only group denied the 'privilege' of having a national Communist party at that time – were not. It is uncertain whether even pro-Communist Serbs would have so readily agreed to Tito's blueprint for the territorial division of Yugoslavia, were it not for his assurances that the boundaries were irrelevant anyway. It was claimed that they would be treated merely as administrative lines between federal units under the same state roof. No debate was ever allowed on the issue of internal borders, although many questions remained unanswered. Just over one percent of all inhabitants of the Republic of Serbia were Croats, while in 1948 – even after the

Ustaša genocide – the Serbs accounted for 17 percent of the population of Croatia. Ethnically devoid of balance, those boundaries had a dubious basis in history. They had never been subjected to a popular plebiscite, let alone to the process of negotiation, signature and ratification by the representatives of the peoples affected by them.

One consequence of Tito's division of Yugoslavia (below) was to split the Serbs into four federal units, leaving a third of them outside the confines of the Republic of Serbia. Furthermore, within Serbia two autonomous provinces were created, thus diminishing that republic's coherence even further. 'Serbia-proper' (or 'Inner Serbia,' *Uža Srbija*) was effectively reduced to the boundaries of the Kingdom before the Balkan Wars of 1912-13. No other federal republic had autonomous provinces carved out of its land, although the same set of ethnic, historical, cultural, and geographic principles would have dictated the granting of the same status to Istria or Dalmatia, let alone the Krajina. Communist Yugoslavia was built not on a-nationality or supra-nationality, but on territorial adjudications

which would have been impossible at any point between 1918 and 1941. The Serbs of western Yugoslavia, who had provided the core fighting force of the Partisan movement (as well as some of its most competent enemies) were dismayed by Tito's territorial arrangements. At the First Congress of Serbs in Croatia, held in Zagreb in September 1945, they were told, neither for the first nor for the last time, that those arrangements did not matter since the Yugoslav state remained in place: "The boundaries of our federal units do not cut up or divide the Serbian people, but provide firm links that tie together all Serbs in Yugoslavia."[254] The new regime was not, of course, officially anti-Serb; but its newly-promulgated principle of equal contribution to victory and equal suffering for it, the corrolary of 'brotherhood and unity,' had as its chief practical consequence a massive official coverup of Ustaša crimes. A massive ideological *Gleichschaltung* was soon under way. The Party 'line' was clearly spelled out in the Resolution adopted by the Congress of Serbs in Croatia in September 1945:

> Firm and unshakeable brotherhood with the Croatian people, forged in the joint struggle and suffering, is the guarantee of a happy and fulfilled life of the Serbs in Croatia... The mortal enemies of our peoples, especially Pavelić's Ustašas and the Četniks of Draža Mihailović, should be punished and all traces of Fascism extinguished... We pay a brotherly tribute to the Croatian people, for it could not be led astray by Pavelić and the Ustašas, but fought instead jointly with us for our common freedom.[255]

Dušan Brkić, chairman of the Communist-created Main Board of Serbs in Croatia who tabled the Resolution, admitted many years later that he was perfectly aware of its surreal qualities, but "that was the only way we were able to act."[256] Tito's edifice thus came to be built on three fictions: the myth of

---

[254] Momčilo Diklić, *Srpsko pitanje u Hrvatskoj, 1941-1950*. Beograd: Zora, 2004, p. 242.
[255] Daily newspaper *Vjesnik*, Zagreb, October 1, 1945.

Yugoslav nations' equal contribution to the Partisan victory; the myth of all groups' equal suffering under the 'occupiers and their domestic servants'; and the equating of the Četniks with  Pavelić's Ustašas. These three myths were firmly imposed by the Communist authorities in Zagreb, headed by Vladimir Bakarić (pictured with Tito in the 1970's), the undisputed boss of Croatia in the post-war period.

The Serbs in the Croatian Communist Party, indoctrinated in Partisan ranks, provided the middle ranking *apparat* and a disproportionate number of army and police personnel, but not the top-ranking leaders. They were in the forefront of enforcing ideological rigidity among their own people, by imposing collectivization of agriculture in the Serb-majority areas and preventing the rebuilding of Orthodox churches demolished by the Ustaša regime (or even ordering the demolition of those that had been spared). In the name of 'brotherhood and unity,' they even opposed the desire of local Serbs to exhume the bodies of Ustaša victims from mass graves and mountain pits for proper funeral. Consequently the process of de-Nazification never took place in Yugoslavia. This has been, and still is, a paramount factor of Croatian society and politics.

The Krajina Serbs emerged from the Second World War as a devastated community. Decimated by genocide and years of fighting, pauperized, devoid of traditional local leaders and intelligentsia, the rural population literally faced starvation in 1945-1946. According to the incomplete data compiled in 1945 by ZAVNOH (Croatia's Communist-controlled government,

---

[256] Diklić (2004), p. 245.

Zemaljsko antifašističko vijeće narodnog oslobodjenja Hrvatske), over 50,000 Serb households were destroyed.

Croatian Communist authorities devised a plan to resettle tens of thousands of homeless Serbs not by rebuilding their houses and villages in the Krajina, but by physically relocating them to Vojvodina and housing them in the confiscated properties that had belonged to the expelled German minority (*Volksdeutsche*). The priority was given to Partisan veterans and their families. In 1945-1947 some 60,000 Krajina Serbs were resettled in the northern Serbian province under the colonisation program.[257] Additional thousands of families made the move of their own accord and were not covered by official statistics. The Serb-Croat ethnic balance, already altered through massive bloodletting in 1941-1945, thus had continued to shift under Tito's Communists: by the time of the 1948 census the Serbs constituted only 14.5 percent of Croatia's population. The cultural balance was shifting, too. Primary education in many Serb villages after 1945 was more rudimentary than in a hundred years preceding the occupation of Yugoslavia in 1941. Croatian government minister Zvonko Brkić warned, four years after the war's end, that the shortage of qualified teaching staff left tens of thousands youngsters uneducated:

> Today we have 330 schools that are closed because they have no teachers, which means that 40,000 children are not attending school... [because] we have no staff, but also in some places... because we have no school buildings.[258]

The Croat top echelon of the Party-state structure neglected the economic development of the Krajina. Of 35 factories built in Croatia in 1945-1949, not one was situated in a Serb-majority area.[259] At the same time, state requisitions of agricultural

---

[257] Ibid., p. 255.

[258] Report to the Third Plenum of the Central Committee of the Communist Party in Yugoslavia, held in Belgrade 29-30 December 1949.

[259] Diklić, op. cit., p. 319.

produce from the Krajina farmers escalated to the point where some had no seed left for the following year's sowing. In May 1950 the inability of Serb peasants to deliver impossibly high quotas of foodstuffs resulted in a disobedience movement in Kordun, led by Partisan veterans Mile Devrnja and Milan Božić. It soon acquired the character of a rebellion and was brutally suppressed. Devrnja, Božić and 15 other alleged ringleaders were shot. Dozens of people were sentenced to long jail terms. The elimination of the remaining prominent Serb cadres from the Croatian party leadership, headed by Dušan Brkić, followed soon thereafter on trumped-up charges of '*Informbiro* [pro-Soviet] deviations' – a deadly serious accusation in the aftermath of Stalin's break with Tito in 1948.

Over the ensuing two decades the regime relied extensively on the Krajina-Serb lower and middle-ranking *nomenklatura*, notably during the 'Croatian Spring' of 1970-1971. This created the illusion of influence and the semblance of a stake in the political order. In reality the Serbs in Croatia lacked both. Their cultural and political institutions – such as the Club of Serb Deputies in the Croatian assembly – were abolished. They lacked leaders and strategy. They were singularly ill-prepared for the crisis of the Yugoslav state that became acute within a decade of Tito's death in 1980. The roots of that crisis and the ensuing wars of 1991-1995 were to be found in 35 years of Tito's autocracy (1945-1980). Hailed by the West for decades after 1948 as a 'national,' user-friendly Communist, Tito had devised in his lifetime a political system designed to perpetuate his personal power by keeping Yugoslavia's national Communist Party hierarchies permanently at odds with each other... with himself as the final arbiter. Apprehensive of all potential rivals to the point of paranoia, under the 1974 Constitution Tito devised an unworkable, rotating collective decision-making system. In the aftermath of his death in early 1980, lacking the single source of final authority, this system contributed to Yugoslavia's slide into disintegration and war.

Tito's brand of federalism was inherently unstable: eight million Serbs, with 40 percent of the total population, effectively had one-eighth of the voting power in the rotating collective bodies under the Constitution of 1974. This was the context  within which the eventual rise of Slobodan Milošević (l.) needs to be understood. An uninspiring and relatively obscure apparatchik devoid of any discernible national sentiment, he emerged in the late 1980s as the Serbs' leader. He would not have been able to do so had he not relied on a deep sense of dissatisfaction among a majority of Serbs of all social classes.

Yugoslavia's internal boundaries were a legacy of Stalin's Comintern, which inspired them, and of Tito's autocratic communism, which enforced them. In 1990-1991 Croatia's resurgent nationalists insisted on preserving those boundaries as the only sacrosanct part of the otherwise despised Yugoslav legacy.

Rise and Demise of the Republic of Serb Krajina

The Serb-Croat conflict of the 1990s grew from elements which should now be familiar. The genocide attempted by Croatian Quislings in 1941-1945 was still in vivid collective memory in 1991. It shaped the determination of the Krajina Serbs not to live under a post-communist Croatian government which took some pains to revive the symbolism, discourse, and even some methods of the Ustaša state. The internal history of Communist Croatia also played a role. Croatia kept the Krajina in 1945 but thereby kept its Serbian Question. The Serbs in Croatia may have had little real clout under Tito and after him, but the Communist *apparat* and the police were disproportionately Serb. This was resented by Croats just as Serb privileges had been resented before 1881, and Serb identity thereafter. As the Croatian Party (*Savez komunista Hrvatske*, SKH) became more nationalistic this was consequential; when Communists failed, this nationalism detonated. The Serbs were identified as the origin of the Communist revolution.

In 1990-1991 the Krajina Serbs, Communists and all others, had the memory of the genocide as a salient feature of their outlook. Their fears were kindled by the government of Franjo Tudjman and his Croatian Democratic Community (*Hrvatska demokratska zajednica*, HDZ), which came to power in 1990 after the first multiparty election since Second World War. It was composed of hard-line nationalists with strong émigré connections. Tudjman readily affirmed that the NDH reflected "centuries-old aspirations of the Croat people."[260] The violations of the rights of Serbs in Croatia began soon after the HDZ electoral victory in April 1990. Thousands of Serbs were soon fired from their jobs, or else forced to sign humiliating 'declarations of loyalty' to the new government in Zagreb.

---

[260] Speech at the First HDZ Convention, February 26, 1990. *Defense & Foreign Affairs Strategic Policy,* January 1993.

Next came clandestine distribution of weapons to 'reliable Croats' in the villages, members of the ruling party. Nocturnal shots fired at the windows of Serb apartments, Ustaša slogans spray-painted on Serb-owned houses and businesses, threatening late-night telephone calls, all became the order of the day in the summer of 1990. Within months over one-hundred-thousand Serbs, mainly women, children, and old people, left their homes and sought refuge in Serbia.

On May 30, 1990, the newly-founded Serb Democratic Party (SDS), led at that time Jovan Rašković, decided to break all ties to the Croatian parliament. Yet Rašković did not trust Milošević and sought to avoid the escalation of what was still political confrontation into armed violence. Events were an omenous course nevertheless. In June the Serbs established the Association of Municipalities of Northern Dalmatia and Lika in Knin. The Serbian National Council was founded in July 1990 to co-ordinate opposition to Croatian independence. Its position was that if Croatia were to secede from Yugoslavia, then the Serbs should have the right to secede from Croatia. Milan Babić, a dentist from Knin, was elected president of the Council. In August 1990 a referendum was held in the Krajina affirming Serb 'sovereignty and autonomy' within Croatia. As expected, it was declared illegal and invalid by the

Croatian government. Also in August, barricades of logs were placed across roads leading to Serb-majority areas. This effectively cut Croatia in two, separating the coastal region of Dalmatia from the rest of the country.

Franjo Tudjman (l.) and his followers were undeterred: a new Croatian constitution was passed in December 1990. It treated Serbs as an ethnic minority by abrogating their previous status as a constituent nation of the Republic of Croatia. In the words of Lord Peter Carrington, the EU negotiator, this was tantamount to "igniting the barrel of gunpowder." Babić's administration responded by announcing the creation of the Serbian Autonomous Region of Krajina (*Srpska autonomna oblast*, SAO Krajina) on 21 December 1990. On 1 April 1991, it declared that it would secede from Croatia. Other mainly Serb communities, in western and eastern Slavonia, announced that they would join the SAO Krajina.

Tudjman's government staged a referendum on independence on 19 May 1991. On 25 June 1991, Croatia and Slovenia both declared their independence from Yugoslavia. In Slovenia the Yugoslav People's Army (*Jugoslovenska narodna armija*, JNA) attempted, without any clear policy or political guidance, to defend some sort of Yugoslav authority. In Croatia bloody clashes between insurgent Serbs and Croatian security forces broke out almost immediately, leaving dozens dead on both sides. At this point the Serbian cry was 'Yugoslavia'. The European Community (after December 1991, the European Union) and UN attempted to broker ceasefires and peace settlements. After Brussels decided to recognize Tito's borders as international frontiers, however, such efforts were to no avail.

The Yugoslavia's divorce should have reflected the nature of its 'marriage' in 1915. Yugoslavia came into being with the approval of the international community – a voluntary union of its three initial constituent peoples: Serbs, Croats, and Slovenes. Prior to 1918, only Serbia and Montenegro were sovereign states: the rest of Yugoslavia was incorporated into Austria-Hungary. They joined Serbia in union as peoples, not as 'states.' The right to secession remained vested in the constituent peoples of Yugoslavia (as distinct from national minorities), and not in Tito's arbitrarily delineated republics. EU negotiator Lord David Owen thus conceded that Tito's internal boundaries were arbitrary and that their redrawing should have been countenanced at the outset of the crisis in 1990-1991:

Incomprehensibly, the proposal to redraw the republics' boundaries had been rejected by all eleven EC countries... [T]o rule out any discussion or opportunity for compromise in order to head off war was an extraordinary decision. My view has always been that to have stuck unyieldingly to the internal boundaries of the six republics within the former Yugoslavia... as being those for independent states, was a folly far greater than that of premature recognition itself.[261]

This outcome flowed from the decision of the Foreign Ministers of the European Community on 16 December 1991, and was given a legal basis in the Opinions issued by the Badinter Arbitration Commission established by the European Community four months earlier. A wide-scale war broke out four months eaerlier, in August 1991. This time the Krajina Serbs had the benefit of JNA officers and equipment, and they fought with conviction and enthusiasm. Over the following months a large area, amounting to a third of the Republic of Croatia, was controlled by the Serbs.

On 19 December 1991, the SAO Krajina proclaimed itself the *Republic of Serbian Krajina*. On 26 February 1992, the SAO Western Slavonia and SAO Slavonia, Baranja and Western Srem were added to the RSK. The Serb Army of Krajina (*Srpska vojska Krajine*) was officially formed on 19 March 1992, its officer corps consisting entirely of the former YPA personnel. The self-proclaimed Republic of Serbian Krajina consisted of a large section of the historical Military Frontier (see map opp. p.), as well as parts of northern Dalmatia with a majority or a plurality of Serbian population, including the city of Knin which became its capital. It covered an area of 17,000 square kilometers, but it was strategically vulnerable, politically unconsolidated, and economically weak.

A ceasefire agreement was signed by Presidents Tudjman and Milošević in January 1992, paving the way for the

---

[261] David Owen. The Balkan Odyssey. London: Mariner Books, 1997.

implementation of a UN peace plan put forward by former U.S. Secretary of State Cyrus Vance. Under the Vance Plan, four United Nations Protected Areas (UNPAs) were to be established in the Krajina. On 21 February 1992, the creation of the United Nations Protection Force (UNPROFOR) was authorized by the UN Security Council for an initial period of one year. The agreement effectively froze the front lines for the next three years. The two sides had fought each other to a temporary standstill.

The partial implementation of the Vance Plan drove a wedge between the governments of the Krajina and Serbia, the RSK's principal backer and supplier of fuel, arms and money. Milan Babić strongly opposed the Vance Plan but was overruled by the RSK assembly. On 26 February 1992, after a long and arduous meeting with the leaders of Serbia in Belgrade, Babić refused to relent and was forced to resign. He was replaced as President by Goran Hadžić, a Milošević loyalist destined to become, many years later, one of the last two fugitives from The Hague tribunal. Hadžić signed the Vance Plan, which implied

the recognition of Croatian sovereignty. Babić (l.) remained involved in politics as a much weaker figure. The position of the Krajina eroded steadily over the following three years. On the surface, the RSK had all the symbols of a state: an army, parliament, president, government and ministries, currency and stamps. But it was surrounded by hostile territory. On two sides lay Croatia, and though the Bosnian Serb Republic gave the RSK some protection on the third side, Krajina was itself all but split in half by enemy territory. There was only one road from Knin to the outside word, and that lay through the very narrow Posavina corridor in northern Bosnia.

The RSK economy was wholly dependent on support from Serbia, however, and Serbia itself was under sanctions and suffering from hyper-inflation. The economic situation soon became disastrous. By 1994, only 36,000 of the RSK's 430,000 citizens were employed. With few natural resources of its own and no access to its natural markets, it had to import most of the goods and fuel it required. Agriculture operated at little more than a subsistence level. Professionals went to Serbia or abroad to escape the hardship.

The government apparatus in Knin was staffed mostly by recycled Communist cadres and riddled with corruption. The region became a haven for black marketeering, including illicit arms sales to the Muslim forces in the Bihać pocket. It was becoming clear by the mid-1990s that without a peace agreement, or more energetic support from Belgrade, the RSK was not economically viable. In Serbia, however, it was seen as an unwanted economic and political burden by Milošević. To his frustration, the Krajina Serb assembly continued to reject his demands to settle the conflict by accepting the principle of Croatian sovereignty.

The RSK's weakness adversely affected its armed forces. Since the 1992 ceasefire agreement, Croatia had spent heavily on importing weapons and training with assistance from American contractors. In contrast the Krajina forces had grown steadily weaker, with its soldiers poorly motivated, trained and equipped. Only 55,000 of them had to cover a front of some 400 miles in Croatia and 65 miles along the border with the Bihać pocket in Bosnia. With 16,000 soldiers stationed in eastern Slavonia, fewer than 40,000 were left to defend the Republic's heartland of Lika, Banija, Kordun, and Northern Dalmatia. By the summer of 1995 not more than 30,000 of them were ready for duty. They faced a far stronger Croatian army. Political divisions between Hadžić and Babić led to tensions between their supporters; Babić himself was assaulted in an incident in Benkovac.

In January 1993 the revitalized Croatian army attacked the Serbian positions around Maslenica in southern Croatia, which curtailed their access to the sea at Novigrad and reopened the vital Adriatic highway. In a second offensive, in September 1993, the Croatian army overran the Medak pocket in southern Lika, committing shocking and well documented atrocities against the unarmed civilians trapped in the area. When Canadian peacekeepers moved into the Medak Pocket, according to the official Ottawa government account, they could hardly have imagined the horror that awaited them:

> They had arrived too late to help the Serbs in the Medak Pocket, but they had forced their way in before the Croatian Special Police could complete their clean-up. Every building had been burned or flattened by mines. Now they understood the truckloads of wood they had seen the Croats trucking in - tinder to light the sturdy stone and mortar farmhouses of the Medak. Everywhere there were shell casings, accompanied by a similar number of disposable latex gloves, indicating that the Croats had been moving bodies to hide evidence. Grisly, burned corpses were found,

29 in all. Hundreds of Serbs went missing, and were never to return. Thousands had been displaced from their homes, which were systematically razed. Even the farm animals that could not be taken had been shot.[262]

The crimes in the Medak Pocket heralded what was to come in the rest of the Krajina. Croatian preparations took almost two years, and proceeded with the support of Germany and the United States, political as well as military. In November 1994 the United States and Croatia signed a military agreement and U.S. intelligence agents set up an operations center on the Adriatic island of Brač. Reconnaissance aircraft were launched from the Center to spy on the Serbs. The Pentagon also contracted Military Professional Resources, Inc. (MPRI) to train the Croatian military. U.S. satellite and spy plane intelligence was furnished to the Croatian military. Following the anticipated failure of the international plan for reintegration (Z-4), the beginning of the end of the RSK came in the first week of May of 1995, when Croatian forces gained control of western Slavonia (Operation Flash), to Belgrade's conspicuous indifference. Finally on August 4, 1995, *Operation Storm* was launched by the Croatian army and police. It was a massive, brutal, and well announced onslaught. It was not resisted by the Krajina high command on orders from Belgrade.

The political objectives of the Croatian state leadership in launching the attack had always been suspected. They became evident years later, when the War Crimes Tribunal at The Hague released a transcript of Tudjman's meeting with his top military commanders and civilian aides at the island of Brioni on July 31, 1995. "We have to inflict such blows," Tudjman announced, "that the Serbs will to all practical purposes disappear":

---

[262] National Defence Canada, 2PPCLI, Medak Pocket History <http://www.army.forces.gc.ca/2PPCLI/RH-United_Nations.asp> For a detailed account of atrocities in the Medak pocket, see Scott Taylor and Brian Nolan, *Tested. Metal*. Ottawa: Esprit de Corps Books, 1998.

[I]t is important that those [Serbian] civilians set out, and then the army will follow them, and when the columns set out they will have a psychological impact on each other ... This means giving them a way out, while pretending to guarantee their civil rights etc... Kinkel has promised that Germany will support us, but we will have to inform them ahead of time.[263]

As Croatian troops launched their assault on August 4, U.S. NATO aircraft destroyed Serbian radar and anti-aircraft defenses. Following the elimination of Serbian anti-aircraft defenses, Croatian planes carried out attacks on Serbian towns and positions. The roads were clogged with escaping civilians. Croatian aircraft bombed and strafed refugee columns.

Several thousand Serbs lost their lives during the exodus, or else were killed by the Croatian forces if they stayed behind. It was the biggest act of ethnic cleansing in post-1945 Europe. A few thousand remained, mostly the elderly, in an area inhabited by half a million people a century ago. It was not the first mass migration produced by war in the Balkans, but it was among the largest – on par with the Volksdeutsche exodus of 1944-1945 –

---

[263] ICTY Case No. IT-02-54-T, Exhibit No. PC11A of June 26, 2003.

and the first to result from a military action *specifically designed* to cause it.

Most of the refugees ended up in Serbia and the Serbian part of Bosnia (Republika Srpska). Massacres continued for several weeks after the fall of Krajina. UN patrols discovered numerous fresh unmarked graves and bodies of murdered civilians well after the 'Storm' was over. A suppressed EU report stated, "The corpses, some fresh, some decomposed, are mainly of old men. Many have been shot in the back of the head or had throats slit, others have been mutilated... Serb lands continue to be torched and looted."[264] Following a visit to the region the Zagreb Helsinki Committee reported that virtually all Serb villages had been destroyed: "In a village near Knin, eleven bodies were found, some of them were massacred in such a way that it was not easy to see whether the body was male or female."[265]

The war in remains controversial, many years after its end in 1995. To the Croats, its causes were in the program of a 'Greater Serbia,' pursued and elaborated for a century and a half that separated Ilija Garašanin in the 1840s and Slobodan Milošević in the 1990s. It was a war of Serbian aggression and Croatian Defence of the Motherland, plain and simple. It was also a war, it is often implied yet seldom openly stated in Croatian sources, between an outpost of the 'Western' civilization and a relic of an inherently incompatible and indubitably more primitive 'Byzantine' one.

To the Serbs the war was above all a reaction to what they perceived as intolerable provocation, an existential response to the revamping of Ustašism in rhetoric, symbols, and substance. In their view, they were reacting to Tudjman's escalating political ploys in Zagreb and his minions' terrorist acts on the ground. The establishment of autonomous regions, and the

---

[264] "Croats Burn and Kill with a Vengeance." Robert Fisk, *The Independent*, 4 September 1995.

[265] "Helsinki Committee Reports on Krajina Operations." Hartmut Fiedler, Österreich 1 Rundfunk, 21 August 1995.

subsequent proclamation of the Republic of the Serbian Krajina, was seen as an act of rebellion by most Croats and as necessary response by most Serbs.

All along President Tudjman acted as if he wanted Dr. Jovan Rašković's (r.) restrained approach to be discredited, in the eyes of his followers, by Croat intransigence. He needed someone more like Rašković's rival Milan Babić – a firm advocate of the Krajina Serbs' sovereignty – to carry out his long-desired *Gleichschaltung* of the Croatian society and to provide a pretext for the final act of the drama that he had envisaged all along. Tudjman's strategic vision behind that final act, a Serb-free Croatia, is no longer in doubt. While circumstantial evidence had always been there, the transcript of the Brioni meeting on July 31, 1995, provides the smoking gun. As if to confrim this, a week later, at a victory rally in Knin, Tudjman announced, "There can be no return to the past, to the times when [Serbs] were spreading cancer in the heart of Croatia, a cancer that was destroying the Croatian national being." He then went on to speak of the "ignominious disappearance" of the Krajina Serbs, "so it is as if they have never lived here!"

Former U.S. Ambassador in Zagreb Peter Galbraith, testifying at The Hague, dismissed claims that Croatia had engaged in ethnic cleansing, "because most of the population had already fled when the Croatian army and police arrived." But Galbraith was being disingenuous. All along Tudjman's objectives included ethnic cleansing on a grand scale. Those objectives were stated with brutal clarity at a meeting he had with his closest aides on 23 August 1995, in the aftermath of Operation Storm:

Tudjman: "One should proceed with the view that a military force can be a most effective means for solving the internal needs of the state. Considering the situation we face with the liberation of occupied territories, the demographic situation, it is necessary for military command precisely to become one of the most efficient components of our state policies in solving the demographic situation of Croatia. [...] We have the fortunate situation that the liberation demands a distribution of military units that would simultaneously solve the demographical [aspect]."[266]

Croatia celebrates August 5 as *Victory and Homeland Thanksgiving Day*. In reality there was hardly any fighting. Belgrade ordered a retreat. The Krajina leaders obeyed. A handful of Croatian officers (such as General Ante Gotovina, l. with Tudjman in Knin, August 1995) were indicted by the ICTY

at The Hague for command responsibility for the atrocities committed by Croatian forces against the civilian Serb population. The key leaders and masterminds – starting with Franjo Tudjman, who died in bed in 1999 – remained immune. The crime itself, not unlike the horror that preceded it in 1941-1945, remains unacknowledged and unatoned for.

---

[266] *Feral Tribune*, Split, July 18, 2003.

The Aftermath

It has been the frequent fate of the Krajina Serbs to be ill-treated and betrayed by distant masters, and to be used as cannon fodder in hopeless battles. But nothing the Habsburgs in Vienna or the Senate of Venice did was quite so inglorious as their betrayal by the regime in Belgrade in 1995.

It was almost unthinkable that the Krajina Serbs should not take up arms against a regime in Zagreb which was reviving the symbols, slogans and atmosphere of the 1941 Ustaša state. It was almost as unthinkable that they would be left in the lurch by Serbia, which they trusted even when those ruling it provided ample evidence that they were unworthy of such trust. The outcome of their struggle was disastrous, not because of their lack of stamina and determination, but because of political decisions made on their behalf in distant centers of power.

Throughout their history, the Krajina Serbs have lived under governments implicitly or overtly hostile to their interests and even their identity.

Under Austria and Venice – both of whom they served in countless battles – they had to defend their Orthodox faith, inseparable from their sense of who they are, against distant state authorities sometimes supportive of their dearly paid privileges, but never fully reconciled to their schismatic ways.

In the decade before the First World War they tried to adopt the propositional principles of civic nationhood and to discard their forefathers' ethno-religious corporatism, but Croatian political nationhood proved to be a singularly infertile soil on which to plant the civic seed.

In the Kingdom of Yugoslavia they were disoriented by the ideology of 'Yugoslavism' and by the lack of a clear framework for social or political action that would allow them to pursue their specific interests, let alone prepare them for the nightmare of 1941-1945.

During those four years the Krajina Serbs were subjected by the Ustaša regime to deadly terror of devastating proportions and unimaginable brutality. The bloodbath was unprecedented even by the grim Balkan standards and the first attempted genocide in modern Europe.

Under Tito and his successors they were either recruited as the shock troops of revolutionary desperation or attacked as the dupes of Royal reaction. Victorious or defeated, they were deprived of any means of promoting and defending their group interests and denied an opportunity to do so within the framework of self-governing political entities. But those with a Partisan medal could enjoy, through the Tito era, a few individual privileges in a system which still distrusted Croatian nationalism. Free elections in 1990 stripped away even these crumbs.

Under President Franjo Tudjman the Serbs were subjected to immediate, systematic discrimination and escalating violence reminiscent in style and substance of the horrors of the Second World War.

Deprived of external support, the Krajina Serbs were finally subjected to a premeditated campaign of ethnic cleansing. This campaign was carried out with the approval and active support of the leaders of what represents itself as 'international community.' Until the very end the peasant-warriors' destiny was to be an object of some distant and often hostile power's policy.

The Krajina Serbs were rarely masters of their own destiny, except in their collective fidelity to Orthodox Christianity which remained intact until the Communists imposed their dominance. In secular things their achievements were ultimately for others. The kings and commissars, who despised what they patronized, designed no safe place for their loyalties.

What remains, for the few who survive in place and the many refugees, is the record. Few regiments in any army have such battle honours. They fought too may battles for their own good, as is the way of good regiments, for the soldier serves the political values of high command. But they often had enemies worth opposing – the Ottomans, the King of Prussia, Napoleon Bonaparte, the Nazis...

In the end they tried to fight for their own interests and identity, and so they made their last stand in 1991. But they did this in the name of Yugoslavia, at a time when the powers that judge states and nations judged differently than in 1918 and 1945. So they obeyed orders one last time.

But it's not over. In the Balkans it never is.

Afterword

Michael M. Stenton

The Western Balkans can be seen as a large upland hinterland of Adriatic coast, a hinterland connecting northern Greece, Albania, Montenegro, most of Serbia, Bosnia and Croatia. Vlachs had driven their livestock through this upland hinterland for centuries. Much of the land was remarkably inaccessible until recent times. It was beyond the rule of ancient and medieval states and was a refuge for rebels and resisters until recent times. It was an upland universe of contiguous, thinly-populated areas – historically not unlike the Scottish Highlands, but an order of magnitude larger. Into this almost stateless zone the Ottoman state pushed remorselessly in the 15th and 16th centuries, establishing its control of towns, valleys and fortresses, and offering new religion or new taxes to the new subjects.

The Ottoman intrusion made the peoples of this upland realm both more mobile and more important. Of course, Christian peasants could submit and stay on the good land of the river valley that Ottoman commanders could seize and tax. By 1700 these settled peasants might, or might not, be recognisably Albanian, Serbian, Croatian. But the rest had upland options. Mountain air made a man free. More exactly, it offered a distinctive freedom to the head of an extended family of successful stock-herders. They were free from tax and free to move, free to buy and sell. There were freedoms for the young men who were fit enough, clever enough, and tough enough to keep moving and trading... and canny enough to pay one coin to officials whose office was to collect two. They were free of Ottoman beys and pashas and Croat-Hungarian magnates. Wherever they went they were accompanied by the Orthodox hedge priests who could endure their lifestyle, or – in fewer places – by the Franciscan brothers who matched their ability to serve the people.

What is usually known as the Habsburg Military Frontier, or the Vojna Krajina, was a long strip of territories which followed the Habsburg-Ottoman Border from the Adriatic coast at Senj, south of Istria, to the Pannonian plain north of Belgrade and thence into Transylvania. It was created in its essentials even before the Habsburg House of Austria took control of it in 1521-1526; it was settled with Christian refugees from Turkish conquest who received land for military service; and it lasted in one form or another until the Ottoman Empire lost Bosnia and Bulgaria in 1878. It was a political-military expedient which created a warlike, difficult settler population that was deliberately isolated from the other parts of Croatia and Hungary. The Border provided an effective riposte to Ottoman raiding because it developed its own system of raids, ransomes and plunder. It was indispensable before 1683, the second Ottoman siege of Vienna, and it was still necessary for at least another century.

The customs and loyalties of the Vojna Krajina are reminiscent of the Anglo-Scottish Border before 1603, and they changed even more slowly. By Mozart's time the Border had largely served its purpose as a barrier to Islamic expansion, but it lasted until the late nineteenth century because the military skills were still useful in Austria's wars against France or Prussia. The history of Hungary-Croatia before 1914, and of Yugoslavia from 1918 until its demise in 1991-1995, are commentaries on the Border's residual importance.

Tito, the Communist victor of the civil war of 1941-1945, might have made the Croatian Krajina – with the Bosanska Krajina on the Bosnian side of the Border – a homeland republic for the Western Serbs who provided the fighting core of his Partisan army, or at least an autonomous area. But he was a Croat, and he did neither. Franjo Tudjman, Tito's general who became anti-Communist president of Croatia, provoked the Krajina Serbs into their final passage of arms in 1991. The

Republika Srpska Krajina was almost emptied when the Croatian Army, trained and assisted by the United States, secured control in 1995. The region had been no less deserted in the late 15th and early 16th century when the Border was put together.

In this book disputes between Serbs and Croats were described at some length. There are said to be two views about ancient Balkan hatreds, one reprehensibly nationalist and the other pleasingly sane: that is, antipathy is either age-old or it is factitious and modern.

The first view discerns a contest that is endemic and, for good measure, incorrigible. But this opinion need not detain us.

The pleasingly sane view is that Croatia and Serbia began to quarrel in 1918, when they quarrelled within and about the new Yugoslavia without which they would have had nothing to quarrel about. In a narrow sense this view is true of pre-1914 Serbia. It is not, however, true of all Serbs, and it is not true of Croatia. One may indeed refuse to accept that any conflict is immutable, still less genetic, ineradicable, essential or, more recently, 'anthropo-geographical.' But, on the territory of today's Croatia, there is a Serb-Croat quarrel which happens to be rather old. It is certainly not modern in origin: Croatian hostility to the Military Border can be traced back at least to the early 17th century. Iit became worse, not better, with time and ended up by infecting Yugoslav politics. It is a long story. Indeed, had there not been a pre-existing Serb-Croat problem in Croatia, Yugoslavia might even have been a success story. The longevity of the 'hatred' – an unsuitably narrow term – is neither 'ancient' (it was unknown before the early modern era) nor modern. It was an outcome of the Ottoman conquest which pushed people around so violently that the trouble caused is still not exhausted. The nationalist malefactors of the Romantic era and afterwards did have material to work on.

Nevertheless, with sufficient perspective, it is difficult not to see the Serbo-Croat quarrel as belonging to a civilizational divide lying where it is commonly supposed to lie. As late as 1915, Admiral Troubridge, commanding His Britannic Majesty's guns at Belgrade, could write 'Europeans,' meaning a set of peoples none of whom lived in the Balkans. In his approval of Serbian courage and patriotism and in his disapproval of Serbian foolishness there is more than prejudice, irritation, or even accurate observation; there is a steady, adult recognition of an Other which is encountered as much as constructed.

In Zagreb there were people who felt the same but in a more pointed way: the Croats were perhaps Slavic, certainly European, while the other Slavs, those defined by Orthodox faith, were something else. In Britain and America, the Irish were once spoken of in like fashion though the words used were different. The now conventional or fashionable labels for this perception – anti-Catholic bigotry or racial prejudice – say too much and too little. The term more to the point is *civilizational*. The English and their cousins had strong patterns of life and expectation which could assimilate some foreign differences with equanimity, but experienced other differences with allergic shock. Now that the Irish are assimilated – even, it seems, in Ireland – the Anglo-Saxons (race was evident, but was not what mattered) can affirm modern virtue by renouncing old prejudice.

This was roughly what Yugoslavia was meant to make possible. Assimilation would remake a people. There might be a mutual confession of sins: in a fraternal, unified context, sophisticated, modern South Slavs would laugh at their former selves. A racial-linguistic unity would restore a unity that the empires, or perhaps the Churches, had pulled asunder. There were three attempts at Yugoslav oneness: the first during part of King Alexander's reign between the wars; the second being the imposition of communist anti-nationalism after the Partisan revolution; and the third in the era of devolved power just before (1974-1980) and just after Tito's death. The first was brief, the second was cancelled and replaced by the third.

Some observers will always feel that it was only the precise political frame of Yugoslavia that failed – because it was never settled, never quite right, not democratic in time – but that the Yugoslav formula itself was sound. (If so, Yugoslavia would remain an option for the distant future.) But Yugoslavia 'as history' did not achieve enough assimilation to subvert the past. Ireland may have been assimilated, but it was despite her best intentions. It was not assimilated to anything political until the European Union appeared as a non-British vehicle for assimilation. Irish nationality won the contest with Britain, after a fashion, and so came in the end to accept the loss of what was irretrievably lost – her language and her customary law.

In another continent and another context it may be said that Pakistan needs India to define itself: India does not. Indeed, it is the knowledge, in Pakistan, that India could envisage herself perfectly well without even thinking of Pakistan that feeds the extremely dangerous, neurotic Pakistani apprehension that India intends to find a way to actualize the assumption of absence. Croatia, Dr. Trikovic suggests, was for a long time in an analogous position. Croatia was not, of course, as sudden a concoction as Pakistan – far from it. But Croatia felt internally threatened and attracted by Serbia, while Serbia could be, more or less, cheerfully indifferent to Croatia.

Croatia, with its former Military Border, was burdened and blessed with a Serb population which had a different nationality, and this formed a Serbian Question which became a preoccupation bordering on obsession. Before 1914, by contrast, Serbia had no Croatian Question. This imbalance in Serb-Croat relations counted for as much as the various flavors of ideological nationalism. The Military Border explains how and why this is so.

In the 19th century both Serbs and Croats made, from time to time, exaggerated and impossible territorial claims. But the Serbians did have a substantial population of fellow Serbs living on Croatian territory. Once the Habsburg empire collapsed Serbia could not be expected to ignore Bosnia with its Serb plurality, or the Vojvodina with its Serb majority; or to ignore the question of how much of the Krajina could or should be taken as Serbia's national territory. Yugoslavia became the only way to prevent Serbia from taking its pick of former South Slav lands. To this extent, Yugoslavia was a Croatian political choice, however painful, which cannot be explained at all without the Krajina and Croatia's Serbian Question.

Croatia clung to its Austro-Hungarian status and helped to defeat radical reconstruction after 1848. Serbia grew from a cluster of rebel counties in the *pashalik* of Belgrade; it survived on its wits until the two empires started to topple and presented inevitable problems. Little Serbia, before 1912, was confident about its power to assimilate new popultions – rightly and wrongly confident. Serbian expansion 1804-1878 had been growth from a micro-state to a small state. It had been limited and assimilation had been largely confined to Serbs. But over-reach was already evident in 1912-1913. Macedonian gains were maximized, and Bulgaria recruited as a permanent enemy, to 'compensate' for the Austrian refusal to allow Serbia to take northern Albania. The principle here was not language, religion or good sense, it was prestige and a crude conception of power.

Croatia in the nineteenth century was bound more tightly to Budapest then at any time since the *Pacta Conventa* of the early 12th century. Its struggle was political and legal. Until the late 19th century it could no more to annex Dalmatia than Serbia could touch Syrmia. Croatia was, in a sense, pessimistic about its Serbs of the Military Frontier – long before 1914 – and it needed stiff doses of national ideology to suppress the doubts. Some potions were Yugoslavist (there was a good deal of pan-Slav or Serb-Croat co-operation in Dalmatia), but others were concocted from theorized refusals to accept that the Serbs were really Serbs; or even if they were, that they could or should be allowed to remain Serbs.

In Yugoslavia no one could win. Even if Croatia had made the Yugoslav state after 1918 – if, that is, Serbo-Croatia could have been designed just as R.W. Seton-Watson would have wished – it is doubtful if Serbia, with a confident personality at its zenith, could have been assimilated quickly enough to make any integrated Yugoslav system work. Croatia, as small as it was (or might be), and with all the disadvantages of having fought loyally for the wrong side in 1914-1918, could neither assimilate not be assimilated. Serbia, though bigger, was poor and bled white by warfare and disease. It was not rich enough or strong enough or attractive enough to assimilate Croatia with its a more developed economy and sense of 'millenium-long' (*tisućletna*) civilizational superiority. This was not an accident of Croatian politics nor a mere curlicue of vile ideology, it was something inevitable. It was an aspect of what Croatia belonged to by instinct and encounter – however embedded in dreary conceit and nationalist artifice. Only statesmanship and sympathy or a very high order could have solved the problems.

If, as nearly happened, Serbia had been taken from the Ottomans by the Habsburgs after 1688 and assimilated, Balkan history and the story of modern Europe would have been different. To say the First World War could not have started as it did, would be both true and absurd. All the decisions about South Slav borders would have been Viennese, and Vienna would have had an even stronger motive to see beyond the fatal 'Austro-Hungarian' experiment of 1867. South Slav politicians, if necessary, might have managed the situation better and got straight down to bargaining about essentials: about borders. No territorial adjudication or dispensation is a certain solution when it takes place; but it puts down roots if it lasts, and fortune can help it to last – as the twenty aggrieved societies of the German *Bund der Vertriebenen* (League of the Expelled) know to their cost. Without a geographically defined Serbia and Croatia – amongst other states and territories – there could be no safe and stable Habsburg empire. The same would be true of any West Balkan successor state.

Serbia and Croatia, as this book shows, are not naturally equal. That the Serbs were more numerous, that the Croats were better technicians, that Belgrade may have been more dynamic and cosmopolitan than Zagreb, are minor points in this inequality. That the Croats had more Latin and less Greek is more relevant. What Croatia was part of in 1914 is evident; but what Serbia was to become was not. The Italo-Byzantine renaissance that could be glimpsed in the Serbian medieval monarchy could not be recovered. Having rejected the Turks and Islam, Serbia needed a new paradigm. There did not have to be a dramatic alliance or political-constitutional act driving this assimilation, however. Simply surviving quietly, doing business, running schools, sending students abroad, without any grand gestures at all, would have been an eminently feasible option.

A federal Balkan state of Serbia, Bulgaria, Macedonia and (perhaps) Greece was already a lost cause by 1914. Without Constantinople it lacked any meaningful centre, and Constantinople, though as magical as ever, was already too Turkish and still much too poor to be effective as a capital of a resurrected Christian monarchy. (The Allies occupied the City in 1919 but they did not know what to do with it and distrusted each other too badly to form an intention, civilized or not. It was secured on behalf of a secularized Turkey.) The entire south Balkan space, without an industrial base, lacked strength. Russia, though powerful at moments, was never as present in the Balkans as feared in the West, and it was in any case excluded by Bolshevism 1917-1941.

Serbia lacked a civilizational hinterland strong enough to serve the Yugoslav project. The trend of her assimilation was westwards; after its enlargement in 1912-1913 Serbia had just enough cultural resources and identity for itself, but not for something much bigger. After the killing of King Aleksandar Obrenović in 1903 and after the display of Serbian anger at the annexation of Bosnia-Herzegovina in 1908, the rejection of Serbia by Vienna was understandable; but it was mistaken as well as ill-fated. Whether Vienna was exceptionally foolish is another matter. There are few countries in Europe that were not wounded and shrivelled by blunders in the suicidal war of 1914.

Serbia in 1918 was expected to make further contact with 'Europe,' and found that *Yugoslavia* was the recommended vehicle for this contact. In the inter-war years, however, it was Serbia's misfortune, as manager of the Yugoslav project, that Europe was economically inert. There was, of course, a possible

Soviet assimilation available in 1945, but it was almost immediately rejected by Yugoslavia. Elsewhere it was infertile even when it could not be rejected. The European Union is the recommended vehicle today, and Serbia – resembling Croatia in 1918, albeit arguably on worse terms – desires membership as much to deflect harm as for any other reason.

A Serbian Yugoslavia, without Croatia-Slavonia, was possible in 1918, but seemed reckless. It might still have been too big for its own good. But the difficulties would have been far fewer and slower to mature. In the event, Croatia was incorporated by consent of a kind. Once inside it was technically, and morally, very difficult for Serbian politicians to renounce the Serbs (or Serbians) of Srem, Slavonia, Croatia and Dalmatia: the former Vojna Krajina. It is unfair to dismiss Yugoslavia as a mere pretext for 'Greater Serbia.' But *Velika Srbija*, once contained in the Yugoslav box, made it equally difficult to deal with Croatia. The Krajina Serbs had been granted something they could scarcely dream of before 1914. Their former 'regiments' had become a set of Yugoslav constituencies, as well as a measure of Serbian national achievement. Both combined to postpone Croatian autonomy between the wars, and then react against its various geopolitical forms in 1939-45 and 1991-95.

No Yugoslav people was likely to demand less than something close to its full territory. The Serbs were trapped into an appearance of responsibility for what was as much imposed on them as it was on others. Yugoslavia was a country desired by the few, not the many. It would have been possible, before 1914, on Austrian terms if Vienna had felt able to break with Hungarian privileges. But Vienna refused to base its imperial survival on the loyalty of South Slavs and therefore, in a sense, chose to be afraid of little Serbia. The one province that pre-1908 Serbia wanted above all was Bosnia, which had then a Serbian plurality. If ever Bosnia were gained, it would bring the Serbian state right up to the entire length of the old Military Frontier. Fear of this unlikely outcome tempted Austria to war; its imminence drew Croatia into Yugoslavia.

Having made Yugoslavia the Serbs had to re-imagine Serbia, but they did not since it seemed not to be strictly necessary. Having failed to make Croatia before 1914, the Croats had to contribute to the raw Yugoslavia that Serbia had delivered, and had to imagine a viable compromise. But the repertoire of national demands was already well established before 1914: Croatian rule in the Military Border and the annexation of Dalmatia. Furthermore, most Croats who liked the Yugoslav ideal saw Zagreb as the capital of a South-Slavia of former Habsburg lands which would include Bosnia and Vojvodina. Serbia's role would be to applaud and assist. If there was in 1918 an outcome as implausible as this, it was an undifferentiated Yugoslavia with all ambitions renounced.

Yugoslav solidarity did have its moments. It defended Dalmatia and Istria against Italy and Slovenia against Austria. But in the long term, it was the price Serbia paid for her short time attempting the impossible. Royal Yugoslavia did not create any sort of Serbia, great or small, and Communist Yugoslavia was founded on the Communist Party doctrine that 'greater-Serbian nationalism' was the glue that must not hold the state together. For Croatia, Yugoslavia was, in 1918 and again in 1945, the least unpromising shelter from the storm of defeat. Twice, the Serbs as Yugoslavs saved the Croats from paying the full price of choosing the wrong side in a great war. But it was impossible to repay the kindness without betraying the national purpose that the kindness protected. Some Serbs saw this, but after the fatal months in 1918-1919 the die was cast and tragedy made probable.

Geopolitics has explanatory force. Croatia, whatever its quarrels with Hungarians and Austrian Germans before 1914, could not be kept inside Yugoslavia if Hungary and Germany were there to help her get out again. The pull of the North was irresistible once Magyar cupidity and German weakness were past. Germany was too weak to help in 1919-1933, and unwilling to do so in 1933-1941, but in April 1941 the Magyars and Germans plunged into Yugoslavia to a roar of approval in

Zagreb. Between 1945 and 1989 the Cold War imposed a new set of restraints, but in 1991 in they went again. Weapons were smuggled across the Hungarian border. *Danke Deutschland* was the response from Zagreb for the heavyweight push for recognition of Croatia's secession that shocked Europe as well, it is said, as the German diplomatic service. Chancellor Helmut Kohl was not the Austrian corporal's revenant, and his motives were different. But motives are not the point. Events would have placed a similar temptation in the way of almost any conceivable German state, whether in the 1940s or the 1990s. Hitler's specific wartime motive and Kohl's sudden susceptibility to the *Bund der Vertriebenen* cannot disguise the gravitational likelihood of the Croatian apple falling off the Yugoslav tree whenever it was shaken. Linguistic affinitude is not enough to make a people or even, very much, an opportunity for a people, although the splutter of success in Italy did look like a winning formula.

This book is an attempt to bring together in one short volume episodes of European and South Slav history which are known of, when recalled at all, only in fragmentary form. At its heart is a story of political-religious toleration which created something and then stopped, leaving a half-tolerated zone of rivalry as a dangerous bequest to modern times.

The history of the Krajina and its people is not the history of a country, not even a vanished country. It is much bigger than the history of a province, however. It is an element in the story of most of the great wars in Europe from the Ottoman offensives after the fall of Constantinople to the last decade of the twentieth century.

Dr. Stenton is a lecturer at Britannia Royal Naval College, Dartmouth, and the author of *Radio London and Resistance in Occupied Europe: British Political Warfare 1939-1943* (Oxford University Press, 2000)

Sources and Bibliography

A. Primary sources

1. German documents on microfilm, listed and catalogued in the Guides to German Records Microfilmed at Alexandria, Virginia (Washington DC: National Archives Records Office):

a. Microcopy T-501, Records of German Field Commands, Occupied Territories and Others. Rolls 250, 256, 264-268, 351 and 352 deal with various aspects of the occupation and resistance in the Balkans.

b. Microcopies T-311...T-315, Records of Army Groups E and F (Heeresgruppen E, F in rolls 175, 176 and 197, mainly relevant to the closing stages of the war) and Records of German Field Commands.

2. Politisches Archiv, Auswärtiges Amt, PA/AA): Office of the Minister (Büro RAM, i.e. Reichsaussenminister - Kroatien); Office of the Secretary of State (Büro Staatssekretär - Jugoslawien Bd 3, Kroatien Bd 1-4). All on NA Microfilm T-120, Rolls 120, 197, 199, 200, 208 and 212.

3. The War Archive in Vienna (Kriegsarchiv Wien, KAW) contains the papers of Glaise von Horstenau (B/67) and Alexander Loehr (B/521).

4. Published collections: *Akten zur Deutschen Auswärtigen Politik 1918-45.*(ADAP) E, 1 (Göttingen, 1969). 2 (1972). *Documents on German Foreign Policy 1918-45* (DGFP) D, 12 vols, (London, 1962)

5. The Federal Archive – Military Archive in Freiburg (Bundesarchiv – Militärarchiv in Freiburg, BA/MAF) has the official papers of Glaise, Loehr and other German generals in the Balkans.

6. George O. Kent, *A Catalog of Files and Microfilms of the German Foreign Ministry Archives, 1920-1945.* Stanford, CA: Hoover Institution, 1966, Vol. 3.

7. Paul N. Hehn (ed.). *The German Struggle against Yugoslav Guerillas in World War II: German Counter-Insurgency in Yugoslavia 1941-1943.* East European Quarterly, Boulder. Distributed by Columbia University Press, New York 1975.

8. International Military Tribunal. *The Trial of Major War Criminals (Proceedings).* Vol. 10. Nuremberg: IMT, 1946. Contains the interrogation of Ribbentrop in 1946, with information on the Axis policy in Yugoslavia.

9. National Archives, Washington D.C.: microfilmed records of the Italian High Command (Comando Supremo) and the Second Army Command (Comando 2. Armata) classified as Microcopy T-821. Rolls 53, 54, 64, 66, 70, 232, 285-290, 294, 297, 298, 395, 398-400, 410, 448, 474, 497 and 503 contain material on the relations of the Italian Army with the Četniks and the NDH.

10. *Documenti diplomatici italiani.* IX, 2 (Rome, 1958). 3 (1959).

11. National Archives, Washington D.C., Record Group 59 DD. 860H.00 and 860H.01 for reports concerning Croatia from the U.S. Legation in Belgrade, the Consulate in Zagreb and U.S. diplomats in Budapest until mid-1941.

12. Public Records Office (PRO) London, FO/371. Foreign Office documents relevant to Yugoslav affairs during the Second World War.

13. Arhiv Saveznog sekretarijata za spoljne poslove (ASSIP): Ministry of Foreign Affairs of the Independent State of Croatia (Ministarstvo vanjskih poslova Nezavisne Države Hrvatske, MVP NDH).

14. ASSIP, Royal Yugoslav Government in Exile, Ministry for Foreign Affairs (Ministarstvo inostranih poslova, F-1, F-2, F4); and Presidency of the Council of Ministers (Predsedništvo Ministarskog saveta, F-1, F-2) have reports on Croatia from Yugoslav diplomats in neutral capitals.

15. Arhiv Jugoslavije (AJ). Fond Milana Stojadinovića (the papers of Milan Stojadinović). Contains documents on the Yugoslav-Italian relations in the late 1930s and on the Croat question at home.

16. Fond izbegličke vlade (Royal Yugoslav Government in Exile documents) deposited in the Yugoslav Archive in Belgrade (AJ). Material covered in: Krizman, Bogdan, and Petranović, Branko. *Jugoslovenske vlade u izbeglištvu.* 2 vols. (1941-43, 1943-45). Belgrade-Zagreb: Arhiv Jugoslavije/Globus, 1981.

17. Institute of Military History, Belgrade (Vojnoistorijski institut, V.I.I.; fond VII/NDH). Abundant material on the NDH in boxes (*kutije*), including statements by captured officials after the war.

18. V.I.I. *Zbornik dokumenata i podataka o Narodno-oslobodilačkom ratu naroda Jugoslavije.* 13 vols in 128 parts. Belgrade: Vojnoistorijski institut 1949. Arranged regionally and topically. The documentary source for the Partisan version of war in Yugoslavia. Contains many Ustaša documents and translations of German and Italian ones.

B. Secondary Sources

Aarons, Mark and Loftus, John. *The Unholy Trinity.* New York: St. Martins, 1991.

Anfuso, Filippo. *Roma, Berlino, Salo (1936-1945).* Milan: Edizione Garzanti, 1950.

Banac, Ivo. *The National Question in Yugoslavia: Origins, History, Politics.* Ithaca and London: Cornell University Press, 1984.

Barriot, Patrick & Crépin, Eve. *On assassine un peuple: les Serbes de Krajina.* Paris: L'Age d'Homme, 1995.

Basta, Milan. *Agonija i slom NDH.* Belgrade, 1971.

Bataković, Dušan T. "The National Integration of the Serbs and Croats: A Comparative Analysis." *Dialogue* (Paris), No. 7-8, September 1994.

Biber, Dušan. "Ustaše i Treći rajh. Prilog problematici jugoslovensko-nemačkih odnosa 1933-1939." *Jugoslovenski istorijski časopis*, 2-1964.

Boban, Ljubo. *Maček i politika Hrvatske seljačke stranke, 1928-1941.* Two volumes. Zagreb: Liber, 1974.

Bracewell, C.W. *The Uskoks of Senj: Piracy, Banditry and Holy War in the sixteenth-century Adriatic* Cornell University Press, 1992.

Broucek, Peter. *Ein General im Zweilicht. Die Erimerungen Edmund Glaise von Horstenau.* Vienna-Cologne-Graz: Boehlhaus Nachf., 3 Vols (1980, 1983, 1988). Vol. 3 includes Glaise's Zagreb diary.

Cannistraro, Pilip (ed.). *Historical Dictionary of Fascist Italy.* Westport, Connecticut-London: Greenwood Press, 1982.

Ciano, Galeazzo. *Diario 1937-43.* Edited and with a preface by Renzo De Felice. Milan: Rizzoli, 1980.

"Croatia," in *Shoah Resource Center.* Jerusalem: The International School for Holocau-st Studies at Yad Vashem, 2005.

Deakin, William. *The Brutal Friendship: Mussolini, Hitler and the Fall of Italian Fascism.* New York: Harper and Row, 1962.

- *The Embattled Mountain.* London - New York - Toronto, 1971.

Diklić, Momčilo. *Srpsko pitanje u Hrvatskoj, 1941-1950.* Beograd: Zora, 2004

Djilas, Milovan. *Wartime.* New York: Harcourt Brace Jovanovich, 1977.

Djuretić, Veselin. *Saveznici i jugoslovenska ratna drama: Izmedju nacionalnih i ideoloških izazova*. 2 vols. Belgrade: SANU, 1985.

Dragnich, Alex N. *The First Yugoslavia: Search for a Viable Political System*. Stanford, California: Hoover Institution Press, 1983.

- *Serbs and Croats: The Struggle in Yugoslavia*. New York: Harcourt, Brace. 1992.

Dvorniković, Vladimir. *Karakterologija Jugoslavena*. Beograd: Gregorić, 1939.

Falconi, Carlo. *The Silence of Pius XII*. Boston: Little, Brown and Co., 1970.

Fortis, Abbe Alberto. *Travels Into Dalmatia*. New York: Cosimo Classics, 2007. A contemporary reprint of an 18th century classic.

Fricke, Gert. *Kroatien 1941-1944: Die "Unabhaengige Staat" in der Sicht des Deutschen Bevollmaechtigen Generals in Agram, Glaise v. Horstenau*. Freiburg/i. Breisgau: Rombach Verlag, 1972.

Gavranić, Pero. *Politička povjest hrvatskog naroda od prvog početka do danas*. Zagreb 1895.

Gligorijević, Branislav. "Politički život na prostoru RSK (1918-1941)" in *Republika Srpska Krajina*, Belgrade 1996.

Hagen, Walter. *Die Geheime Front*. Wien: Niebelungen Verlag, 1950. In English: *The Secret Front - the Story of Nazi Political Espionage*. London: Weidenfeld and Nicholson, 1953. "Hagen" is the alias of a former German intelligence officer, Wilhelm Hoettl.

Hammel, E.A. "Demography and the Origins of the Yugoslav Civil War." *Anthropology Today* 9 (1): 4-9 (February 1993), Royal Anthropological Institute of Great Britain and Ireland.

Hlinicka, Karl. *Das Ende auf dem Balkan 1944/45: Die Militaerische Raeumung Jugoslawiens durch die Deutsche Wehrmacht*. Goettingen: Musterscheudt, 1970.

Hollins, David. *Austrian Frontier Troops, 1740-98*. Oxford: Osprey Publishing, 2005.

Hory, Ladislaus, and Broszat, Martin. *Der kroatische Ustascha-Staat, 1941-1945*. Stuttgart: Deutsche Verlags-Anstalt, 1964.

Hoptner, Jacob B: *Yugoslavia in Crisis, 1934-1941*. New York: Columbia University Press, 1962.

Horvat, Josip. *Zivjeti u Hrvatskoj: Zapisi iz nepovrata.* Zagreb: Liber, 1983.

Istorija srpskog naroda, Beograd: Srpska književna zadruga, 10 vols.

Ivanović, Vane. *Memoirs of a Yugoslav.* New York and London: Harcourt Brace Jovanovich, 1977.

Janković, Djordje. *Tradicionalna kultura Srba u Srspkoj Krajini i Hrvatskoj.* Beograd: Etnografski muzej, 2000.

Jareb, Jere. *Pola stoljeca hrvatske politike.* Buenos Aires: Knjižnica Hrvatske Revije, 1960.

Jelić-Butić, Fikreta. *Ustaše i Nezavisna Država Hrvatska 1941-1945.* Zagreb: Globus, 1977.

Jukić, Ilija. *The Fall of Yugoslavia.* New York: Harcourt Brace Jovanovich 1974.

Kazimirović, Vasa. *NDH u svetlu nemačkih dokumenata i dnevnika Gleza fon Horstenau 1941-1944.* Belgrade: Narodna knjiga, 1987.

Kiszling, Rudolf. *Die Kroaten: Der Schichsalweg eines Südslawenvolkes.* Graz-Cologne: Verlag Hermann Boehlhaus, 1956.

Krestić, Vasilije. *Istorija Srba u Hrvatskoj i Slavoniji, 1848-1914.* Beograd: Politika, 1992.

- *Through Genocide to Greater Croatia,* Belgrade: BIGZ, 1997.

Krizman, Bogdan. *Korespondencija Stjepana Radića, 1885-1918.* Zagreb Zagreb: Sveučilište – Institut za hrvatsku povijest, 1972.

- *Ante Pavelić i ustaše.* Zagreb: Globus, 1987.

- *NDH izmedju Hitlera i Mussolinija.* Zagreb: Globus, 1980.

- *Ustaše i Treći Reich.* Two volumes. Zagreb: Globus, 1983.

Kukuljević Sakcinski, Ivan. *Književnici u Hrvatah u prvoj polovini XVII vieka.* Zagreb 1868.

Lederer, Ivo. *Yugoslavia at the Paris Peace Conference.* New Haven and London: Yale University Press, 1963.

Lowe, C.J. and Marzari, F. *Italian Foreign Policy, 1870-1940.* London and Boston: Routledge and Kegan Paul, 1975.

Martin, David. *The Web of Disinformation: Churchill's Yugoslav Blunder.* San Diego and New York: Harcourt, Brace, Jovanovich, 1990.

Mažuran, I. *Popis naselja i stanovnistva u Slavoniji 1698. godine*, vol. 2, JAZU, Osijek, 1988.

Milaš, Bishop Nikodim. *Documenta spectantia historiam Dalmatiae et Istriae a XV usgue ad XIX saeculum.* Zara 1894.

Milazzo, Matteo J. *The Chetnik Movement and the Yugoslav Resistance.* Baltimore and London: The Johns Hopkins University Press, 1975.

Miletić, Antun. *Koncentracioni logor Jasenovac 1941-1945.* Beograd: Narodna knjiga, 1986.

Miller, Nicholas J. *Between Nation and State: Serbian Politics in Croatia Before the First World War.* University of Pittsburgh Press, 1997.

Neubacher, Hermann. *Sonderaufrag Südost 1940-1945. Bericht eines fliegenden Diplomaten.* Goettingen: Muster-Schmidt-Verlag, 1957.

Novak, Viktor. *Magnum Crimen: Pola vijeka klerikalizma u Hrvatskoj.* Zagreb, 1948.

Orlow, Dietrich. *The Nazis in the Balkans: A Case Study of Totalitarian Politics.* University of Pittsburgh Press, 1968.

Paris, Edmund. *Genocide in Satellite Croatia: A Record of Racial and Religious Persecutions and Massacres.* Chicago, 1962.

Pavlinović, Mihovio. *Misao hrvatska i misao srbska u Dalmaciji, od godine 1848 do godine 1882.* Zadar, 1882.

Pavlovich, Paul. *History of the Serbian Orthodox Church.* Toronto: Serbian Heritage Books, 1989.

Pavlowitch, Stevan. *Unconventional Perceptions of Yugoslavia 1940-1945.* East European Monographs. New York: Columbia University Press, 1985.

Petrovich, Michael Boro. *History of Modern Serbia, 1804-1918.* New York: Harcourt, Brace, Jovanovich, 1976.

Plećaš-Nitonja, Nikola. *Požar u Krajini.* Chicago 1975.

Plenča, Dušan. *Kninska ratna vremena 1850-1946.* Zagreb: Globus, 1986.

Porphyrogenitus, Constantine. *De Administrando Imperio.* Dumbarton Oaks Texts, 2009.

Jovan Radonić and Mita Kostić. *Srpske privilegije od 1690 do 1792.* Belgrade: Naučna knjiga, 1954.

Rendulic, Lothar. *Gekämpft, gesiegt, geschlagen.* Welsermühl Verlag, Wels und Heidelberg, 1952.

Ribar, Dr. Ivan. *Iz moje političke suradnje, 1901-1965.* Zagreb: Naprijed, 1965.

Roberts, Walter R. *Tito, Mihailović and the Allies 1941-1945.* (2nd ed.). Durham, North Carolina, 1987.

Roksandić, Drago. *Srbi u Hrvatskoj od 15. stoljeća do naših dana.* Zagreb: Vjesnik, 1991.

Rothenberg, Gunther E. *The Austrian Military Border in Croatia, 1522-1747.* Urbana: University of Illinois Press, 1960.

- *The Military Border in Croatia 1740-1881.* Chicago and London: The University of Chicago Press, 1966.

Šišić, Ferdo. *Povijesti hrvatskoga naroda.* Zagreb, 1916.

- "O stogodišnjici Ilirskog pokreta." *Ljetopis Jugoslavenske akademije,* Zagreb, Vol. 49-1936.

Srbi u Hrvatskoj: Naseljavanje, broj i teritorijalni razmeštaj. Belgrade: Univerzitet u Beogradu, 1993.

Starčević, Ante. *Razgovori.* Djela, Vol 3. Zagreb 1894.

Steinberg, Jonathan. "Types of Genocide: Croatians, Serbs, and Jews, 1941-1945," in David Cesarani, *The Final Solution: Origins and Implementation.* Routledge 1996.

Stillman, Edmund. *The Balkans.* New York: Time-Life Books, 1967.

Stenton, Michael. *Radio London and Resistance in Occupied Europe: British Political Warfare 1939-1943.* Oxford University Press, 2000.

Stojadinović, Milan. *Ni rat ni pakt: Jugoslavija izmedju dva rata.* Buenos Aires: El Economista, 1963.

Sufflay, Milan. *Hrvatska u svjetlu svjetske historije i politike.* Zagreb, 1928.

Taylor, Scott & Nolan, Brian. *Tested Metal.* Ottawa: Esprit de Corps, 1998

Tomasevich, Jozo. *The Chetniks.* Stanford University Press, 1975.

Trifkovic, Srdja. *Ustaša: Croatian Separatism and European Politics, 1929-1945.* London: The Lord Byron Foundation, 1998.

- "Rivalry Between Germany and Italy in Croatia, 1942-1943." *The Historical Journal*, Vol. 34, No. 4 (1993).

- "Yugoslavia in Crisis: Europe and the Croatian Question 1939-41." *European History Quarterly.* Vol. 23 (1993), No. 4, pp. 529-561.

- "The First Yugoslavia and Origins of Croatian Separatism." *East European Quarterly.* Vol. 24, No 3, September 1992, pp. 345-370.

Van Creveld, Martin. *Hitler's Strategy 1940-1941: The Balkan Clue.* Cambridge University Press 1973.

Vaníček, František. *Specialgeschichte der Militärgrenze: Aus Originalquellen und Quellenwerken geschöpft.* Vienna: Kaiserlich-Königliche Hof- und Staatsdruckerei, 1875.

Voinovitch, Louis. *Dalmatia and the Yugoslav Movemen.* London: George Allen & Unwin, 1920.

Vucinich, Wayne. *Serbia between East and West.* Stanford, California: Stanford University Press, 1954.

West, Rebecca. *Black Lamb and Grey Falcon.* Penguin Classics, 2007.

Wilson, Peter H. *The Thirty Years War: Europe's Tragedy.* Cambridge, MA: The Belknap Press, 2009.

Winnifrith, T. J. *The Vlachs: The History of a Balkan People,* London: Palgrave MacMillan, 1987.

Wolff, Larry. *Venice and the Slavs: The Discovery of Dalmatia in the Age of Enlightenment.* Stanford, CA: Stanford University Press, 2001.

The Author

Srdja (Serge) Trifkovic has a BA in international relations from the University of Sussex, a BA in political science from the University of Zagreb, and a doctorate in history from the University of Southampton. In the course of a long career combining journalism with academia he has worked for the BBC in London, the Voice of America in Washington D.C., and as foreign affairs editor of *Chronicles* magazine (1999-2009). His previous books in English include:

Defeating Jihad: How the war on terrorism may yet be won, in spite of ourselves. Boston, MA: Regina Orthodox Press, 2007.

Peace in the Promised Land: A Realist Scenario (editor & contributor). Rockford, IL: Chronicles Press, 2006.

The Sword of the Prophet. Islam: History, Theology, Impact on the World. Boston, MA: Regina Orthodox Press, 2002.

Ustaša: Croatian Separatism and European Politics, 1929-1945. London: The Lord Byron Foundation, 1998.

* * * * *

The Lord Byron Foundation for Balkan Studies

www.Balkanstudies.org

was founded by the late Sir Alfred Sherman in 1994 as a non-partisan research center devoted to studying the Balkan Peninsula in all its aspects. The Foundation's research, publications and conferences are designed to correct the current trend of public commentary, which tends, systematically, not to understand events but to construct a version of Balkan rivalries that fits daily political requirements. The Foundation is named after a great Western poet who gave his life in the fight to free Balkan Christians from Islamic rule. This choice reflects its belief in the essential unity of our civilization.

The work of The Lord Byron Foundation is based on the acceptance that the cause of tolerance in a perennially troubled region can never be advanced by misrepresentation or by the sentimental lapse of seriousness that often characterizes Western discourse on the region.